CHEAT SHEET

Dummies 101: Excel For Windows 95

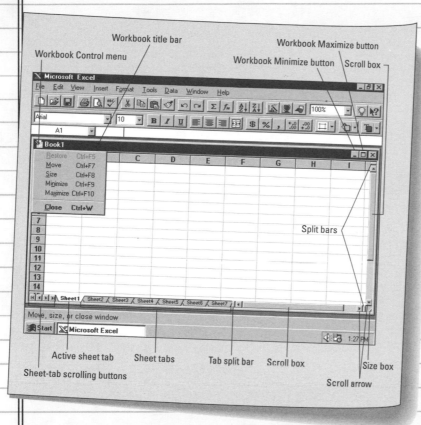

Workbook Control menu
Workbook title bar
Workbook Maximize button
Workbook Minimize button
Scroll box

Restore	Ctrl+F5
Move	Ctrl+F7
Size	Ctrl+F8
Minimize	Ctrl+F9
Maximize	Ctrl+F10
Close	Ctrl+W

Split bars

Active sheet tab   Sheet tabs   Tab split bar   Scroll box   Size box
Sheet-tab scrolling buttons   Scroll arrow

Standard Toolbar

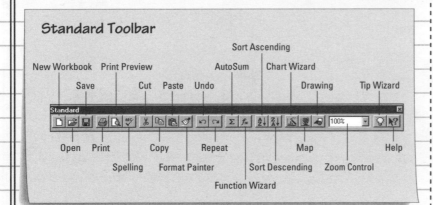

New Workbook   Print Preview   AutoSum   Sort Ascending   Chart Wizard
Save   Cut   Paste   Undo   Drawing   Tip Wizard

Open   Print   Copy   Repeat   Map   Help
Spelling   Format Painter   Sort Descending   Zoom Control
Function Wizard

Formatting Toolbar

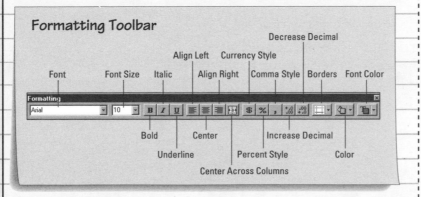

Decrease Decimal
Align Left   Currency Style
Font   Font Size   Italic   Align Right   Comma Style   Borders   Font Color

Bold   Center   Increase Decimal
Underline   Percent Style   Color
Center Across Columns

Excel For Windows 95
Function Key Template —
© 1996 IDG Books Worldwide, Inc.

Dummies 101:™ Excel For Windows® 95

	F1	F2	F3	F4	F5	F6	F7	F8	F9	F10	F11	F12
(Alone)	Answer Wizard	Edit Cell and Activate Formula Bar	Paste Name	Repeat Last Action or Absolute	Go To	Next Pane	Spell Check	Extend Mode	Calculate Workbook	Menu Bar	Create Chart on Chart Sheet	Save As Dialog Box
Shift+	Contextual Help	Cell Note	Function Wizard	Repeat Find or Go To	Find	Previous Pane		Add Mode	Calculate Worksheet	Context Menu	Insert Worksheet	Save Workbook
Ctrl+		Info Window	Define Name	Close Window	Restore Workbook Window	Next Workbook	Move Workbook Window	Size Workbook Window	Minimize Workbook Window	Maximize Workbook Window	Insert Macro Sheet	Open Dialog Box
Ctrl+Shift+			Create Names			Previous Workbook						Print Dialog Box

Shortcut Keys in Excel for Windows 95

Shortcut key	What it does
Ctrl+'	Turn on and off formula view
Ctrl+1	Format Cells dialog box
Ctrl+2	Add or remove bold
Ctrl+3	Add or remove italic
Ctrl+4	Add or remove underline
Ctrl+5	Add or remove strikethrough
Ctrl+6	Show or hide objects
Ctrl+7	Show or hide Formatting toolbar
Ctrl+8	Show or hide outline symbols
Ctrl+9	Hide selected rows
Ctrl+0 (zero)	Hide selected columns
Ctrl+- (minus)	Delete cells
Ctrl+= (equal)	Calculate workbook
Ctrl+Shift+~(tilde)	General number format (1100.5)

More Cool Shortcut Keys in Excel for Windows 95

Shortcut key	What it does
Ctrl+Shift+!	Comma number format (1,100.50)
Ctrl+Shift+@	Time number format (1:30 PM - 24-hour clock)
Ctrl+Shift+#	Date number format (01-11-55)
Ctrl+Shift+$	Currency number format ($1,100.50)
Ctrl+Shift+%	Percent number format (110050%)
Ctrl+Shift+^	Scientific number format (1.10E+03)
Ctrl+Shift+&	Outline border
Ctrl+Shift+(	Unhide rows
Ctrl+Shift+)	Unhide columns
Ctrl+Shift+_	Remove Borders
Ctrl+Shift++(plus)	Insert cells

DUMMIES 101:™
EXCEL FOR
WINDOWS® 95

by Greg Harvey

IDG
BOOKS
WORLDWIDE

IDG Books Worldwide, Inc.
An International Data Group Company

Foster City, CA ✦ Chicago, IL ✦ Indianapolis, IN ✦ Braintree, MA ✦ Southlake, TX

Dummies 101:™ Excel For Windows® 95

Published by
IDG Books Worldwide, Inc.
An International Data Group Company
919 E. Hillsdale Blvd.
Suite 400
Foster City, CA 94404

Library of Congress Catalog Card No.: 96-75123

ISBN: 1-56884-630-4

Printed in the United States of America

10 9 8 7 6 5 4 3 2 1

1M/RS/QT/ZW/IN

Distributed in the United States by IDG Books Worldwide, Inc.

Distributed by Macmillan Canada for Canada; by Computer and Technical Books for the Caribbean Basin; by Contemporanea de Ediciones for Venezuela; by Distribuidora Cuspide for Argentina; by CITEC for Brazil; by Ediciones ZETA S.C.R. Ltda. for Peru; by Editorial Limusa SA for Mexico; by Transworld Publishers Limited in the United Kingdom and Europe; by Al-Maiman Publishers & Distributors for Saudi Arabia; by Simron Pty. Ltd. for South Africa; by IDG Communications (HK) Ltd. for Hong Kong; by Toppan Company Ltd. for Japan; by Addison Wesley Publishing Company for Korea; by Longman Singapore Publishers Ltd. for Singapore, Malaysia, Thailand, and Indonesia; by Unalis Corporation for Taiwan; by WS Computer Publishing Company, Inc. for the Philippines; by WoodsLane Pty. Ltd. for Australia; by WoodsLane Enterprises Ltd. for New Zealand.

For general information on IDG Books Worldwide's books in the U.S., please call our Consumer Customer Service department at 800-762-2974. For reseller information, including discounts and premium sales, please call our Reseller Customer Service department at 800-434-3422.

For information on where to purchase IDG Books Worldwide's books outside the U.S., contact IDG Books Worldwide at 415-655-3021 or fax 415-655-3295.

For information on translations, contact Marc Jeffrey Mikulich, Director, Foreign & Subsidiary Rights, at IDG Books Worldwide, 415-655-3018 or fax 415-655-3295.

For sales inquiries and special prices for bulk quantities, write to the address above or call IDG Books Worldwide at 415-655-3200.

For information on using IDG Books Worldwide's books in the classroom, or ordering examination copies, contact the Education Office at 800-434-2086 or fax 817-251-8174.

For authorization to photocopy items for corporate, personal, or educational use, please contact Copyright Clearance Center, 222 Rosewood Drive, Danvers, MA 01923, or fax 508-750-4470.

is a trademark under exclusive license to IDG Books Worldwide, Inc., from International Data Group, Inc.

About the Author

Greg Harvey is a product of the great American Midwest. Born in the Chicagoland area in 1949 (thus his saying "I'm only as old as China" — Red China, that is) in the dark ages of the Cold War before the age of McDonald's, MTV, and, certainly, personal computers. On the shores of Lake Michigan, he learned his letters and numbers and showed great promise in the world of academia (quickly achieving Red Bird reading status, after being put back as a Yellow Bird due to an unforeseen bout of chicken pox at the start of the school year). After earning many gold stars along with a few red ones, he graduated from Roosevelt School (named for Teddy, not that socialist Delano) in 1963.

During his stint at Thornridge High School in the perfectly boring Chicago suburb of Dolton, Illinois (named for Tom Dolton, the gunslinger?), he found great solace in Motown music (thanks, Phil!) and the drama department (to this day, he can recite every line from the play *Auntie Mame* verbatim). Bored with what passed for academic studies, he went through high school in three years. Looking back on these formative years, Greg was sure thankful for the great tunes and Auntie's philosophy, "Life's a banquet, kid, and some poor suckers are starving."

In 1966 (ah, the Sixties), he entered the University of Illinois at Urbana, Illinois, where he was greatly influenced by such deep philosophers as Abby Hoffman and Mahatma Gandhi. In the summer of 1968, he purchased his first pair of handmade sandals (from Glen, a hippie sandal maker who'd just returned from the Summer of Love in San Francisco).

During his college years, he became quite political. He holds the distinction of being one of a handful of men and women to attend the "camp-out" protest against women's dorm curfews (back then, not only were dorms not sexually integrated, but women were locked up at 11:00 p.m. on weeknights and 1:00 p.m. on weekends) and the last one to leave after all the others went back to their dorms. During his subsequent college years, he became a regular at the Red Herring coffee house, the veritable den of SDS activity on campus.

In addition to anti-war protests, Greg attended various and sundry classes in the Liberal Arts (such as they were in the last half of the 20th century). In the end, he took a major in Classical Studies (Ancient Greek and Latin) and a split minor in American History and French. (Greg showed a facility for foreign language, probably stemming from the fact that he's always had a big mouth.) In the course of his classical studies, he was introduced to his first computer-based training, learning basic Latin with a CAI program called (what else but) PLATO!

At the beginning of 1971 (January 12, in fact), Greg migrated west from Chicago to San Francisco (with flowers in his hair). Deciding that it was high time to get a skill so that he could find a real job, he enrolled in the Drafting and Design program at Laney College in Oakland. After that, he spent nine years working over a hot drafting table, drawing (by hand, mind you) orthographic and perspective plans for various and sundry engineering projects. During his last engineering gig, he worked with a proprietary CAD software package developed by Bechtel Engineering that not only generated the drawings but kept track of the materials actually needed to create the stuff.

In 1981, following his engineering career, Greg went back to school at San Francisco State University, this time to earn his secondary teaching credential. Upon completion of his teacher training, he bought one of the very first IBM personal computers (with 16K and a single 160K floppy disk!) to help with lesson preparation and student bookkeeping. He still vividly remembers poring over the premier issue of *PC World* for every piece of information that could teach him how to make peace with his blankety-blankety personal computer.

Instead of landing a teaching job at the high school or community college (because there weren't any at the time), Greg got a job with a small software outfit, ITM, that was creating an online database of software information (well ahead of its time). As part of his duties, Greg reviewed new software programs (such as Microsoft Word 1.0 and Lotus 1-2-3 Release 1) and wrote articles for business users.

After being laid off from this job right after the Christmas party in 1983 (the first of several layoffs from high-tech startups), Greg wrote his first computer book on word-processing software for Hayden Books (as a result of a proposal that he had helped to write while still employed full-time at ITM). After that, Greg worked in various software-evaluation-and-training jobs. After a few more high-tech software-testing-and-evaluation jobs in Silicon Valley, Greg turned to software training to get, as he put it, "the perspective of the poor schmoe at the end of the terminal." During the next three years, Greg trained a whole plethora of software programs to business users of all skill levels for several major independent software training companies in the San Francisco Bay area.

In the fall of 1986, he hooked up with Sybex, a local computer book publisher, for which he wrote his second computer training book, *Mastering SuperCalc*. And the rest, as they say, is history. To date, Greg is the author of over 30 books on using computer software, with the titles created under the ...*For Dummies* aegis for IDG being among his all-time favorites.

In mid-1993, Greg started a new multimedia publishing venture, Media of the Minds. As a multimedia developer, he hopes to enliven his future computer books by making them into true interactive learning experiences that will vastly enrich and improve the training of users of all skill levels.

ABOUT IDG BOOKS WORLDWIDE

VIII
WINNER
Eighth Annual
Computer Press
Awards 1992

IX
WINNER
Ninth Annual
Computer Press
Awards 1993

IDG
BOOKS
WORLDWIDE

Welcome to the world of IDG Books Worldwide.

IDG Books Worldwide, Inc., is a subsidiary of International Data Group, the world's largest publisher of computer-related information and the leading global provider of information services on information technology. IDG was founded more than 25 years ago and now employs more than 7,700 people worldwide. IDG publishes more than 250 computer publications in 67 countries (see listing below). More than 70 million people read one or more IDG publications each month.

Launched in 1990, IDG Books Worldwide is today the #1 publisher of best-selling computer books in the United States. We are proud to have received 8 awards from the Computer Press Association in recognition of editorial excellence and three from Computer Currents' First Annual Readers' Choice Awards, and our best-selling *...For Dummies®* series has more than 19 million copies in print with translations in 28 languages. IDG Books Worldwide, through a joint venture with IDG's Hi-Tech Beijing, became the first U.S. publisher to publish a computer book in the People's Republic of China. In record time, IDG Books Worldwide has become the first choice for millions of readers around the world who want to learn how to better manage their businesses.

Our mission is simple: Every one of our books is designed to bring extra value and skill-building instructions to the reader. Our books are written by experts who understand and care about our readers. The knowledge base of our editorial staff comes from years of experience in publishing, education, and journalism — experience which we use to produce books for the '90s. In short, we care about books, so we attract the best people. We devote special attention to details such as audience, interior design, use of icons, and illustrations. And because we use an efficient process of authoring, editing, and desktop publishing our books electronically, we can spend more time ensuring superior content and spend less time on the technicalities of making books.

You can count on our commitment to deliver high-quality books at competitive prices on topics you want to read about. At IDG Books Worldwide, we continue in the IDG tradition of delivering quality for more than 25 years. You'll find no better book on a subject than one from IDG Books Worldwide.

John J. Kilcullen

John Kilcullen
President and CEO
IDG Books Worldwide, Inc.

IDG Books Worldwide, Inc., is a subsidiary of International Data Group, the world's largest publisher of computer-related information and the leading global provider of information services on information technology. International Data Group publishes over 250 computer publications in 67 countries. Seventy million people read one or more International Data Group publications each month. International Data Group's publications include: **ARGENTINA:** Computerworld Argentina, GamePro, Infoworld, PC World Argentina; **AUSTRALIA:** Australian Macworld, Client/Server Journal, Computer Living, Computerworld, Digital News, Network World, PC World, Publishing Essentials, Reseller; **AUSTRIA:** Computerwelt, PC TEST; **BELARUS:** PC World Belarus; **BELGIUM:** Data News; **BRAZIL:** Annuário de Informática, Computerworld Brazil, Connections, Super Game Power, Macworld, PC World Brazil, Publish Brazil, SUPERGAME; **BULGARIA:** Computerworld Bulgaria, Networkworld/Bulgaria, PC & MacWorld Bulgaria; **CANADA:** CIO Canada, ComputerWorld Canada, InfoCanada, Network World Canada, Reseller World; **CHILE:** Computerworld Chile, GamePro, PC World Chile; **COLUMBIA:** Computerworld Colombia, GamePro, PC World Colombia; **COSTA RICA:** PC World Costa Rica/Nicaragua; **THE CZECH AND SLOVAK REPUBLICS:** Computerworld Czechoslovakia, Elektronika Czechoslovakia, PC World Czechoslovakia; **DENMARK:** Communications World, Computerworld Danmark, Macworld Danmark, PC World Danmark, PC World Danmark Supplements, TECH World; **DOMINICAN REPUBLIC:** PC World Republica Dominicana; **ECUADOR:** PC World Ecuador, GamePro; **EGYPT:** Computerworld Middle East, PC World Middle East; **EL SALVADOR:** PC World Centro America; **FINLAND:** MikroPC, Tietoverkko, Tietoviikko; **FRANCE:** Distributique, Golden, Info PC, Le Guide du Monde Informatique, Le Monde Informatique, Reseaux & Telecoms; **GERMANY:** Computer Business, Computerwoche, Computerwoche Extra, Computerwoche Focus, Electronic Entertainment, GamePro, I/M Information Management, Macwelt, PC Welt; **GREECE:** GamePro, Macworld & Publish; **GUATEMALA:** PC World Centro America; **HONDURAS:** PC World Centro America; **HONG KONG:** Computerworld Hong Kong, PCWorld Hong Kong, Publish in Asia; **HUNGARY:** ABCD CD-ROM, Computerworld Szamitastechnika, PC & Mac World Hungary, PC-X Magazine; **INDIA:** Computerworld India, PC World India, Publish in Asia; **INDONESIA:** InfoKomputer PC World, Komputek Computerworld, Publish in Asia; **IRELAND:** ComputerScope, PC Live!; **ISRAEL:** PC World 32 BIT, People & Computers; **ITALY:** Computerworld Italia, Computerworld Italia Special Editions, Lotus Italia, Macworld Italia, Networking Italia, PC Shopping, PC World Italia, PC World/Walt Disney; **JAPAN:** Macworld Japan, Nikkei Personal Computing, SunWorld Japan, Windows World Japan; **KENYA:** East African Computer News; **KOREA:** Hi-Tech Information/Computerworld, Macworld Korea, PC World Korea; **MACEDONIA:** PC World Macedonia; **MALAYSIA:** Computerworld Malaysia, PC World Malaysia, Publish in Asia; **MEXICO:** Computerworld Mexico, GamePro, Macworld, PC World Mexico; **MYANMAR:** PC World Myanmar; **NETHERLANDS:** Computable, Computer! Totaal, LAN Magazine, Macworld, Net Magazine; **NEW ZEALAND:** Computer Buyer, Computerworld New Zealand, MTB, Network World, PC World New Zealand; **NICARAGUA:** PC World Costa Rica/Nicaragua; **NIGERIA:** PC World Africa; **NORWAY:** Computerworld Norge, Computerworld Privat, CW Rapport Klient/Tjener, CW Rapport Nettverk & Telecom, CW Rapport Offentlig Sektor, IDG's KURSGUIDE, Macworld Norge, Multimedia World, PC World Ekspress, PC World Nettverk, PC World Norge, PC World's Produktguide, Windows Spesial; **PAKISTAN:** Computerworld Pakistan, PC World Pakistan; **PANAMA:** GamePro, PC World Panama; **PARAGUAY:** PC World Paraguay; **P. R. OF CHINA:** China Computerworld, China Infoworld, Computer & Communication, Electronic Product World, Electronics Today, Game Camp, PC World China, Popular Computer Week, Software World, Telecom Product World; **PERU:** Computerworld Peru, GamePro, PC World Profesional Peru, PC World Peru; **POLAND:** Computerworld Poland, Computerworld Special Report, Macworld, Networld, PC World Komputer; **PHILIPPINES:** Computerworld Philippines, PC Digest, Publish in Asia; **PORTUGAL:** Cerebro/PC World, Correio Informático/Computerworld, Mac•In/PC•In Portugal; **PUERTO RICO:** PC World Puerto Rico; **ROMANIA:** Computerworld Romania, PC World Romania, Telecom Romania; **RUSSIA:** Computerworld Rossiya, Network World Russia, PC World Russia; **SINGAPORE:** Computerworld Singapore, PC World Singapore, Publish in Asia; **SLOVENIA:** MONITOR; **SOUTH AFRICA:** Computing S.A., Network World S.A., Software World; **SPAIN:** Computerworld España, COMUNICACIONES WORLD, Dealer World, Macworld España, PC World España; **SWEDEN:** CAP&Design, Computer Sweden, Corporate Computing, MacWorld, Maxi Data, MikroDatorn, Nätverk & Kommunikation, PC/Aktiv, PC World, Windows World; **SWITZERLAND:** Computerworld Schweiz, Macworld Schweiz, PCtip; **TAIWAN:** Computerworld Taiwan, Macworld Taiwan, PC World Taiwan, Publish Taiwan, Windows World; **THAILAND:** Thai Computerworld, Publish in Asia; **TURKEY:** Computerworld Monitör, MACWORLD Turkiye, PC WORLD Turkiye; **UKRAINE:** Computerworld Kiev, Computers & Software Magazine, PC World Ukraine; **UNITED KINGDOM:** Acorn User, Amiga Action, Amiga Computing, Amiga, Appletalk, CD Powerplay, CD-ROM Now, Computing, Connexion, GamePro, Lotus Magazine, Macaction, Macworld, Open Computing, Parents and Computers, PC Home, PC Works, The WEB; **UNITED STATES:** Cable in the Classroom, CD Review, CIO Magazine, Computerworld, Computerworld Client/Server Journal, Digital Video Magazine, DOS World, Electronic, InfoWorld, I-Way, Macworld, Maximize, MULTIMEDIA WORLD, Network World, PC World, PUBLISH, SWATPro Magazine, Video Event, WebMaster; **URUGUAY:** PC World Uruguay; **VENEZUELA:** Computerworld Venezuela, GamePro, PC World Venezuela; and **VIETNAM:** PC World Vietnam   10/17/95

Dedication

To all my Excel students who taught me what should go in this book.

Acknowledgments

Let me take this opportunity to thank all of the wonderful people, both at IDG Books Worldwide and at Harvey & Associates, whose dedication and talent combined to get this book out into your hands in such great shape.

At IDG Books, I want to give special thanks to Colleen Rainsberger for her many great suggestions for this book and, especially, for her strong representation of my views to the development team (also known as *the committee*), Milissa Koloski and Diane Steele for their strong support and encouragement, and Diana Conover, Diane Giangrossi, and the production staff in Indianapolis.

At Harvey & Associates, many thanks go to Michael Bryant for working on updating the exercises for Excel for Windows 95 and to Carol Beebe for editing the manuscript to make sure that it was legible and for testing out the exercises in each lesson to ensure that the steps were complete, accurate, and (most importantly) clear to someone who had never used Excel for Windows 95 before.

Thanks to Access Technology for designing the *Dummies 101* series disk.

(The Publisher would like to give special thanks to Patrick J. McGovern, without whom this book would not have been possible.)

Credits

**Executive Vice President
and Publisher**
Milissa L. Koloski

Associate Publisher
Diane Graves Steele

Brand Manager
Judith A. Taylor

Editorial Managers
Kristin A. Cocks
Mary Corder

Product Development Manager
Mary Bednarek

Editorial Executive Assistant
Richard Graves

Editorial Assistants
Constance Carlisle
Chris Collins
Kevin Spencer

Assistant Acquisitions Editor
Gareth Hancock

Production Director
Beth Jenkins

Production Assistant
Jacalyn L. Pennywell

**Supervisor of
Project Coordination**
Cindy L. Phipps

Supervisor of Page Layout
Kathie S. Schnorr

Supervisor of Graphics and Design
Shelley Lea

Pre-Press Coordination
Tony Augsburger
Patricia R. Reynolds
Todd Klemme
Theresa Sánchez-Baker

Media/Archive Coordination
Leslie Popplewell
Melissa Stauffer
Jason Marcuson

Project Editor
Colleen Rainsberger

Editors
Diana R. Conover
Kelly Ewing
Diane Giangrossi

Technical Reviewer
Pamela Toliver

Project Coordinator
J. Tyler Connor

Graphics Coordination
Gina Scott
Angela F. Hunckler

Production Page Layout
Shawn Aylsworth
Brett Black
Cameron Booker
Linda Boyer
Dominique DeFelice
Maridee Ennis
Anna Rohrer

Proofreaders
Christine Sabooni
Carl Saff
Robert Springer

Indexer
Richard S. Shrout

Cover Design
Kavish + Kavish

Contents
at a Glance

Files at a Glance

ABC 123

Practice files

Practice folder
- Bo-Peep Client List
- Fuzy Wuzzy Media-Annual Sales
- MGE 1996 Qtr 1 Sales
- MGE Addresses (final)
- MGE Annual Sales
- Simon's Pie Shoppes 96 P&L
- Simon's Pie Shoppes Q1 96 Sales
- Sprat Diet Centers 96 P&L

Completed files

Unit 1 folder
- Data Series
- MGE Quarterly Sales

Unit 2 folder
- MGE Quarterly Sales (afmt)
- MGE Quarterly Sales (fmt)

Unit 3 folder
- Bo-Peep Client List (print)
- MGE Annual Sales (pg)

Lab 1 folder
- MGE Quarterly Sales (fmt)

Unit 4 folder
- MGE Quarterly Sales (afmt)
- Price Table (names)
- Price Table (values)
- Price Table

Unit 5 folder
- J&J Trauma Centers 96 P&L
- MGE 96 P&Ls
- MGE Quarterly Sales (notes)
- MGE Quarterly Sales (totals)
- Mother Hubbard 96 P&L
- Simon's Pie Shoppes Q1 96 Sales (sp)

Lab 2 folder
- MGE 96 P&Ls (totals)

Unit 6 folder
- MGE Quarterly Sales (chart)

Unit 7 folder
- Bo-Peep Client List (deleted)
- Bo-Peep Client List (edited)
- Bo-Peep Client List (filter rec)
- Bo-Peep Client List (filter state)
- Bo-Peep Client List (sort alpha)
- Bo-Peep Client List (sort date)
- Bo-Peep Client List (sort zip)
- MGE Addresses (filter name)
- MGE Addresses (filter state)
- MGE Addresses (filter zip)
- MGE Addresses (sort co)
- MGE Addresses (sort zip)
- MGE Addresses

Lab 3 folder
- MGE Quarterly Sales (chart)
- Bo-Peep Client List (filter date)

Table of Contents

Introduction

Welcome to *Dummies 101: Excel For Windows 95!*

Excel for Windows 95 is the latest and greatest version of the premier spreadsheet program available on IBM and IBM-compatible personal computers. In addition to its spreadsheet capabilities, Excel also includes easy-to-use charting and database management features.

Dummies 101: Excel For Windows 95 is a set of lessons that teach you the basics of using the Excel spreadsheet. The lessons in this book also teach you how to use the program to produce charts and maintain simple databases. This book presupposes no prior experience with Excel and only a modicum of experience with Windows 95. (You must at least know how to start your computer and get the Windows 95 Taskbar up and running.)

Each lesson contains hands-on exercises that you can complete at your own pace. In doing these exercises, you practice using all the fundamental Excel for Windows 95 features as you create projects of the kind that you can expect to be creating in actual work situations (you know, on the job, for big money!).

This book is organized into three parts. Part I covers the rock-bottom fundamentals of creating a spreadsheet in Excel. Part II extends your basic spreadsheet skills by teaching you how to edit the spreadsheet. Part III takes you beyond the spreadsheet by introducing you to charting spreadsheet data and building databases.

Each of the three parts contains between two and three units that are related in some way to each other. In turn, each unit consists of between two and six lessons. These lessons introduce the topic and features that you will learn by doing the accompanying exercises. Each lesson contains between one and six exercises that you are expected to complete before beginning the next lesson.

At the end of each unit, you will find a quiz that you can take to test your knowledge of the features that you learned in the unit and further exercises that you can use to try out the skills that you should have gained in that unit. At the end of each part, you will find a review section that summarizes the various tasks that you learned in the units in that part, a test that checks your knowledge of all the material covered in the units in that part, and a lab assignment that will test how well you can apply what you've learned to real-world tasks (tasks that you would be expected to perform on a real-world job).

Using This Book

Notes:

The *Dummies 101* series offers a self-paced, skill-based course for the "rest of us" who learn better by doing rather than hearing. As such, you are expected to use this book while you're at your computer with Excel running under Windows 95, and you are expected to complete *all* the exercises in each lesson before you go on to the next lesson. You must do the exercises in sequence because the exercises in each lesson build upon the knowledge and skills that you get in the lessons and exercises that have come before. If you skip a lesson or some of its exercises, you may well find yourself lost, confused, or otherwise unprepared for the stuff that you're doing in later exercises.

You should figure on spending a minimum of 50 to 60 hours in completing all the exercises and lab assignments in this book. Of course, you don't have to do all the exercises in one week-long sitting. (You'd have to be *really* jazzed on Excel or *really* desperate for work to do that!)

You can complete a lesson here and a lesson there, as time permits, until you've completed the whole book. You might also consider doing just the first two parts (the parts that teach all about using the Excel spreadsheet) during one initial, concentrated period, leaving the third part until time permits.

You can expect to start working with Excel *for real* after successfully completing the units in Part I. You can expect to perform reasonably well doing Excel spreadsheet work after successfully completing the units in Part II. The stuff in the units in Part III, while rounding out your Excel skills, can be completed at a later time when you have either the opportunity to continue your Excel studies or the need to know how to do nonspreadsheet tasks such as making charts and building databases.

After you have successfully completed this entire book with its 119 exercises, 7 unit quizzes, 3 lab assignments, and 3 part tests, I assure you that you'll possess a thorough fundamental knowledge of Excel for Windows 95 as well as all the essential skills necessary to use the program on a daily basis to produce, edit, and print basic spreadsheets, charts, and databases. In fact, many times you'll find that not only do you possess a more thorough basic knowledge and higher skill level than do your coworkers (who've never had the benefit of such a structured beginning course in Excel), but you also know more of the shortcuts than they do, and you are more aware of the most efficient ways to get essential tasks done with Excel.

A Word about Doing the Exercises

As you would expect in a hands-on course, the exercises in this book are full of step-by-step instructions. Sometimes, I will give you keyboard instructions for performing the steps, while other times I will give you mouse instructions. This mix-and-match approach is quite intentional because I want you to be familiar with both systems when you're learning a new feature. (After you start working with Excel for Windows 95 on your own, *you* can decide which approach feels more comfortable and decide if you want to stick with one over the other.)

When you see a keyboard instruction such as "press Ctrl+C" or "press Alt+F4" in a step, you need to understand that you keep the first key (the key listed before the plus sign — *Ctrl* or *Alt* in these examples) depressed while you press the second key (the *C* key or function key *F4* in these examples). Then, after both keys are depressed, you can release them — either at the same time or one at a time. What you don't want to do, however, is to try to depress both keys simultaneously because (more often than not) this action results in your hitting the second key before the first, which can end up giving you a far different result than was intended!

In terms of understanding mouse instructions, you only have to know a click, a double-click, and a secondary mouse click. (A secondary mouse click is often referred to as *right-clicking the mouse*.) You also must know how to drag through a selection with the mouse pointer (just keep the primary mouse button depressed while you move the mouse pointer through the cells or list of items to be selected).

Many steps will indicate that you need to type something in a text box or a cell of a spreadsheet. The stuff that you type will appear in *italic* type (which looks just like the word *italic* in this sentence). When you see italic type in a step, you type the letters, numbers, or whatever appears in italics *without* bothering to put that text into italics. In other words, the use of italics is just a convention to help indicate what characters you need to type. At the end of the step, your text should match that text shown in italics except that *your* text will be in regular type instead of italic type.

To help you in getting through the steps in an exercise, I've tried to use the text surrounding the steps to describe what's coming up next. Despite my best attempts to keep you informed, you may find places in the exercises when you're suddenly not sure that you're on the right track. Many times, this reaction occurs because you're anticipating a particular result at the end of a step, and the result that you're anticipating won't actually take place until you complete the very *next* step in the exercise.

Because this kind of self-doubt is such a common problem, I urge you to try to get through each entire exercise instead of second-guessing your present course and stopping at some step along the way. That way, even if you don't "see the magic" (or achieve the described result) after you finish — and you end up having to redo the exercise — you can at least eliminate not-having-hung-in-there-and-completed-all-the-steps-in-the-exercise as being the culprit.

Special Icons and Features in the Book

To help you identify different types of information in the text, the editors of this series have developed the following nifty features and icons that you'll soon be encountering:

Prerequisites   This area appears at the beginning of each unit, telling you what things you should have done before you start its lessons.

Progress Check   This area tells you what tasks you should be able to perform before you move on to the next lesson.

on the test

This icon indicates something that you really, really need to know before you start using Excel on your own (although the topic or feature may or may not actually come up on the unit quiz or the part test).

extra credit

This icon indicates a section that contains additional information that you might need to know when you start using Excel on your own.

heads up

This icon warns you about something that can go wrong unless you're really careful (so be careful!).

Getting Started: What You Need to Do

Before you begin using *Dummies 101: Excel For Windows 95*, you need to make sure that your computer is set up correctly and that you've installed the sample files that come on the disk found at the end of this book.

Before you can use these course materials, you must have Microsoft Excel 7.0 (running under Microsoft Windows 95) installed on your computer. It does not matter whether Excel 7.0 has been installed as part of the Microsoft Office for Windows 95 suite of programs or all by itself.

If you are running Excel 5.0 under Windows 95, you will not be able to use these course materials to their full advantage because Excel 5.0 cannot read the long filenames supported by Windows 95 (long filenames that are used both in the sample files and in the files that you create in the exercises) and will therefore render them as gibberish in the Open and Save As dialog boxes on your screen. My strong advice to you is to upgrade your copy of Microsoft Excel from Version 5.0 for Windows 3.1 to Version 7.0 for Windows 95 before you attempt to do any of the exercises contained in this book.

Installing the Dummies 101: Excel For Windows 95 sample files

If you've got Excel 7.0 installed on your computer under Windows 95, then all you have to do before you get started with the course is install the sample files located on the disk that comes with this book. As part of this installation process, you will create a personal folder where you will save the work that you create when doing the exercises in each lesson. When naming this personal folder, you are no longer limited to only eight characters, so type away! (I named mine *Greg Harvey*) If more than one person will be doing the course and using the same practice and completed files on your hard disk, be sure that each person chooses a unique name for his or her personal folder.

To perform this installation and create this personal folder, you simply follow these easy steps:

1 **Start your computer, click the Start button on the Windows 95 Taskbar, and click Run on the Start menu to open the Run dialog box.**

2 **Remove the disk from the back cover of this book and insert it into your floppy disk drive.**

3 **In the Open drop-down list box in the Run dialog box, type *a:\install* (or type *b:\install* if you put the disk in your B floppy drive), click File on the menu bar, and then click the OK button or press the Enter key.**

4 **Follow the directions on-screen.**

Accept the settings that the installation program suggests. If you have any problems, call the IDG Books Worldwide Customer Support number: 800-762-2974.

How to use the sample files

After the sample files are installed and you've created the personal folder (or *folders*, if more than one person will perform the exercises), you are ready to roll. The Files at a Glance page in this book shows you all the files and folders that are copied into the Excel 101 folder on your hard disk. You will use the practice files in the Practice folder to complete the exercises in the upcoming lessons.

You can use the completed files, copied into the various unit and lab folders, to check the work that you create when doing the exercises. To compare a file that you've created against its completed counterpart, you simply select the folder for that unit or lab assignment and then open the file in Excel (you'll learn how to open files in Excel in the first lesson in Unit 2).

You can also use these completed files to continue your Excel for Windows 95 studies in the event that the workbooks that you created in earlier exercises are lost. Rather than go back to Lesson 1-1 and re-create all your work, you can open whatever files are to be used in the lesson that you're about to do from the unit or lab folder that immediately precedes the lesson that you're about to do.

Later on, if you want, you can uninstall (remove) all the *Dummies 101* files. Follow the disk's on-screen instructions. Be careful, though: Once you choose the uninstall option, those files are gone, and the only way to get them back is to run the installation program again.

Notes:

Creating the Spreadsheet

Part 1

In this part . . .

Part I forms the core of the Excel for Windows 95 course. Part I is made up of three units that cover the absolute basics that you must have under your belt in order to have any claim to knowing the program. Unit 1 teaches you the art of creating new spreadsheets. Unit 2 teaches you the art of formatting spreadsheets. Unit 3 teaches you the skill of printing spreadsheets. Master the lessons in these three units, and you will be well on your way to learning how to use Excel for Windows 95.

Entering the
Spreadsheet Data

Objectives for This Unit

✓ Starting Excel with a blank workbook from either the taskbar or by using shortcuts

✓ Opening a blank workbook from within Excel

✓ Moving the cell pointer to any cell in the workbook

✓ Entering the different types of data in a cell

✓ Doing data entry within a preselected cell selection

✓ Totaling columns and rows of values with AutoSum

✓ Saving and naming your Excel workbook

✓ Entering a series of entries with AutoFill

✓ Creating a custom AutoFill list

Prerequisites

▶ Microsoft Excel for Windows 95 installed on hard disk

▶ Excel 101 folder created on hard disk to store practice files

▶ Personal folder created in Excel 101 folder (such as c:\Excel 101\gregh) to store the practice workbooks you create

As boring and mundane as the topic of data entry may sound at first, no single topic is more important to your mastery of the program. When you build a new spreadsheet, the vast majority of the time is consumed by just getting the darned data entered into your spreadsheet.

The goal of Unit 1 is to make you comfortable doing all types of data entry in a new worksheet. After studying this unit, you should be able to open a blank workbook in Excel and begin entering the data required by your new spreadsheet. You should also be able to save that spreadsheet data in a disk file so that you'll have access to it in future Excel work sessions.

Lesson 1-1

Starting Excel and Opening a New Workbook

workbook is the
basic document or
file in Excel. Each
new workbook you
open contains 16
blank worksheets
that you can use in
creating your new
spreadsheet

Before you can learn how to enter data in a new spreadsheet, you have to learn how to open a new workbook to contain that spreadsheet. Every time you start Excel, the program automatically opens a brand new, completely blank *workbook* where you can start creating your new spreadsheet.

Because you have to know how to start Excel before you can do anything with the program, you may as well start out by learning the different methods you can use to open a new Excel workbook. You can start Excel from three possible places in Windows 95: the Taskbar, the Microsoft Office Shortcut Bar, or from an Excel shortcut that you can create on your desktop. However, in any case, you need to have your computer turned on and the Windows 95 desktop on your computer screen before you can start Excel.

Exercise 1-1: Starting Excel from the Taskbar

Assuming that Windows 95 is up and running and the Taskbar is displayed on your desktop, start Excel with a new workbook by following these steps:

1 **Click the Start button on the Taskbar; then move the mouse pointer up until you highlight Programs on the Start menu.**

2 **Move the mouse pointer over and down until you highlight Microsoft Excel on the continuation menu; then click to start Excel.**

Excel will start loading, during which time you see the Microsoft Excel for Windows 95 splash screen. When the program finishes loading, Excel appears with a blank workbook called Book1, as shown in Figure 1-1.

Starting Excel with the Microsoft Office Shortcut Bar

If your computer has Microsoft Office for Windows 95 installed and the Microsoft Office toolbar is displayed at the top of the Windows desktop (as shown in Figure 1-2), you can start Excel with a new workbook just by clicking the Microsoft Excel button (the one with the italicized XL icon on it).

If you don't see the Microsoft Excel button on the Microsoft Office Shortcut Bar, you can add it by clicking the Office Logo button located on the left end of the Shortcut bar and then choosing the Customize command on its shortcut menu. Next, click the Buttons tab of the Customize dialog box. A list box appears with the programs that you can add or remove from the Shortcut Bar. Locate the Microsoft Excel check box and click it before you click OK or press Enter. Windows 95 then adds the Microsoft Excel button to the Office Shortcut Bar, and you can simply click this button to begin starting Excel with a new workbook.

Excel button on
Microsoft Office
Shortcut Bar

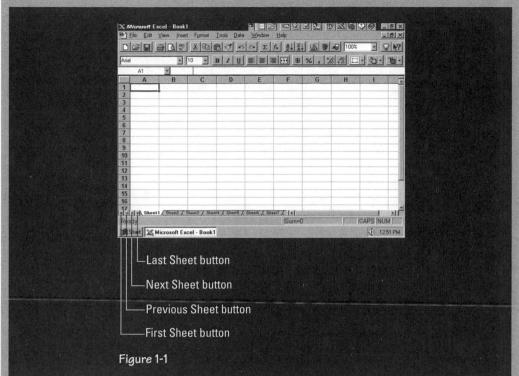

Last Sheet button

Next Sheet button

Previous Sheet button

First Sheet button

Figure 1-1

Figure 1-1: When you start Excel, you get a new workbook named Book1.

Notes:

Starting Excel by creating an Excel shortcut

Most of the time, you will start Excel from the Taskbar because the Taskbar automatically appears when you first start Windows 95. However, some occasions may arise (especially if you are not using Microsoft Office and, thus, the Office Shortcut Bar) when you may find starting Excel from a shortcut that you have created on your desktop very convenient.

Exercise 1-2: Creating an Excel shortcut

To create an Excel shortcut on your desktop, do this little exercise:

1 **If you started Excel from the Taskbar, exit Excel by holding down the Alt key as you press function key F4 (this process is normally written as Alt+F4).**

To create an Excel shortcut, you must first find the Excel program file on your hard disk.

2 **Click the Start button on the Taskbar and move the mouse pointer up until you highlight Find on the Start menu.**

3 **Move the mouse pointer to highlight Files or Folders from the Find continuation menu and click to open the Find dialog box.**

Next, you need to locate the Excel program called EXCEL.EXE on your hard disk. This file appears as Excel (without the .*EXE*) in the Find dialog box. (The file EXCEL.EXE is opened whenever you double-click the Microsoft Excel program icon in the Taskbar or Microsoft Office Shortcut Bar.)

Figure 1-2: Click the Microsoft Excel button to start the program from Microsoft Office Shortcut Bar.

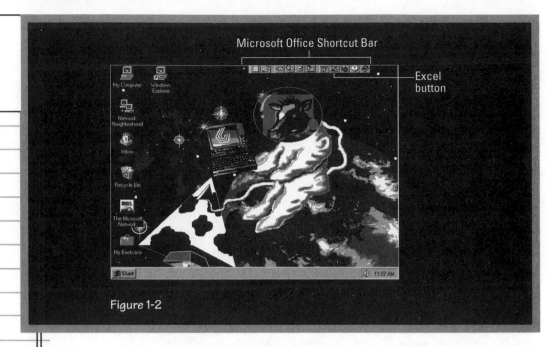

Figure 1-2

Notes:

4 **Type *excel.exe* in the Named list box and click Find Now or press Enter.**

Windows 95 searches your hard disk and locates the Excel program file. The Excel icon appears in a list box of the Find dialog box along with other information about this file. You can be sure that you have the right file by checking that *Application* is listed in the Type column in this list box.

5 **Click the Excel icon in the list box and drag it to your desktop; then click the Close button on the Find dialog box to close the Find dialog box.**

Your new Shortcut to Excel icon appears on the desktop.

6 **Double-click the Shortcut to Excel icon on the desktop to open Excel.**

Starting Excel by opening an existing workbook

You can open Excel along with an existing Excel workbook file by locating the workbook's file icon with the Windows Explorer and then double-clicking its icon. (You can always tell when you're looking at an Excel workbook file icon in the Windows Explorer list because the Excel workbook file icon has a tiny Excel logo on its left side.)

When you double-click a workbook file icon, Windows first checks to see whether Excel is already running before it opens the file. If the program is not running, Windows automatically opens Excel before loading the workbook and displaying it on your screen.

Opening a new workbook within Excel

Every time that you open Excel, the program automatically opens a new workbook with 16 blank worksheets, any of which you can use in creating your new spreadsheet. If you need to open a new workbook from within Excel, you can do so by any of the following ways:

> ◆ Click the New Workbook button on the Standard toolbar.
>
> ◆ Choose <u>N</u>ew on the <u>F</u>ile pull-down menu.
>
> ◆ Press the shortcut keys Ctrl+N.

When you open a new workbook from within Excel, the program gives the new workbook a temporary filename using the next available number.

Exercise 1-3: Opening a bunch of blank workbooks

Now it's time to practice using the various methods for opening new workbooks in Excel with this exercise:

1 **With Book1 active in Excel, click the New Workbook button on the Standard toolbar to open a second workbook.**

Excel responds by opening a second new, blank workbook called Book2.

2 **Click the <u>F</u>ile menu and then click <u>N</u>ew on the pull-down menu.**

Doing this opens the New dialog box with the Workbook icon selected on the General tab.

3 **Click OK (or press Enter) to close the New dialog box and open another workbook.**

Excel responds by opening another new, blank workbook with the temporary name of Book3.

Press Ctrl+N to open yet a fourth workbook.

Pressing Ctrl+N also opens the New dialog box with the Workbook icon on the General tab selected.

Click OK or press Enter to open yet another blank workbook.

Excel responds by opening another new, blank workbook with the temporary name of Book4.

Exercise 1-4: Switching between the open workbooks

Excel makes switching between the workbooks you have open easy with the Window pull-down menu. To see how to switch from one workbook to another, try the following exercise:

1 **Switch to Book2 by clicking the <u>W</u>indow menu and then clicking the <u>3</u> Book2 menu option near the bottom of the menu.**

When you choose this option, Excel switches to the first new workbook you opened (indicated by the appearance of Book2 on the program title bar).

2 **Switch to Book3 by pressing Alt+W to open the <u>W</u>indow menu and then pressing 2 to choose the <u>2</u> Book 3 option.**

Doing this switches to the second new workbook you opened, indicated by the appearance of Book3 on the program title bar.

New Workbook button

Notes:

Progress Check

If you can do the following, you've mastered this lesson:

❑ Start Excel from the Windows Taskbar.

❑ Open a new workbook in Excel.

❑ Switch between the open workbooks.

❑ Close the open workbooks.

3 **Switch to Book1 by clicking the <u>W</u>indow menu to open it and then pressing 4 to choose the <u>4</u> Book 1 option.**

Doing this switches to the first new workbook, the workbook that automatically opened when you started Excel (indicated by the appearance of Book1 on the program title bar).

You can also switch between open workbooks by pressing Ctrl+F6 or by pressing Ctrl+Shift+F6. Pressing Ctrl+F6 activates the next open workbook down in the list shown on the Window pull-down menu (or the workbook at the very top of this list when the workbook at the bottom is the one currently selected). Pressing Ctrl+Shift+F6 activates the previously open workbook in the list (or the workbook at the very bottom of this list when the workbook at the top is the one currently selected).

Closing workbooks

Before you leave Lesson 1-1 behind, you should learn to close the workbooks that you open up. As with almost everything else in Excel, you can close the open workbooks in a number of ways:

▶ Click <u>C</u>lose on the <u>F</u>ile pull-down menu.

▶ Press Ctrl+W.

▶ Double-click the workbook window's Control menu (the little Excel icon button that's immediately to the left of <u>F</u>ile on the menu bar when the workbook is full size or on the workbook title bar to the left of the workbook title when the window is less than full size).

▶ Press Ctrl+F4.

Exercise 1-5: Closing up the open workbooks

The following exercise gives you practice with most of the methods for closing the workbooks that you just learned how to open up:

1 **Use the <u>W</u>indow pull-down menu to switch to Book4.**

2 **Click the <u>F</u>ile menu; then click the <u>C</u>lose command to close this workbook.**

Excel closes Book4, revealing Book1. If you had made any changes to the worksheets in Book4, Excel would have prompted you to save these changes before it had closed this workbook.

3 **Use the Window pull-down menu to switch to Book3.**

4 **Press Ctrl+F4 to close the Book3 workbook.**

As soon as you press this shortcut combination, Excel immediately closes Book3, which reveals Book1 underneath it.

5 **Use the Windows pull-down menu to switch to Book2.**

6 **Press Ctrl+W to close Book2.**

Doing this closes the Book2 workbook and reveals the very last open workbook, Book1, which Excel automatically opened for you when you started the program. You should keep this workbook open as you work through the exercises in Lesson 1-2.

Moving the Cell Pointer   Lesson 1-2

All right! Now that you're an expert at opening and closing new workbooks (to say nothing of switching between them), you're ready to move on to the fascinating topic of how to move around and between the worksheets of a workbook. Each worksheet of the workbook (and remember that 16 worksheets are included in each new workbook) is divided by column and row gridlines into little boxes formally known as *cells*. You enter all your spreadsheet data into these cells.

on the test

The layout of your final spreadsheet is determined by which data you put into which cells of the worksheet. As you're about to discover, in order to put specific data into a particular cell, you must first make that cell the *current* or *active* cell in the worksheet. To activate a cell, put the *cell pointer* in the cell that's about to be blessed with your data.

To help you keep track of your position in the worksheet, Excel displays a frame on the left side and on the top of the workbook that identifies each column and row. Columns of the worksheet are identified by letters of the alphabet (of which only columns A through I are displayed when you first open a new workbook). Rows of the worksheet are identified by numbers (of which only rows 1 through 18 are shown when you first open a new workbook, depending on your screen size). Each cell of the worksheet is given a unique *cell address* made up of its column letter followed by its row number (such as cell A1, A2, B1, and so on).

You can immediately tell which cell is current in a worksheet by looking at the cell-address indicator that appears at the far left of the *formula bar,* which is located directly above the frame that has the column-letter identifications. As you move the cell pointer to a new cell, this cell-address indicator changes to show the address of the current cell.

Moving the cell pointer with the mouse

In Excel, you can move the cell pointer (and thereby select a new cell) either with the mouse or with the keyboard. To select a new cell with the mouse, simply position the mouse pointer (which appears as a white cross within the worksheet) somewhere on the cell and click the primary mouse button. Excel responds by repositioning the mouse pointer in the cell that you clicked, and the cell-address indicator is updated with the new current cell address.

Exercise 1-6: Changing the active cell with the mouse

Try selecting cells with the mouse by doing the following exercise:

1 **Make cell E2 current by positioning the white-cross mouse pointer in row 2 of column E and then clicking the primary mouse button.**

As soon as you click the mouse, the cell pointer appears in the cell of the second row of column E, and the cell-address indicator reads E2.

2 **Next, make cell D12 current by positioning the white-cross mouse pointer in row 12 of column D and then clicking the primary mouse button.**

cell with the cell pointer is always the current or active cell

cell address is made up of the letters of the cell's column followed by the number of the cell's row

☒

white-cross mouse pointer

Notes:

As soon as you click the mouse, the cell pointer appears in the cell of the twelfth row of column D, and the cell-address indicator reads D12.

3 **Now, make cell I15 active by positioning the white-cross mouse pointer in row 15 of column I and then clicking its cell.**

As soon as you click the mouse, the cell pointer appears in the cell of the fifteenth row of column I, and the cell-address indicator reads I15.

Scrolling the worksheet

The only problem with using the mouse to select cells is that the cell that you want to make active must be visible on-screen before you can click it. For example, if I were to ask you to make cell T30 current with the mouse, you'd be stuck because you can't position the white-cross pointer in the thirtieth row of column T when neither row 30 nor column T are visible on-screen.

To bring new portions of the worksheet into view on-screen, you can use the horizontal and vertical *scroll bars* located on the right and bottom of the workbook window. These scroll bars have *scroll arrows* pointing in opposite directions and *scroll boxes* that indicate the relative position of the view of the screen currently displayed. To scroll new *rows* of the worksheet into view, you can either drag the scroll box in the vertical scroll bar up and down, or you can click the up- and down-arrow scroll buttons. To scroll new *columns* of the worksheet into view, you can drag the scroll box in the horizontal scroll bar to the left and right, or you can click the left- and right-arrow scroll buttons.

In Excel for Windows 95, the scroll box in each scroll bar is dynamic so that if you hold down the down-arrow button in the vertical scroll bar or the right-arrow scroll button in the horizontal scroll bar, the scroll box becomes smaller and smaller as you whiz through more and more worksheet rows and columns. After you've covered more territory (and the scroll boxes have become smaller), you can move back quickly from your present position to the top or left edge of the worksheet by dragging the scroll box.

To help you keep your place as you drag the scroll box, Excel for Windows 95 uses a new feature called *scroll tips*. As you drag the scroll box in either the vertical or horizontal scroll bar, a small scroll-tips window pops up in the worksheet area. This scroll-tips window keeps you informed of the first row or column address that will appear at the top or left edge of the worksheet when you release the mouse button.

Exercise 1-7: Selecting cells in hidden parts of the worksheet

Using the scroll bars can take some getting used to, so here's a little exercise designed to get you accustomed to using the mouse to select cells that are not automatically displayed when you first open a new workbook:

1 **Position the mouse pointer on the right-arrow scroll button in the horizontal scroll bar (where the mouse pointer assumes the arrowhead shape); then click the primary mouse button and hold it down. Release the mouse button as soon as you can see columns AA, AB, and AC on your screen.**

If columns AA, AB, and AC go whizzing by and off the screen before you know what hit you, just click the left-arrow scroll button and hold the mouse button down until these columns come back into view.

Note two things before you go on to the next step. First, notice that Excel has to double up on the column letters after it reaches column Z (thus the AA, AB, AC, and so on). Second, notice that the cell pointer is nowhere to be found on the screen. (It's still back in cell I15, which is the last cell that you selected.)

2 **Select cell AB7 by clicking its cell on the screen.**

The cell pointer appears in the cell that you clicked, and (if it was the right cell) cell address AB7 appears in the cell-address indicator on the formula bar.

Next, you can scroll down to bring up rows that are further down in the worksheet.

3 **Position the mouse pointer on the down-arrow scroll button in the vertical scroll bar (where the mouse pointer assumes the arrow-head shape); then click the primary mouse button and hold it down. When row 77 appears as the first row in the workbook window, release the mouse button to stop the vertical scrolling.**

Did you notice the cell pointer floating up and off the workbook window as you did the vertical scrolling? To select a new cell in this section of the worksheet, you would still need to reposition the cell pointer by clicking its cell with the mouse pointer.

4 **Make cell AE86 current by clicking its cell in the workbook window.**

As soon as you click this cell, the cell pointer magically appears in the worksheet, and the cell address (AE86) appears at the beginning of the formula bar.

5 **To make cell A1 active again, first drag the vertical scroll box up until Row:1 appears in the scroll-tips window; then drag the horizontal scroll box left until Column:A appears in the scroll-tips window; and finally, click this first cell of the worksheet.**

Moving the cell pointer with the keyboard

Scrolling is great for bringing new parts of your spreadsheet into view on-screen. However, you still have to remember to click a cell in the newly visible area if you want to make that cell active. By repositioning the cell pointer with the keyboard, you can combine the act of making new cells active and scrolling new sections of the worksheet into view.

Table 1-1 gives you a rundown on how the most common cursor keys move the cell pointer. After you've had a chance to look over the keystrokes in this table, you can practice using these keystrokes in Exercise 1-8.

when you scroll to a new section of the worksheet, Excel leaves the cell pointer behind

Notes:

Table 1-1	Keys for Moving the Cell Pointer
Key	**Cell Pointer Moves To**
→ or Tab	Cell to the immediate right
← or Shift+Tab	Cell to the immediate left
↑	Cell up one row
↓	Cell down one row
Home	Cell in column A of the current row
Ctrl+Home	First cell (A1) of the worksheet
Ctrl+End or End, Home	Cell in the worksheet at the intersection of last column that has any data in it and last row that has any data in it (for example, the last cell of the so-called *active area* of the worksheet)
PgUp	Cell one screenful up in the same column
PgDn	Cell one screenful down in the same column
Ctrl+→ or End, →	First occupied cell to the right in the same row that is either preceded or followed by a blank cell
Ctrl+← or End, ←	First occupied cell to the left in the same row that is either followed or preceded by a blank cell
Ctrl+↑ or End, ↑	First occupied cell above in the same column that is either followed or preceded by a blank cell
Ctrl+↓ or End, ↓	First occupied cell below in the same column that is either preceded or followed by a blank cell
Ctrl+PgUp	Last occupied cell in the next worksheet of the workbook
Ctrl+PgDn	Last occupied cell in the previous worksheet of the workbook

Exercise 1-8: Using the keyboard to move a cell at a time

In this exercise, you practice moving the cell pointer around and between empty worksheets. Note that some of the keystrokes outlined in Table 1-1 work only when you're dealing with a worksheet that contains spreadsheet data. You can practice using these keys later on, after you've had a chance to do some data entry so that you have data to work with.

Before you attempt this exercise, make sure that the cell pointer is once again in cell A1.

1 Make cell C3 active by pressing the → key twice to move to cell C1 and the ↓ key twice to move to cell C3.

As you press the → and ↓ keys, keep your eye on the cell-address indicator. Notice how the cell-address indicator is updated each time you press one of these keys. Note also that, to get to cell C3 from cell A1, you could just as well have pressed the ↓ key twice to move to cell A3 and then the → key twice to reach cell C3.

2 Make cell F3 current by pressing the Tab key three times.

Pressing the Tab key is equivalent to pressing the → key to move the cell pointer to the right one cell at a time.

3 Make cell D3 current by holding the Shift key down while you press the Tab key twice.

Pressing Tab while the Shift key is held down (sometimes referred to as the *Backtab key combo*) is equivalent to pressing the ← key to move the cell pointer to the left, one cell at time.

4 Make cell D25 active by holding down the ↓ key until the cell pointer reaches this cell.

If you overshoot row 25 as you zoom down column D (which you probably will, unless you're tapping the ↓ key), just press the ↑ key until you get back up to the right cell.

Exercise 1-9: Using the keyboard to make larger moves

Now that you've had a chance to practice moving one cell at a time with the keyboard, it's time to practice with keys that make bigger jumps in the worksheet:

1 Make cell A25 current by pressing the Home key on the cursor keypad.

Pressing the Home key moves the cell pointer to the very beginning of the row that it's in, no matter how far right in the row the cell pointer happens to be.

Oddly enough, pressing the End key does not move the cell pointer to the end of its row. In Excel (as in Lotus 1-2-3), pressing the End key puts the program into a special END mode in which the program dutifully waits for you to press one of the four arrow keys on the cursor keypad.

When you press an arrow key after pressing the End key, Excel jumps the cell pointer to the first cell that has something in it and is either preceded or followed by a blank cell. In Unit 2, you get a chance to see how valuable this feature is when you need to move quickly from one end of a table of data to another.

Just know, for now, that if you press the End key and then press an arrow key, Excel jumps the cell pointer to the very boundary of the worksheet in the direction of the arrow key. (Excel makes this jump because no occupied cell is available for the pointer to land on before it reaches the very edge of the worksheet.) You can use this End-plus-the-arrow-keys trick to see how large a worksheet really is.

2 Move the cell pointer to the last column of the worksheet in row 25 by pressing (*and then releasing*) the End key *before* pressing the → key.

Wow! Cell IV25 should now be the active cell, and you should see a lot of unfamiliar and slightly strange columns (like IN, IO, IP, IQ, and such). Column IV, at the extreme far-right edge of the Excel worksheet, is the 256th column (using the double-letter system for identifying columns beyond column Z).

hold down an arrow key to whiz through the cells in one direction; tap the arrow key to fine-tune the cell pointer's position

Next, go ahead and use End plus the ↓ key to find out how many total rows are in the worksheet.

3 **Move the cell pointer to the last row of the worksheet in column IV by pressing (*and then releasing*) the End key *before* pressing the ↓ key.**

Whew! Cell IV16384 should now be the current cell. Cell IV16384 just happens to be the address of the very last cell of any worksheet you work with in Excel. And for you trivia lovers, a worksheet with 256 columns (column A through IV) and 16,384 rows gives you a total of 4,194,304 cells to work with!

As you may have noticed in looking over the keystrokes in Table 1-1 (you did look them over, didn't you?), Excel offers an alternative to pressing and releasing the End key before pressing an arrow key to scurry from one end of a table of data to the other (or to the very ends of the worksheet, in this case). Excel's alternative involves pressing the Ctrl key *as* you press an arrow key. I prefer the Ctrl-plus-arrow-key method to the End-then-arrow-key method because the former feels smoother to me.

Try this method for yourself in the next step as you jump from column IV back to column A in row 16,384.

4 **Move the cell pointer directly to cell A16384 by pressing *and holding down* the Ctrl key until you've had a chance to press (*and release*) the ← key.**

Hey, that was slick. Get more practice with this method by taking a ride around the four corners of the worksheet.

5 **Hold down the Ctrl key and then press ↑ to move to cell A1. Next, continue to hold down the Ctrl key as you press the → key to move to cell IV1, the ↓ key to move to cell IV16384, and finally, the ← key to move once again to cell A16384.**

Now you're having fun! Try this once-around-the-worksheet tour again, but this time take a counterclockwise tour.

6 **Hold down the Ctrl key and then press → to move to cell IV16384. Next, continue to hold down the Ctrl key as you press the ↑ key to move to cell IV1, the ← key to move to cell A1, and finally, the ↓ to move back down to cell A16384.**

You'll want to know one more keystroke combo as you work with Excel: Ctrl+Home. These two little keystrokes move the cell pointer back to cell A1 (the *home cell*) from any other cell in the worksheet, just like that!

7 **Move the cell pointer to cell A1 by pressing and holding down the Ctrl key until you've had a chance to press and release the Home key.**

And there you are: back home in cell A1, all safe and sound.

Moving the cell pointer with the Go To feature

Scrolling the worksheet (either with the scroll bars or with the keystrokes you've just learned) is fine if you're just *cruising* the worksheet in search of spreadsheet data whose cell addresses are not yet known. I have a much better way to get to where you want to go in a worksheet when you *do* know the address of the cells that hold this data. You can use the Go To feature. This feature can be accessed either by selecting the Go To command on the Edit pull-down menu (not recommended) or by pressing the function key F5 (highly recommended).

Either way, Excel responds by displaying the Go To dialog box (similar to the one shown in Figure 1-3). Enter the address of the cell to which you want to send the cell pointer in the Go To dialog box's Reference text box. As soon as you click the OK button or press Enter (highly recommended), Excel jumps the cell pointer to whatever address it finds in that Reference text box.

Exercise 1-10: Making a cell active with Go To

All you need is just a little practice with the Go To feature to see how it enables you to jump from one cell to any other in the worksheet with ease.

1 **Make cell F700 the current one by pressing F5 and then typing *f700* in the Reference text box of the Go To dialog box before you press Enter.**

Boom! Assuming that you typed *f700* (using zero, and not the letter O), the cell-address indicator on the formula bar should have read F700 almost immediately after you pressed the Enter key. Just think how long it would have taken to scroll to this place in the worksheet either with the scroll bars or with the nifty cell-pointer keystrokes that you've learned!

That jump was so easy, why don't you try it again, this time moving the cell pointer to cell BA2500.

2 **Make cell BA2500 the active cell by pressing F5 again. This time type *ba2500* in the Reference text box of the Go To dialog box before you press Enter.**

You may have noticed that, when you opened the Go To dialog box with F5 this time, the Reference text box contained the cell reference $A$1. (This display is Excel's way of noting the cell that you came from to get to cell F700. The dollar signs in the address denote an *unchanging* or *absolute address* rather than big money.) As soon as you start typing the new cell address (ba2500) in the Reference text box, the old $A$1 cell address in this text box is completely replaced by the characters that you type.

If you open the Go To dialog box again (which is just what I'm going to have you do in Step 3), you can see the cell address $F$700 in the Reference text box, and $F$700 is also listed right below $A$1 in the Go to list box.

Because Excel keeps adding the address of the cell you just came from to the Reference text box of the Go To dialog box, you can return to the cell from whence thou came simply by pressing Enter. Try it.

3 **Return the cell pointer to cell F700 by pressing F5 to open the Go To dialog box and then immediately pressing the Enter key.**

Bam! No sooner do you press Enter than you are back in cell F700. And guess what? Excel added cell address $BA$2500 to the Reference text box in the Go To dialog box so that you can return to the place from which you came just by pressing F5 and Enter. Try it.

4 **Return the cell pointer to cell BA2500 by pressing F5 (to open the Go To dialog box) and then immediately pressing Enter.**

You've now used the Go To dialog box to set up a relay between cell F700 and cell BA2500. To jump back and forth between these cells, all you need to do is press F5 and Enter.

5 **Press F5 and Enter to jump to cell F700; then immediately press F5 and Enter again to return to cell BA2500.**

Notes:

Figure 1-3: Press F5 to move the cell pointer with the Go To dialog box.

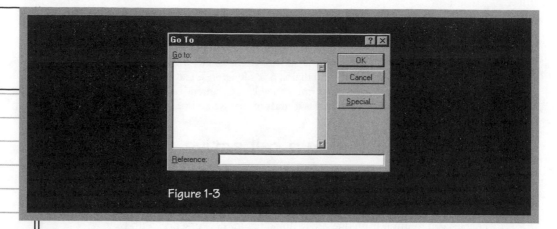

Figure 1-3

Just like playing Ping-Pong, you can jump between these two cell addresses forever. Although doing this seems like a pretty mindless activity now (in an empty worksheet), remember this handy little technique should you need to jump back and forth between two tables of data located in different parts of the worksheet (so that you can, for example, compare information on the two separate tables).

6 **Return the cell pointer back home to cell A1 by pressing Ctrl+Home.**

Moving between the sheets of the workbook

As you learned at the beginning of this unit, each workbook that you open contains 16 blank worksheets, and each worksheet has 256 columns and 16,384 rows. To make moving from worksheet to worksheet easy, each workbook window is equipped with *sheet tabs* (which show the number of the worksheet as Sheet1, Sheet2, and so on) and *sheet tab scrolling buttons*. The sheet tabs are located at the bottom of the workbook window, immediately left of the horizontal scroll bar. The sheet tab scrolling buttons are located immediately left of the sheet tabs.

To show you which worksheet is active (current), Excel makes the active worksheet's sheet tab white and displays that worksheet's number in bold type. The white sheet tab appears to be part of the active worksheet (in contrast to the gray sheet tabs of the nonactive worksheets that appear as though they're behind the active sheet). To make a new worksheet active, you click its sheet tab. Excel then transforms the clicked sheet tab from gray to white, displays its sheet number in bold, and displays its worksheet with all its spreadsheet data in the workbook window. After a worksheet becomes active, you can use any of the techniques that you've learned in this lesson to move the cell pointer to the cells that require data entry or editing.

If the tab for the worksheet that you want to use is not displayed at the bottom of the workbook window, you can use the sheet tab scrolling buttons to bring its tab into view. Table 1-2 shows you the four sheet tab scrolling buttons and indicates what each button does when it is clicked.

Table 1-2	The Sheet Tab Scrolling Buttons
Button	**Function**
⏮	Scrolls to first Sheet1 tab (or whatever sheet happens to be the first one in your workbook)
◀	Scrolls the previous sheet tab into view
▶	Scrolls the next sheet tab into view
⏭	Scrolls to Sheet16 tab (or whatever sheet happens to be the last one in your workbook)

Note that scrolling new sheet tabs into view is not the same as making that sheet active. To select a new worksheet and make it active, you must *still* click its sheet tab after scrolling it into view.

Instead of scrolling a worksheet's tab into view and then clicking the tab to make the worksheet active, you can press Ctrl+PgDn to select the next worksheet or Ctrl+PgUp to select the previous worksheet. When you use these keystrokes, Excel activates each worksheet in succession, positioning the cell pointer in the cell that it occupied the last time that you made that worksheet current.

Finally, if you click the secondary mouse button on any of the four sheet tab scrolling buttons, a context menu (listing all the sheets in the workbook) appears. Click the desired sheet name to activate it.

☑ **Progress Check**

If you can do the following, you've mastered this lesson:

❑ Make new cells current with the mouse.

❑ Make new cells current with the keyboard.

❑ Use the Go To feature to make a new cell current.

❑ Move back and forth between the sheets of your workbook.

Adding Data to a Cell   Lesson 1-3

Now that you're an expert on moving the cell pointer to the cells where you want to place your spreadsheet data, you're ready to learn how to enter that data. As I told you in Lesson 1-2, the cell pointer must be in the cell where you want the data to appear *before* you start to enter the data. Here's another precondition to data entry: The program must be in Ready mode (as evidenced by the word *Ready* at the far left of the status bar — the lowest bar in the Excel program window, just above the Windows 95 Taskbar). This precondition is not often a problem because the program stays in Ready mode *unless* you select some sort of Excel command *or* the program is busy doing something for you. Should you ever have difficulty in making a cell entry, keep in the back of your mind that the problem could be that Excel is no longer in Ready mode, so Excel is not ready to accept your data entry. In this situation, you'll find that pressing Esc to cancel out of the other modes is usually the way to return the program to the Ready condition.

Excel, like other data processing computer programs, differentiates between two fundamental types of data that you can enter in the current cell: *text* (also known as *labels*) and *values*.

Text, as you would imagine, is used for spreadsheet headings as well as nonnumeric data spreadsheet entries (such as product descriptions, client names, and the like). Values are used for any numeric entries in the spreadsheet (such as monthly income, quarterly losses, and the like).

before you enter data, check to see if the cell pointer is in the right cell and that the status bar reads Ready

Normally, letters or a combination of punctuation, letters, and (in some cases) numbers compose text. For example, if you were to enter item numbers like AVI478, AVI479, and AVI480, Excel would treat them as text entries. Values can be composed of whole numbers between 0 and 9 (known as *digits*) or a combination of digits and certain allowable punctuation marks, such as a hyphen (-) to indicate a negative value, a period (.) to indicate a decimal point, a comma (,) to separate thousands, and a dollar sign ($) to signify moolah, *dinero*, you know, bucks.

One more thing about the two types of Excel entries: When you make a *text* entry in a cell, Excel automatically aligns the entry with the left edge of the cell; whereas when you enter a *value* in a cell, Excel aligns it with the right edge of the cell. This default left-cell alignment versus right-cell alignment of text and values has interesting repercussions that you'll discover as you perform the exercises in this lesson.

Exercise 1-11: Entering the title for the spreadsheet

In this and the following exercise, you practice making the most common types of text entries (that is, entering the headings required by your spreadsheet). With this exercise, you start the process of creating a simple worksheet that charts the first quarter sales for a (highly) fictional company called Mother Goose Enterprises Incorporated. This corporation encompasses a number of interesting companies, such as Jack Sprat Diet Centers, Jack and Jill Trauma Centers, and my favorite: Little Bo-Peep Pet Detectives.

The first entry that you'll make will be in cell A1, where you'll put the spreadsheet's title, *Mother Goose Enterprises 1st Quarter 1996 Sales*. Because this may be your first spreadsheet entry ever, I'll break up the steps a lot more than usual so that you can get a really good idea of what's going on. Before you start, be sure that cell A1 is the active cell. If cell A1 is not current, press Ctrl+Home and make it so. (I always admired the way that Captain Picard gave orders from the bridge of the USS Enterprise.)

1 **Hold down the Shift key and then type M to start entering the word *Mother* in cell A1.**

As soon as you type capital *M*, a couple of interesting changes (well, at least I think they're interesting!) take place. First, the *M* that you typed appears both in cell A1 and on the formula bar. However, the *insertion point* (the flashing vertical bar) appears only after the *M* in cell A1. Second, three new buttons appear in front of the *M* on the formula bar (not counting the down-arrow button that has been there all along, even though you didn't notice it). These buttons are the Cancel button (with the red *X*), the Enter button (with the green check mark), and the Function Wizard (with the *fx*).

You click the Cancel button if you want to abandon the cell entry that you're making and restore the cell to its previous state. You click the Enter button if you want to complete the cell entry in the active cell.

First try the Cancel button to return cell A1 to its empty state.

2 **Click the Cancel button to get rid of the *M* that you entered in Step 1.**

Note that (as soon you click the Cancel button) the *M* disappears from both cell A1 and the formula bar, and the Cancel, Enter, and Function Wizard buttons have gone *poof* as well. Note, too, that instead of clicking the Cancel button on the formula bar, you could have achieved the same result by pressing Esc.

Cancel button

Okay! Enough of this data-entry, data-cancel stuff: The time has come to get down to work and put the entire spreadsheet title into cell A1. Just keep in mind that the title's kinda long, so keep checking your typing as you go. If you find that you've made typos, press the Backspace key (right above Enter) to delete the aberrant character before you correctly retype the title's characters from that point on.

3   Type *Mother Goose Enterprises 1st Quarter 1996 Sales* and then check your typing either in the cell itself or on the formula bar.

As you can see, this title is a long sucker that extends way beyond the right edge of cell A1. Fortunately, as you're about to find out, Excel allows long text entries to spill over into neighboring cells to the right, provided that those cells remain empty.

4   If the title looks okay, click the Enter button on the formula bar to complete its entry in cell A1.

As soon as you click this button to complete the entry, the cell pointer remains in cell A1 as the long title spills over all the way into part of column E. Note that the title appears not only in the worksheet but also on the formula bar.

Although the title *appears* to be in cells A1 through E1, realizing that it *is* (in fact) entered in only one cell (A1) is important. This distinction is easy enough to prove to yourself.

5   Press Tab or the → key to make cell B1 active.

As soon as you move the cell pointer out of cell A1 into cell B1, the spreadsheet title disappears from the formula bar (thus demonstrating that the formula bar always shows you what's in the current cell and that, when the current cell is blank, the formula bar is blank as well).

Next, see what happens to the spillover of the long title in cell A1 when you enter some text in cell B1.

6   Type *Halt!* in cell B1 and then click the Enter button on the formula bar to complete this cell entry.

Just like magic, entering *Halt!* in cell B1 cuts off the long title in cell A1 (on my monitor, only *Mother Go* remains visible in the cell).

Proving to yourself that making the text entry in cell B1 affected *only* the display of the spreadsheet title without having any effect on its contents is really important, so go ahead and put the cell pointer back in cell A1.

7   Press Shift+Tab or ← to move the cell pointer back into cell A1.

Voilà, as they say in Gai Paris. As soon as you make cell A1 active, the formula bar once again displays this cell's entire content, which happens to be the entire spreadsheet title.

Well, it's time to get rid of the *Halt!* in B1 so that your entire spreadsheet title can once again be seen in the first row of the worksheet.

8   Press Tab or → to move the cell pointer to cell B1; then press Delete to get rid of the text entry in this cell.

Magic time again (eat your heart out David Copperfield), because as soon as you press Delete, Excel removes the text entry from B1 and redisplays the spreadsheet title in A1.

Notes:

Exercise 1-12: Entering the headings for the sales table

Now you need to add the column and row headings to the sales table spreadsheet. These headings identify its financial data. To start, you'll enter the time-period headings in row 2. Then you'll go on and enter the category headings in column A.

1 **Make cell B2 active.**

To do this, you can use any of the techniques that you've learned for moving the cell pointer, such as clicking the cell or using the arrow keys to move there. (Don't use the Go To feature because you have such a short way to go.)

2 **Type *Jan* in cell B2 and then press the → key to complete the entry and move the cell pointer to cell C2, the next cell that requires a heading.**

Instead of clicking the Enter button on the formula bar to complete an entry, you can press whichever of the four arrow keys (←, →, ↑, ↓) is appropriate in order to move the cell pointer to the next cell that requires data entry. Because Excel uses the four arrow keys to complete data entry in a cell and move the cell pointer, you can't use these keys to move the insertion point through the entry you've typed (as you might be tempted to do to fix a typo). Instead, you must use the Backspace key to delete all the characters to the left of the insertion point up to and including the typo when editing an entry *before it's been completed.*

3 **Type *Feb* in cell C2 and then press the → key to complete the entry and move the cell pointer to D2, the cell where you'll enter your next column heading.**

4 **Type *Mar* in cell D2 and then press the → key to complete the entry in that cell and move the cell pointer to cell E2, the cell where you'll enter your last column heading.**

5 **Type *Qtr 1 Total* in cell E2 and then press the ↓ key to complete the entry and move the cell pointer down to row 3.**

Okay, now you're ready to enter, in column A, the row headings that identify the different companies that make up Mother Goose Enterprises.

As these headings go down the rows in the column (from cell A3 through A9), you could press the ↓ key to complete each heading, while at the same time moving the cell pointer down a row to the cell where you need to enter the next heading. Instead, I'm going to have you press the Enter key to complete each entry. In Excel for Windows (this is not the case, by the way, on the Macintosh), pressing the Enter key completes the cell entry and moves the cell pointer to the next cell down.

6 **Press the Home key to move the cell pointer to cell A3, type *Jack Sprat Diet Centers,* and press Enter to complete this entry *and* move the cell pointer down to cell A4.**

7 **Type *J* to start entering the company name in cell A4.**

As soon as you typed the *J* for Jack and Jill Trauma Centers, Excel immediately assumed that you wanted to reenter Jack Sprat Diet Centers and *went ahead and entered this text on the formula bar and in the current cell.* This presumptuous/nifty new feature in Excel for Windows 95 is called *AutoComplete.* Because everything but the *J* is highlighted, you can replace the AutoComplete entry by continuing to type your own entry in the cell. To accept the AutoComplete recommendation, you simply complete the entry.

8 **Type the remainder of the name *ack and Jill Trauma Centers,* in cell A4 and press Enter to complete this row title and move the cell pointer to cell A5.**

9 **Type *Mother Hubbard Dog Goodies* in cell A5; then press Enter to complete this entry and move the cell pointer down to cell A6.**

The *M* in Mother Hubbard triggers the AutoComplete function, which dutifully places Mother Goose Enterprises 1st Quarter 1996 Sales in the current cell. Carry on as before.

10 **Type *Rub-a-Dub-Dub Hot Tubs and Spas* in cell A6; then press Enter to complete this entry and move the cell pointer down to cell A7.**

11 **Type *Georgie Porgie Pudding Pies* in cell A7; then press Enter to complete this entry and move the cell pointer down to cell A8.**

12 **Type *Hickory, Dickory, Dock Clock Repair* in cell A8; then press Enter to complete this entry and move the cell pointer down to cell A9.**

13 **Type *Little Bo-Peep Pet Detectives* in cell A9; then press Enter to complete this entry and move the cell pointer to A10**

14 **Type *Total* in cell A10; then click the Enter box on the formula bar to complete the entry and leave the cell pointer in cell A10.**

extra credit

So you don't want to use the AutoComplete feature?

If you feel that the AutoComplete feature is not particularly useful (or even downright annoying), you can shut it off by Clicking Tools on the menu bar and then Options on the pull-down menu (to open the Options dialog box). Click the Edit tab and then click the Enable AutoComplete for Cell Values check box to remove its check mark. Click OK or press Enter to save this change.

Congratulations! You're now well on your way to completing your first spreadsheet table in Excel. At this point, your sales table should look like the one shown in Figure 1-4. Note that all the column and row entries that you've made (whether or not they spill over the right edges of their cells) are tightly left-aligned with the left edge of their cells.

ABC 123

Figure 1-4: Here's how your sales table should appear with its column and row headings.

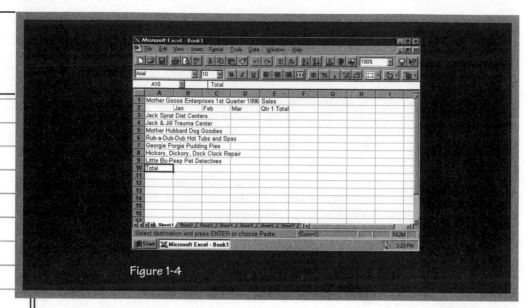

Figure 1-4

Preventing Enter from moving the cell pointer

Because you can always use the ↓ key to complete a cell entry and move the cell pointer, having the Enter key work the same way is (to put it mildly) redundant. I've always thought that the Enter key should complete the cell entry and leave the cell pointer in that cell (thereby offering a keyboard alternative to having to click the Enter box on the formula bar with the mouse). The Excel software engineers at Microsoft obviously don't agree with me, or they would not have made pressing Enter act like pressing the ↓ key rather than like clicking the Enter box on the formula bar.

Fortunately, should you agree with me and want to make pressing the Enter key to complete a cell entry work like clicking the Enter box on the formula bar, you can make this change by following these steps:

1. Click Tools on the menu bar and then click Options to open the Options dialog box.

2. Click the Edit tab in the Options dialog box.

3. Click the Move Selection after Enter check box to remove its check mark.

4. Click OK or press Enter to close the Options dialog box and put your change in effect.

After taking these steps, pressing Enter after typing an entry in a cell will complete the entry without moving the cell pointer.

Doing numeric data entry in a spreadsheet

Entering values in a spreadsheet is much the same as entering text. The biggest difference stems from the fact that you can often accomplish all your data entries from the numeric keypad rather than the standard QWERTY keyboard (assuming, of course, that you're not using a computer — like a laptop — that doesn't have a separate numeric keypad). Also, when entering values in a spreadsheet, you normally don't worry about numeric formatting, which is taken care of (as you will learn in Unit 2) with a separate procedure.

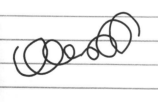

This handy capability frees you to concentrate on entering just the essential numbers and punctuation (meaning dashes for minus signs and periods for decimal points) that make up the values. As you'll soon discover, Excel is quite capable of adding other, nonessential numeric punctuation such as dollar signs and commas to separate thousands. The program's numeric formatting can also add or decrease the number of decimal places displayed in your values and convert values to percentages (complete with the percent sign).

Entering dates and times

You enter dates and times of the day as values rather than as text in your worksheets. You do this so that you can use these entries in formulas that perform arithmetic calculations (such as subtracting one date from another to return the number of days between them or subtracting one time from another to find out how many hours have elapsed).

To enter a date in a cell as a value rather than as text, you enter the date using any of the following date formats:

November 24, 1996

11/24/96 or 11-24-96

11-Nov-96

24-Nov (Excel assumes that its the current year in this date)

Nov-96 (Excel assume that it's the first day of the month in this date)

To enter a time of day in a cell as a value rather than as text, you enter the date using any of the following time formats:

2:15 (Excel assumes that you mean 2:15 AM)

2:15 AM

2:15 PM

14:15 (same as 2:15 PM based on a 24-hour clock)

14:15:10 (for 2:15 PM and 10 seconds)

Exercise 1-13: Entering the values in the sales table

Now it's time to practice numeric data entry by entering the January, February, and March sales figures for the various Mother Goose companies. You will enter these values in a block of cells, starting with cell B3 (where you'll enter the January sales for Jack Sprat Diet Centers) and extending all the way to D9 (where you'll enter the March sales for Little Bo-Peep Pet Detectives).

Note that this block (also known as a *range*) of cells does not include any of the totals required for the sales table, neither those that total the first quarter sales for each company down column E, nor those that total the monthly sales for all companies across row 10. In the next lesson, you will learn how to create and copy the formulas that will total these sales figures both down column E and across row 10.

Notes:

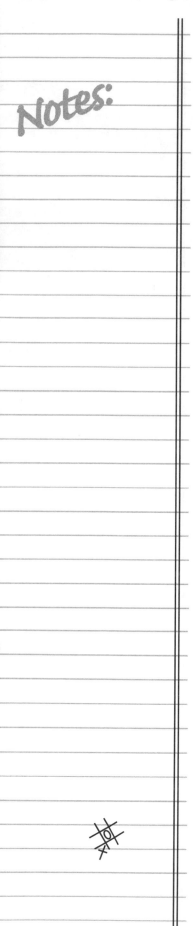

Notes:

When you know you have to do data entry in just a particular range of cells in a worksheet (as you do in this exercise), selecting those cells before you start the data entry is a good idea. By preselecting the range, you can speed up data entry. Preselecting restricts the cell-pointer movement to just that range selected, which lets you put most of your concentration on typing the entries correctly rather than keeping track of which cell is current.

In this exercise, you'll start the data-entry process by selecting the cell range starting in cell B3 and extending to cell D9. The only problem is that you're not really "scheduled" to learn about the various methods for selecting ranges of cells in Excel until Unit 4. But because you have need of a method now, I'll teach you the simplest method for selecting a range, the old shift+click method.

1 **Click cell B3 to make this cell active and then hold down the Shift key and don't release it until after you've clicked cell D9.**

The Shift key extends the selection from the first cell clicked (B3) to the last cell clicked (D9). Now you have the range of cells (written in shorthand as B3:D9, which means B3 through, and including, D9) selected. Note that all the selected cells in this range are highlighted (that is, appear black) except for cell B3. This cell appears white, indicating that it is the active cell within the selected range (that is, the cell which will accept your numeric input). As you learned in Exercise 1-11, although the company name entries in column A appear to be spilling over into the columns on the right, one look at the formula bar will tell you that the current cell is empty.

2 **Type *80138.58* and then press the Enter key to enter this value into cell B3 and move the cell pointer down to cell B4.**

When you do data entry in a preselected cell range, you must not use the arrow keys to complete the entries and move the cell pointer because doing this deselects the range (and breaks down your temporary data-entry barrier) as it moves the cell pointer. Instead, you complete entries either by pressing Enter (which moves the cell pointer down one row) or Tab (which moves the cell pointer over one column).

3 **Type *123456.2* and then press Enter to enter this value into cell B4 and move the cell pointer down to cell B5.**

Continue to enter the January sales values down column B by typing the values and then completing their entry by pressing the Enter key (be sure you finish off the entries with the Enter key and don't go anywhere near the arrow keys).

4 **Enter *12657.05* into cell B5, *17619.79* into cell B6, *57133.56* into cell B7, *168291* into cell B8, and finally, *30834.63* into cell B9.**

When you press Enter to finish off the entry of 30834.63 in cell B9, the cell pointer automatically jumps to cell C3 (the top of the next column of the selected cell range). Now, you're starting to see the magic of doing data entry in a preselected cell range.

Of course, you don't have to do your data entry down each column as you move from left to right across the preselected range; you can do your data entry across the rows from left to right as you move down the selection.

5 **Type *59389.56* in cell C3; then press the Tab key to complete the entry in cell C3 and move the cell pointer one column to the right to cell D3.**

Pressing Tab completes the entry and moves you one cell to the right across the row of the selected range.

6 **Type *19960.06* in cell D3 and press Tab to complete the entry.**

When you press Tab to complete an entry at the end of the row in a selected range, Excel sends the cell pointer back to the cell in the first column of the next row (cell B4, in this case).

7 **Press Tab once to move the cell pointer to cell C4; then type *89345.7* and press Enter to complete this entry and move down to cell C5.**

Complete the rest of the February sales entries in column C by typing the values indicated and then completing their data entry by pressing the Enter key to move down to the cell in the next row.

8 **Type *60593.56* in cell C5 and press Enter, *40635* in cell C6 and press Enter, *62926.31* in cell C7 and press Enter, *124718.1* in cell C8 and press Enter, and finally, *71111.25* in cell C9.**

When you press Enter to complete the entry of 71111.25 in cell C9, the cell pointer jumps up to cell D3 at top of the last column in the selected range.

9 **Press Enter once to move the cell pointer down to cell D4; then type *25436.84* and press Enter to complete this entry and move the cell pointer down to cell D5.**

Complete the remaining March sales entries in column D by typing the values indicated and then completing their data entry by pressing the Enter key to move down to the cell in the next row.

10 **Type *42300.28* in cell D5 and press Enter, *42814.99* in cell D6 and press Enter, *12408.73* in cell D7 and press Enter, *41916.13* in cell D8 and press Enter, *74926.24* in cell D9 and press Enter, and then finally press the ← key to make the cell A3 with the Jack Sprat Diet Centers heading the current cell.**

When you press Enter to complete the entry of 74926.24 in cell D9, Excel moves the cell pointer back to cell B3, the first cell in the selected range (right back where you started from). When you press the ← to make cell A3 active, Excel deselects the cell range B3:D9 where you just completed your data entry.

Pat yourself on the back for having made it through this exercise! At this point, your sales table should look like the one shown in Figure 1-5. You should note a few things about your table before you march on to the grand finale of creating the formulas that total these sales figures. First, note how entering the January sales figures in cells B3 through B6 has cut off the row headings in column A that identify the Mother Goose companies. Also, notice how, although all the values in cells B6 through D6 are right-aligned in their cells, they're not exactly what I'd call lined up in their columns (can you imagine having to add up these columns of numbers in their current state?). I promise that you'll learn how to take care of these problems in Unit 2 because they're all easily-rectified formatting problems. For the moment, however, set aside any concerns you might have about the look of what you've entered and turn your attention to the next lesson where you begin to learn about formulas, the heart and soul of any spreadsheet.

☑ Progress Check

If you can do the following, you've mastered this lesson:

❑ Enter text or a value in a cell and move to the next cell that requires data entry.

❑ Enter text or a value in a cell without moving the cell pointer.

Figure 1-5: Here's how your sales table should appear with its sales figures.

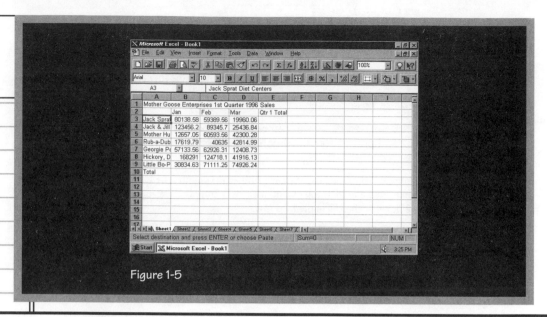

Figure 1-5

Lesson 1-4

Calculating Values with Formulas

Formulas form a special and very important subcategory of the type of data known as *values*. Unlike the values that you learned to enter in Exercise 1-13 of Lesson 1-3 that consist of only numbers and punctuation, *formulas* contain the information that tells Excel what arithmetic operation to perform and which values are to be used in that operation. When you enter a formula in a cell, the *result* of the calculation called for in the formula appears in the cell within the worksheet, while the *contents* of the formula appear on the formula bar (thus the name *formula bar*, in case you were wondering), assuming that the cell pointer is in that cell.

All formulas in Excel must start with the equal sign (=). The equal sign indicates to the program that it is to evaluate and compute the stuff that follows this symbol. If you don't start your formula with an equal sign, instead of calculating the result in a cell, Excel displays the contents of the formula in the cell. For example, if I forget the equal sign and enter

        10+25

in cell C3, all I'll see in cell C3 is

        10+25

(left-aligned as a text entry, I might add). If I do it right, however, and enter

        =10+25

in cell C3, the much-desired answer of

        35

will appear in cell C3.

When designating the arithmetic operations to be performed in your simpler formulas, you'll use a combination of the following symbols:

+ (plus sign) to perform addition between values

– (minus sign or hyphen) to perform subtraction between values

* (asterisk) to perform multiplication between values (gone are the days when you can use ×, the so-called "times" symbol)

/ (forward slash) to perform division between values

^ (caret) to raise one value to the power of another value

More often than not, the formulas that you create in Excel won't even include any explicit values, like the numbers 10 or 25. In place of explicit values, they will contain references to the cells that *contain* such explicit values (like cell A3 or B3). The reason is simple: If you build a formula that refers to the cells that contain the values you want calculated, the result of the formula can be updated simply by modifying the values in those cells. For example, if I enter the formula

=10+25

into cell C3, Excel will display the result, 35, in this cell the same as it would if I were to enter the value 10 in cell A3 and the value 25 in cell B3 and then enter the formula

=A3+B3

in cell C3. However, when built with cell references (as shown in the preceding example) rather than with explicit values, I can have Excel update the calculated result in cell C3 simply by replacing the values in either cell A3 or B3. For example, if I were to replace the value 10 in cell A3 with 25, the formula in cell C3 will be automatically recalculated to display the new result of 50. To affect the same change on the formula with explicit values, I would have to go to cell C3 and edit the formula itself, replacing the term 10 with 25. Whenever possible, you'll want to design your spreadsheets so that you can update their formulas simply by changing values in the cells referenced in the formulas rather than by having to tinker with the formulas themselves.

Beyond the simple formulas that you can create by combining the arithmetic operators covered earlier, Excel offers you a wealth of built-in *functions* that you can use when you need Excel to perform special or complicated calculations. The only trick to using any Excel function in your formulas is that you must specify what values the function is to use in its computations according to the strict order that the function expects these values to follow. This daunting task is greatly simplified with the use of the Excel Function Wizard.

Exercise 1-14: Totaling values with AutoSum

The easiest (and, therefore, the best) way to start experiencing the power of formulas in your spreadsheet is to use the AutoSum button to create formulas that total your first quarter sales figures. The AutoSum button (located on the standard toolbar right below the Excel pull-down menus) not only automatically inserts the Excel SUM function (complete with the equal sign) but also selects the block of cells that the program thinks are most likely the ones that you want totaled. If the program selects correctly, then all you have to do to create the formula in your cell is complete the cell entry, using any of the methods that you've learned (such as the Enter key, arrow keys, or Enter box on the formula bar).

Notes:

AutoSum button

To see how easy the AutoSum button is to use, you'll create two formulas using the SUM function. One formula will be in cell E3, which will total the Jack Sprat Diet Centers sales for January, February, and March in the cell range B3:D3. The second one will be in cell B9, which will total the January sales for all Mother Goose companies in the cell range B3:B9.

1 **Click cell E3 to make it active.**

2 **Click the AutoSum button on the standard toolbar.**

Excel responds by entering =SUM(B3:D3) in cell E3. Notice that cells B3, C3, and D3 are surrounded by a *marquee* (the so-called marching ants) and that the cell range B3:D3 in the formula is highlighted. At this point, you could modify the cell selection and thereby modify which cells are totaled by the SUM function. Because this cell selection is already correct, go ahead and complete the formula entry.

3 **Click the Enter box on the formula bar to complete the SUM formula entry in cell E3.**

As soon as you click the Enter box, Excel calculates the sum of the values in the cell range B3:D3 and displays the result (159488.2) in the cell. Notice, however, that the formula, =SUM(B3:D3), and not the calculated total, appears on the formula bar.

Next, use the AutoSum button to total the January sales in cell B10.

4 **Click cell B10 to make it current.**

5 **Click the AutoSum button on the standard toolbar.**

Excel responds this time by entering =SUM(B3:B9) in cell B10. Notice that cells B3, B4, B5, B6, B7, B8, and B9 are now surrounded by a marquee and that the cell range B3:B9 in the formula is highlighted.

6 **Click the Enter box on the formula bar to complete the SUM formula entry in cell B10.**

You see the calculated total (490130.8) in cell B10 and the =SUM(B3:B9) on the formula bar.

Copying cell entries with the fill handle

Now you have to admit that this task was pretty easy! So easy, in fact, that I bet that you could go on to use the AutoSum button to create the rest of the formulas for totaling the sales values. However, rather than create more formulas with the AutoSum (as easy as that is), I have something better in mind. I'm going to have you copy the formula that you've entered in cell B10 to the right (to cells C10, D10, and E10), and then I'm going to have you copy the formula you've entered in cell E3 down to cells E4, E5, E6, E7, E8, and E9.

To make these formula copies, I'm going to teach you how to use a nifty little mouse pointer called the *fill handle*. First of all, the fill handle only appears when you position the regular white-cross mouse pointer on the lower-right corner of the cell pointer (where you see a really teeny-tiny little box that looks kinda like a growth on the cell pointer). When the fill handle appears, you can drag it in a single direction (left, right, up, or down). As you drag, the cell pointer stretches to include all the cells that you move the mouse pointer through. When you release the mouse button, Excel copies the data that's in the active cell (a formula, in this case) to all the others that are included within the extended cell pointer.

heads up

The only potential problem in using the fill handle to copy something like a formula across rows or down columns of a worksheet is that you can end up deleting the formula if you drag the fill handle back onto the active cell that contains the original formula to be copied. You can always tell when you're dragging the wrong direction because the message

```
Drag inside selection to clear cells
```

will appear at the very bottom of the screen on the status bar. If you're dragging the correct direction (away from the active cell), the message

```
Drag outside selection to extend series or fill;
drag inside to clear
```

will appear in this area instead. If you find yourself about to clear the active cell, start dragging the opposite direction. If you end up actually messing up and clearing the active cell, choose Undo Clear on the Edit menu or press Ctrl+Z right away.

Exercise 1-15: Copying SUM formulas with the fill handle

To finish off the formulas needed in your sales table, you'll use the fill handle to copy them. First, you'll use the fill handle to copy the formula in cell B10 across to the cell range C10:E10, and then you'll use it to copy the formula in E3 down to the cell range E4:E9.

1 **With the cell pointer still in cell B10, position the mouse pointer on the tiny box in its lower-right corner.**

2 **When the mouse pointer changes to the fill handle, drag the fill handle to the right until the boundary of the cell pointer (which appears in light gray) is extended to include from cell B10 through and including cell E10.**

When you release the mouse button, Excel copies the formula from B10 to cells C10, D10, and E10, leaving this entire cell range selected.

3 **Click cell E3 to make it active; then position the mouse pointer on the tiny box in its lower-right corner.**

4 **When the mouse pointer changes to the fill handle, drag the mouse pointer down until the boundary of the cell pointer extends to include from cell E3 through and including cell E9.**

When you release the mouse button, Excel copies the formula in cell E3 to cell E4, E5, E6, E7, E8, and E9 and leaves this cell range selected.

5 **Click cell A1 to make it current and deselect the cell range E3:E9.**

Check your work against Figure 1-6. Does your table have the same monthly and quarterly totals as mine? If so, you're cleared to go on to Lesson 1-5 where you'll save your work. If not, check the values that you've entered in the body of the table. Chances are good that you've entered values different from mine in one or more cells. When you locate a cell with a wrong value, make it current; then enter the correct value as though the cell were still empty. When you complete the entry, Excel will replace your incorrect value with the newly-entered correct value.

☐ + ☐

fill handle

Notes:

☑ **Progress Check**

If you can do the following, you've mastered this lesson:

❑ Create SUM formulas with the AutoSum button.

❑ Copy formulas with the fill handle.

Figure 1-6: Here's how your sales table should appear with its formulas.

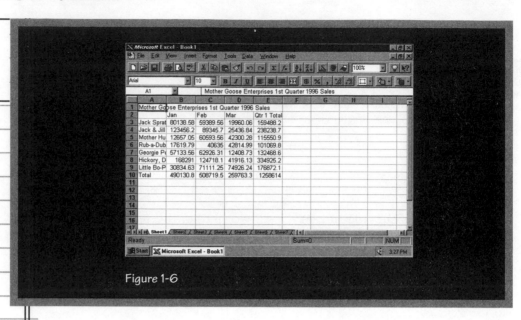

Figure 1-6

Lesson 1-5

Saving Your Sales Spreadsheet

Congratulations! In reaching this point in Unit 1, I think you'll agree that you've reached a real milestone in learning how to create a new spreadsheet. The only problem is that your masterpiece hasn't yet been saved on disk and, therefore, you are in danger of losing the work that you've done should your computer experience a malfunction or should Excel suddenly go south on you. Being able to save your Excel workbooks is one of the most important skills you can learn.

on the test

When you save your spreadsheet for the first time, you need to do a minimum of the following two things:

- ▶ Give the workbook a permanent filename.
- ▶ Indicate where on the hard disk the workbook file is to be stored.

Most of the time, my new Excel students seem to have no problem naming their workbook files, but they have a really hard time paying attention to where on the hard disk they've saved the files.

This inattention leads to the inevitable anguished cry of "I know I saved my workbook last week, but it's not on the hard disk now" at the beginning of Unit 2 when the students need to open the workbook with the Mother Goose Enterprises sales table so that they can begin formatting it. Suffice it to say, going through the trouble of saving your workbook does you little good if you can't find it to open it later.

One of the best new features of Excel for Windows 95 is that you no longer have to obey the old DOS/Windows file-naming conventions. You are not constrained to filenames with no more than eight characters, a three-character filename extension separated from the main name with a period, and no spaces. In fact, you now have the luxury of using up to 256 letters and spaces to name your file.

When determining where on the disk to save your workbooks, keep in mind that whatever folder you want to store your work in must already exist on the hard disk before you try to save the file (the Save As dialog box in Excel does not have a New Folder button — this isn't a Macintosh, you know). To create a folder for your work, you need to use the Windows Explorer with the technique that you learned in your *Dummies 101: Windows 95* course.

Exercise 1-16: Saving your sales table spreadsheet

The time has now come to save your Mother Goose Enterprises sales worksheet. You will save its workbook in your personal folder (the one that you created with either your name, your initials, or your online handle before you began Unit 1) within the Excel 101 folder that contains the practice files that you'll need in later units. If you haven't created an Excel 101 folder and/or your personal folder on the hard disk, refer to the Getting Started section at the beginning of this book before you do this exercise.

1 **Click the File menu and then click the Save command or press Ctrl+S.**

The first time that you choose the Save command, Excel displays the Save As dialog box, displaying the contents of the My Documents folder. Here is where you select the folder (the folder in which the file is to be saved) and name your workbook file. Next, you need to select your personal folder.

2 **Click the Up One Level button to display Hard Disk (C:) in the Save in drop-down list box, double-click the Excel 101 folder to open this folder, and then double-click the icon for your personal folder to open it.**

3 **Replace Book1 as the filename by typing *MGE Quarterly Sales* in the File name text box.**

Next, you need to select your personal folder.

4 **Click the Save button or press Enter.**

MGE Quarterly Sales should appear in the File name list box, and your personal folder should appear in the Save in list box. If this is the case, proceed to step 5.

5 **Click the Save button or press Enter.**

When you press Enter, Excel saves your *MGE Quarterly Sales* workbook file in your personal folder.

After saving your workbook for the first time, you need to continue to save the changes you make to the workbook at regular intervals. When you save subsequent changes by choosing Save on the File menu, clicking the Save button on the standard toolbar, or pressing Ctrl+S, Excel saves the changes without displaying the Save As dialog box. If you need to rename the workbook file and/or save it in a new folder or on a different disk, you must choose the Save As command on the File menu instead.

Notes:

Up One Level button

Recess

Now that your workbook is safely saved in your personal folder on the hard disk, you can take a well-deserved break if you wish. To quit Excel, click the File menu and then click the Exit command (or press Alt+F and then type X). Because you just saved your workbook, Excel will close this document along with the program without prompting you to save your changes. When you're ready to do the Exercise 1-17 in Lesson 1-6, you'll have to start Excel again, using one of the techniques you learned at the beginning of this unit.

Lesson 1-6

Using AutoFill to Enter a Data Series

There's one more topic that needs to be covered before concluding this first unit on entering the spreadsheet data, and that's the use of the *AutoFill* feature. AutoFill uses an initial cell entry in the worksheet to automatically fill out a data series of entries in the cells you select with the fill handle (the same jobber you used to copy your SUM formulas in the sales table).

AutoFill can fill data series based on a variety of initial values, as illustrated in Table 1-3. When you extend the series with the fill handle, Excel increments the series in each subsequent cell selected by one unit (be it a month, day, hour, quarter, and so on). For example, if you select a cell that contains Monday in it and then drag the fill handle down to empty cells in the next three rows, Excel will put Tuesday, Wednesday, and Thursday in those cells.

If you want to increment the series other than by ones, you can do this by entering the first and second entry in the series and then selecting both these two cells before dragging the fill handle. For example, if you want to create a series made up of every other month, you would enter January in one cell and then enter March in the cell immediately below or to the right. Then you would drag through the two cells so that both January and March were selected before dragging the fill handle to the empty cells where you want the other months of the series (May, July, September, and November) entered.

Table 1-3	Examples of Different AutoFill Series
Initial Entry	*Entries Created by AutoFill in the Next Three Cells*
June	July, August, September
Jun	Jul, Aug, Sep
Tuesday	Wednesday, Thursday, Friday
Tue	Wed, Thu, Fri
1/11/96	1/12/96, 1/13/96, 1/14/96
Jan-96	Feb-96, Mar-96, Apr-96
30-Nov	1-Dec, 2-Dec, 3-Dec
10:00 PM	11:00 PM, 12:00 AM, 1:00 AM
8:01	9:01, 10:01, 11:01
Quarter 1	Quarter 2, Quarter 3, Quarter 4

Initial Entry	Entries Created by AutoFill in the Next Three Cells
Qtr2	Qtr3, Qtr4, Qtr1
Q3	Q4, Q1, Q2
Team 1	Team 2, Team 3, Team 4
1st Floor	2nd Floor, 3rd Floor, 4th Floor

extra credit

Copying data rather than filling a series

You can circumvent the AutoFill feature and copy an initial entry that Excel would otherwise consider as an initial value in a data series that should be filled (like the samples shown in Table 1-3). To copy an entry rather than fill a series, you must hold down the Ctrl key as you drag the fill handle. When you hold down the Ctrl key, a tiny plus sign appears above and slightly to the right of the fill handle, indicating that Excel will copy the entry in the active cell when you drag instead of filling the series.

Exercise 1-17: Creating a simple data series

In this and the next exercise, you'll have fun creating a variety of different data series with the AutoFill feature. You'll start off in this exercise creating data series that increment by one unit and then go on in the next exercise to create some that increment by other units.

1 **Open a new workbook in which to create your data series with AutoFill.**

If you have to restart Excel, this new workbook will come up automatically. If you still have your *MGE Quarterly Sales* workbook open, you'll have to click the New button on the standard toolbar or press Ctrl+N and then click OK or press Enter to open a new workbook.

2 **Make cell A2 current and then type *Jan* and click the Enter button on the formula bar.**

By clicking the Enter button rather than pressing an arrow key or the Enter key, you keep the cell pointer in the current cell A2.

3 **Drag the fill handle down column A until you reach cell A14 and then release the mouse button.**

When you release the mouse button, Excel enters the months Feb through Dec in cells A3 through A13 and then enters Jan again in cell A14. Note that the cell range A2:A14 is still selected and cell A2 is still active.

4 **Without deselecting the cell range A2:A14, drag the fill handle in the lower-right corner of the cell pointer up two rows until January and December in cells A14 and A13 become grayed out and November is the last highlighted cell. When this happens, release the mouse button.**

When you release the mouse button, Excel clears the December and January entries from cells A13 and A14, leaving the cells with January through November selected in cell range A2:A12. Now you understand the meaning of the message, "Drag inside selection to clear cells," which appears when you drag in the direction opposite of the one that extends the data series.

Notes:

ABC

Notes:

5 Click cell A2 to deselect range A2:A12, then drag the fill handle to the right until the cell pointer includes cell I2 (that's all the way to column I in row 2), and then release the mouse button.

Excel responds by entering the names of the months Feb through Sep in cells B2 through I2, leaving the cell range A2:I2 selected.

That's enough for the months. Now you'll move on and create some date and time series in worksheet 2.

6 Click the Sheet 2 tab to make the second worksheet active.

7 Click cell B2 and then type *10-1-96* before you click the Enter button on the formula bar.

Note how Excel automatically converts your date from 10-1-96 to 10/1/96 (which the program much prefers for dates that include the number of the month, day, and year).

8 Drag the fill handle to the right until the cell pointer includes cell G2 and then release the mouse button.

As you drag the fill handle, notice how the next entry in the series appears in the cell-address indicator on the formula bar. When you release the mouse button, Excel fills out the date series by entering the dates 10/2/96 through 10/6/96 in cells B3 through G3.

9 In cell A3, type *8:00 AM* and then click the Enter button on the formula bar.

10 Drag the fill handle down until the cell pointer includes cell A12 and then release the mouse button.

When you release the mouse button, Excel fills out the time series by entering the times 9:00 AM through 5:00 PM in cells A3 through A12.

Exercise 1-18: Creating more complex data series

Up to now, all of the data series that you've created have increased by one unit (be it a month, day, or hour). To create a data series that increments by other units (such as every third month, every other day, or every three hours), you need to enter both the initial entry and the next entry that demonstrates the increment you want used in the entire data series. Then you select both entries before you use the fill handle to create data series.

1 Click the Sheet 3 tab to make the third worksheet active.

2 Click cell B2 and then type *Mon* before you press the → key to make cell C2 current.

3 Type *Wed* in cell C2 and then press the ← key to make cell B2 current again.

4 Hold down the Shift key as you press the → key to select both cell B2 and C3.

5 Drag the fill handle to the right until you select cell H2 and then release the mouse button.

When you release the mouse button, Excel creates a data series in the cell range D2:H2 that contains every other day of the week.

For your last data series, you create a number series that counts down from 50 by tens.

6 Click cell A3 and then type *50* before you press the ↓ key to make cell A4 current.

7 Type *40* in cell A4 and then press the ↑ key to make cell A3 current again.

8 Hold down the Shift key as you press the ↓ key to select both cell A3 and A4.

9 Drag the fill handle from A4 down until you select cell A13 and then release the mouse button.

Excel creates a data series in the cell range A5:A13 that counts down by tens (from 30 in cell A5 all the way to -50 in cell A13).

Exercise 1-19: Creating a custom AutoFill list

In Excel for Windows 95, you can create your own data lists that Excel's AutoFill feature can use. To see how easy custom lists are to make, in this exercise, you will create a custom list of the different companies that make up Mother Goose Enterprises.

The easiest way to create a custom list is enter the series in a range of cells and then tell Excel to use that range in putting together the custom list. Because you've already entered the different companies as row headings in the sales table in your *MGE Quarterly Sales* workbook, you can use these entries to create your custom AutoFill list.

First, however, you have to save the data series worksheet and bring back your *MGE Quarterly Sales* file.

1 Click the Sheet1 tab to make the first worksheet with the months data series current, then click cell A1.

2 Click the Save button on the standard toolbar or press Ctrl+S.

3 If necessary, click the Up One Level button to open the Excel 101 folder in the Save in drop down box and then double-click your personal folder before you type *Data Series* as the filename in the File name text box. Then press Enter.

4 If your MGE Quarterly Sales workbook is still open, click the Window menu and then click MGE Quarterly Sales near the bottom of the Window menu. If it's not still open, click the File pull-down menu and then click MGE Quarterly Sales near the bottom of the File menu to open it.

If you need to open your MGE Quarterly Sales workbook and it doesn't appear on the list of four files on the File menu, press Ctrl+O to bring up the Open dialog box. Click the Look in drop down button and then click the Hard Disk (C:) icon in the drop-down menu. Double-click the Excel 101 folder icon in the list box before you double-click the icon for your personal folder. Finally, double-click MGE Quarterly Sales file icon in the Open dialog list box.

5 **In Sheet1 of the MGE Quarterly Sales workbook, click cell A3 and then hold down the shift key as you click cell A9.**

The cell range A3:A9 should now be selected (note that it doesn't matter that company names in this cell range are not completely visible in the worksheet).

6 **Click the Tools menu and then click the Options command (or press Alt+T and then type O).**

7 **Click the Custom Lists tab in the Options dialog box.**

Note that Import List from the Cells text box near the bottom of the dialog box contains the range address $A$3:$A$9 (the cell range that you just selected in the sales table).

8 **Click the Import button near the bottom of the Custom Lists tab.**

As soon as you click the Import button, Excel adds the entries in the selected cell range to the List Entries box, and the first part of the list shows up at the bottom of the Custom Lists box.

9 **Click OK to close the Options dialog box.**

10 **Click cell A1 to make it current and then click the Save button on the standard toolbar or Ctrl+S to save your workbook.**

Now that you've created the Mother Goose companies custom list in Excel, you can use it to fill any or all of the series in any workbook you have open. All you have to do is enter one of its items in a cell and then drag the fill handle in the direction you want filled.

Congratulations! You've made it through Unit 1 (and it wasn't all that hard, now was it?). Okay, I'll grant you that this was quite a bit of material (did you say too much) to take on, especially for your first time using Excel. At this point, you should probably quit Excel (choose Exit on the File menu) and give you and your computer a much deserved rest.

Unit 1 Quiz

Test your knowledge by answering the following questions about the wonderful stuff you learned in Unit 1. For each of the following questions, select the letter of the correct response. (Remember, I'm not above asking questions where more than one response is correct.)

1. **All of the following statements about the cell pointer are true except for?**

   A. Indicates the active cell in the worksheet.

   B. Moves when you move the mouse on your desk.

   C. Moves when you click a new cell with the mouse.

   D. Indicates the cell that will accept your next data entry.

2. Assume that the cell pointer is in cell A1, and you need to move it to cell AJ500. Which of the following methods is the fastest way to get there?

   A. Press PgDn about a hundred times to reach row 500 and then press the → key about a million times to reach column AJ.

   B. Repeatedly click the ↓ scroll arrow button on the vertical scroll bar about a billion times to reach row 500 and then repeatedly click the → scroll arrow button on the horizontal bar about two billion times to reach column AJ.

   C. Click and hold down the ↓ scroll arrow button on the vertical scroll bar until the cell pointer reaches row 500 and then click and hold down the → scroll arrow button on the horizontal bar until the cell pointer reaches column AJ.

   D. Press F5, type AJ500 and then press Enter.

3. To make another worksheet in your workbook active, you can use any of the following methods except for?

   A. Click the next and previous sheet tab scrolling buttons until the worksheet is displayed in the workbook window.

   B. Click the sheet tab of the desired worksheet.

   C. Press Ctrl+PgDn or Ctrl+PgUp until the desired worksheet is displayed.

   D. Click the Window menu and then select the number of the desired worksheet from the bottom of this menu.

4. All of the following statements about text when first entered in a cell are necessarily true except for?

   A. The entry is automatically centered in the cell.

   B. The entry consists of letters only.

   C. The entry cannot be calculated in an arithmetic formula.

   D. If the entry is too long to entirely fit in the cell, its extra text will spill over to cells to the right provided these cells are empty.

5. All of the following statements about a value when first entered in a cell are necessarily true except for?

   A. The entry is automatically right-aligned in the cell.

   B. The entry can be used in any arithmetic formula.

   C. The entry will consist of numbers only.

   D. The entry does not appear the same on the formula bar when its cell is active as its does in the worksheet.

6. To complete a data entry in the cell, you can do any of the following except for?

   A. Click the Enter button on the formula bar.

   B. Press the Enter key.

   C. Press the Esc key.

   D. Press the ↑ key.

7. Which of the following dates would not be entered as a value?

   A. 24-5-96

   B. May 24th, 1996

   C. May 24, 1996

   D. 5-24-96

8. Excel will correctly calculate all of the following cell entries except for?

   A. =A3*B3

   B. =A3*100

   C. 50*100

   D. =50x100

9. Excel will calculate correctly all of the following cell entries except for?

   A. =IV15+IV16

   B. =IX15-IV16

   C. =IV15/IV16

   D. =IV15^IV16

10. If you enter *Item 500* in cell B2 and Item *450* in cell C2 and then select both cells and drag the fill handle to the right to cell D2, when you release the mouse button, what will cell D2 contain?

    A. Item 500

    B. Item 450

    C. Item 400

    D. 400

Unit 1 Further Exercises

In these exercises, you get a chance to apply what you learned in Unit 1 by creating a new worksheet on your own for Mother Goose Enterprises that tracks first quarter projected sales for the corporation's various companies.

Exercise 1-20: Opening the MGE Quarterly Sales and starting a new worksheet

You begin this exercise by opening the MGE Quarterly Sales workbook you created in the exercises in this unit and then starting a new sales table for Mother Goose Enterprises on the second worksheet (Sheet2).

1. If necessary, start Excel as you learned how to do in Lesson 1-1 of this unit.

2. If the MGE Quarterly Sales workbook is still open from working on earlier lessons in Unit 1 but is not active, click the Window menu and then click MGE Quarterly Sales on the pull-down menu.

    If this workbook is not open, click the File menu and then select MGE Quarterly Sales near the bottom of this pull-down menu.

    If MGE Quarterly Sales is not open and is no longer found on the File pull-down menu, press Ctrl+O to bring up the Open dialog box. Click the Up One Level button, double-click the Excel 101 folder, and then double-click your personal folder. Click MGE Quarterly Sales and then click Open or press Enter.

3. Click the Sheet2 sheet tab at the bottom of the MGE Quarterly Sales workbook to make its second worksheet active.

4. Enter the title Mother Goose Enterprises 1st Quarter 1997 Sales (Projected) in cell A1.

5. Use the AutoFill feature you learned in Lesson 1-6 to enter the months Jan, Feb, and Mar in cells B2, C2, and D2, respectively.

6. Enter Qtr 1 Total in cell E2.

7. Type Jack Sprat Diet Centers in cell A3 and then click the Enter button on the formula bar.

8. Use the custom AutoFill list you created in Exercise 1-19 to enter the rest of the Mother Goose Enterprises companies in cells A4:A9.

9. Enter Total in cell A10.

Exercise 1-21: Entering formulas for the Projected Sales table

Now, you're ready to enter formulas that calculate a projected sales increase of five percent for all Mother Goose Enterprises companies and the SUM formulas that total their monthly sales in each column and their quarterly sales across the rows.

1. Click cell B3 to make it current and then type = (equal sign).

    The cell pointer changes to a flashing cursor inside the cell to the right of the equal sign and also inside the formula bar indicating that you need to complete the formula for that cell.

2. Click the Sheet1 sheet tab to make that worksheet current and then click cell B3.

    Notice that =Sheet1!B3 appears in the formula bar and that the cell B3 is surrounded by a marquee (the so-called marching ants). You will use the Jack Sprat Diet Centers January 1996 Sales and the multiplier 1.05 to get the desired five percent increase.

3. Type *(asterisk) the multiplication sign in Excel and followed by the value 1.05 and then click the Enter box on the formula bar to complete the formula and leave the cell pointer in the current cell.

    Sheet 2 becomes the current sheet with the value 84145.51 entered in cell B3. The formula for cell B3 can be seen in the formula bar and should read =Sheet1!B3*1.05.

4. Use the fill handle as you learned in Exercise 1-15 of Lesson 1-4 to copy this formula across to cell D3, encompassing the cell range B3:D3, release the mouse button before you use the fill handle again to drag the cell pointer outline down to row 9, to select cell range B3:D9, and then release the mouse button.

    As if by magic, Excel completes all the projected sales calculations in the new worksheet for all the Mother Goose Enterprises companies. You will now enter the SUM formulas for monthly and quarterly sales totals.

5. Use the AutoSum button as you learned in Exercise 1-14 to create the SUM formula in cell B10 that totals the January sales for all companies.

6. Use the fill handle as you learned in Exercise 1-15 to copy this formula to the right to the cell range C10:E10.

7. Use the AutoSum button to create the SUM formula in cell E3 that totals the Jack Sprat Diet Centers sales for Quarter 1.

8. Use the fill handle to copy this formula down through the cell range E4:E9 and then click cell A1 to deselect the range E3:E9.

    Your completed table should contain the same values as the one in Figure 1-7.

Exercise 1-22: Saving your 1997 Projected Sales worksheet

Now you're ready to save your new first quarter 1997 Projected Sales worksheet as part of your MGE Quarterly Sales workbook.

1. Click the Sheet1 sheet tab to make the MGE 1996 Sales worksheet current.

    Because Excel saves the position of the cell pointer as part of your workbook, you'll position it in cell A1 of sheet1 where you'll want it to be when you next open this workbook.

2. If necessary, click cell A1 in Sheet1 to make its first cell current.

3. Click the Save button on the standard toolbar (the one with the floppy disk icon) or press Ctrl+S.

4. Press Alt+F4 to exit Excel and return to Windows 95.

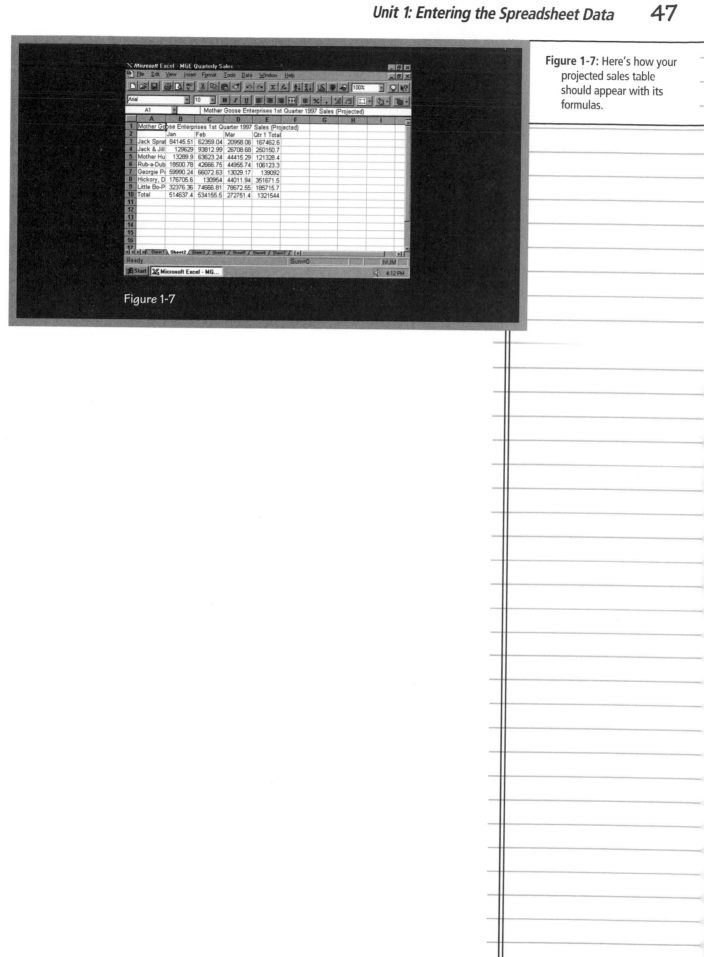

Figure 1-7

Figure 1-7: Here's how your projected sales table should appear with its formulas.

Formatting the Spreadsheet

Objectives for This Unit

✓ Opening an Excel workbook saved on disk

✓ Widening and narrowing columns and rows

✓ Formatting cells with the buttons on the Formatting toolbar

✓ Applying appropriate number formats to spreadsheet values

✓ Creating custom number formats for a worksheet

✓ Creating a style for applying certain formatting

✓ Using AutoFormat to format a table of data

Welcome back. I'm glad to see that Unit 1 didn't scare you off. Trust me when I say that it's going to get easier from here on in. ("Sure," you say, "how could it get any harder?") Having now completed the exercises in Unit 1, you'll probably agree that just knowing how to get spreadsheet data into a worksheet and save it on disk is not enough. The worksheets in your MGE Quarterly Sales workbook are in pretty rough shape: the row headings in column A are all cut off by the values in column B, and the values (both those you entered and those calculated by formula), while all right-aligned in their cells, are still far from lined up with each other.

The goal for this unit is to learn how to take care of these kinds of routine formatting issues so that the spreadsheets that you create are clear and easy to read. Although probably not as crucial as your data entry lessons in Unit 1, the formatting lessons in this unit are nevertheless an important part of mastering Excel. After all, it does you little good to get all that data entered and calculated in your spreadsheet if no one is interested in, or able to read, the information!

Opening the Workbook for Formatting

Before you can make any formatting changes to your workbooks, you have to be able to open them in Excel. Excel for Windows 95 keeps a running list, at the bottom of the File pull-down menu, of the last four workbooks that have been opened. If you've worked with a workbook lately, the easiest way to open it may very well be directly from the File menu.

Of course, you can't always count on the workbook file that you need to open to be one of the last four opened and, therefore, to show up among those listed on the File pull-down menu. Sometimes you'll have to grab the bull by the horns and open the workbook you want to work with from the Open dialog box. The only trick to using the Open dialog box is remembering in which folder on the disk you saved the workbook you want to open and figuring out how to get to and open this folder.

Exercise 2-1: Changing the default file location

In this exercise, you'll change the default file location so that your Excel 101 folder is the one that is automatically open in the Open dialog box. When you first open this dialog box after starting Excel for Windows 95, the program looks for files in the My Documents folder (a default folder that is automatically created when you install Excel for Windows 95).

Although the My Documents folder is a convenient place to store the workbooks you create with the program, you may want to change this default folder to some other one that's more likely to contain your work. For example, while completing the *Dummies 101* course on Excel for Windows 95, you'll be opening or saving workbooks in either your personal folder or the Practice folder found within the Excel 101 folder. To save time in opening and saving files while you're completing this course, you should change the default file location to the Excel 101 folder by doing the following:

1 Start Excel, click **T**ools on the menu bar, and then click **O**ptions on the pull-down menu to open the Options dialog box.

2. Click the General tab in the Options dialog box.

3 Position the I-beam mouse pointer after the *s* in *C:\My Documents* in the **D**efault File Location text box to locate the insertion point at the end of *My Documents;* then backspace to delete the characters *My Documents,* leaving *C:* in this text box.

4 Type *Excel 101* so that the pathname reads *C:\Excel 101* in the **D**efault File Location text box.

5 Click OK or press Enter to close the Options dialog box.

Now that you've changed the default file location from *C:\My Documents* to *C:\Excel 101,* Excel will automatically look in this folder whenever you open the Open dialog box to bring up a workbook for editing. Excel will also look in this folder whenever you use the Save As dialog box to save a new workbook or a copy of a workbook with a new filename or a new location.

☑ Progress Check

If you can do the following, you've mastered this lesson:

❑ Change the default file location with the Options dialog box.

❑ Open your Excel workbook file with the Open dialog box.

After you complete this course and begin working on your own workbook files in another folder, you can then change the default file location (as outlined in the steps above) to that folder where you'll be working.

Exercise 2-2: Opening your MGE Quarterly Sales workbook

In this second exercise, you'll use the Open dialog box to open the MGE Quarterly Sales workbook located in your personal folder so that you can format the data in this workbook.

1 **Click the Open button on the Standard toolbar or press Ctrl+O to display the Open dialog box.**

Because you changed the default file location to your Excel 101 folder, you should see your personal folder along with the Practice folder in the Open dialog list box.

2 **Double-click your personal folder's icon in the Open dialog list box to open it.**

3 **Double-click the MGE Quarterly Sales file icon in the Open dialog list box to open this workbook.**

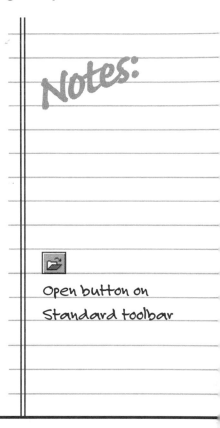

Widening Columns and Rows

Lesson 2-2

on the test

As you've seen in Unit 1, text entries that spill over into cells in neighboring columns to the right are cut off whenever you enter data in these cells. What you haven't seen is how *values* freak out when you add so much number formatting that the values can no longer be displayed in their cells given the current width of their columns (instead of numbers, all you see is a string of ###### in the cells).

The antidote to both of these problems (truncated long text entries and overly formatted values) is to widen the column with the cells that contain these entries. In a new worksheet, all the columns and rows are a uniform size: All columns start out at 8.43 characters wide, while all rows are 12.75 points high.

As you'll learn in the next few exercises, you can widen and narrow any of a worksheet's columns and rows as required by the data in your particular spreadsheet. You can even completely hide columns and rows in a worksheet (which is equivalent to narrowing the column to 0.00 characters wide or the row to 0.00 points high). This technique of hiding columns and rows comes in handy when you have some "sensitive" data in columns or rows of the worksheet that, although you aren't too keen on having displayed or printed in a report, are still required in the calculating of formulas in cells whose results do need to be shown.

In the following three exercises in this lesson, you'll get some experience with widening and narrowing certain individual columns and rows of the MGE Quarterly Sales worksheet. Keep in mind that, although you'll only be applying these techniques to single columns and rows for practice, you can apply any of these techniques to multiple columns or rows, provided that they're selected beforehand.

Why not just spread out the data?

You may be wondering why, when you're dealing with a worksheet 256 columns wide by 16,384 rows long, you don't just space out the data (after, all this a *spread*sheet) so that long text entries can't be truncated by other cell entries. While there are some aesthetic reasons for not skipping any more columns and rows in a table of data than necessary, the most important reason for not doing this is to conserve computer memory.

As you start entering data in new "virgin" columns and rows of the worksheet, Excel needs to reserve entire blocks of computer memory to hold the data that you *might* enter in that area. When you keep your spreadsheet designs tight and use as few blank cells as possible as "spacers" (so as not to use any more columns or rows than necessary), Excel doesn't have to reserve as many memory blocks, thus conserving computer memory and making it possible for you to get more data in a worksheet with the same system resources.

You can always tell how much memory that Excel and the workbooks you have open are using by choosing the <u>A</u>bout Microsoft Excel command at the bottom of the <u>H</u>elp pull-down menu. Then choose the <u>S</u>ystem Info button to open the Microsoft System Info dialog box. Among the many statistics in this dialog box, you will see Available memory listed in KB (kilobytes) and USER memory available listed as a percentage of the total.

Exercise 2-3: Adjusting the column width with AutoFit

Excel's AutoFit feature automatically adjusts the width of a particular column or the height of a particular row based on the longest entry in that column or row. To use this feature, you must position the mouse pointer on the worksheet frame on the right border of the column or lower border of the row that you want to adjust. When you position the mouse pointer on this border, Excel changes the pointer to a double headed arrow. Then, when you double-click the mouse button, Excel adjusts the column or row to the best fit for the data entries that it contains.

Try widening column A in the Mother Goose 1st Quarter 1996 Sales worksheet (Sheet 1) of your MGE Quarterly Sales workbook with the AutoFit feature so that you can see all the company names currently cut off by January sales figures entered in column B:

1 **Position the mouse pointer on the frame on the border between column A and column B.**

2 **When the mouse pointer changes shape from the white cross to the double-headed arrow, click and hold down the mouse button.**

While you hold down the mouse button with the double-headed-arrow mouse pointer, the cell address indicator on the formula bar changes from telling you the current cell address to indicating the current column width (A1 to Width: 8.43, in this case). Also, notice that a thin black line now extends from the mouse pointer down the worksheet in column A.

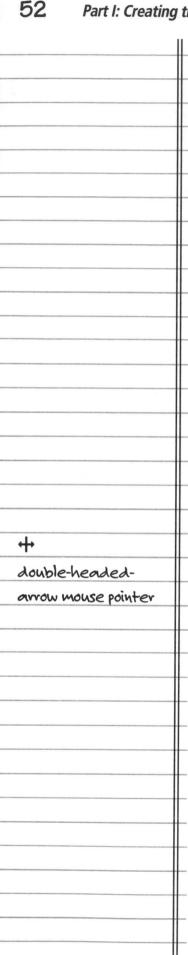

double-headed-
arrow mouse pointer

3 **Release the mouse button.**

As soon as you release the mouse button, the cell address indicator changes back to normal, and the thin black line extending from the mouse pointer down column A disappears.

4 **Now, double-click the border between columns A and B on the frame to widen column A with AutoFit.**

Whoa, Nelly! AutoFit really widened column A, and then some (it actually shot out from 8.43 to nearly 42 characters wide when you did your little double-click on the border number)! Oops, I forgot to remind you that the awfully long spreadsheet title entered in cell A1, Mother Goose Enterprises 1st Quarter 1996 Sales, is the longest entry in column A and would be the one on which the new column width would be based. Sorry!

5 **Press Ctrl+Z to undo your AutoFit command and restore column A to its original default width.**

Exercise 2-4: Adjusting the column width with AutoFit Selection

Obviously, you have to be careful when using AutoFit to adjust the width of a column with a long text entry like the spreadsheet title in cell A1. In this exercise, you'll use a variation of the AutoFit command called AutoFit Selection. When you use AutoFit Selection, Excel adjusts the column width to the best fit for just those cells that are selected in that column.

1 **Click cell A3 to make it current.**

2 **Hold down Shift as you click cell A9 to select the cell range A3:A9.**

3 **Click Format on the menu bar; then move the mouse pointer down to highlight Column on the pull-down menu and to display the Column continuation menu.**

4 **Click AutoFit Selection on the Column continuation menu.**

That's better. This time, Excel widened column A just enough to completely display the longest text entry in the cell selection A3:A9, which is Hickory, Dickory, Dock Clock Repair in cell A8.

Exercise 2-5: Adjusting the column width manually

Of course, you don't have to use AutoFit or AutoFit Selection to adjust the width of a column. You can adjust the width of a column manually by dragging the double-headed mouse pointer until the column is as wide or as narrow as you want it. You can also use the Width command on the Column continuation menu to set the column width to a set number of characters.

In this exercise, you'll get a chance to manipulate the width of column A by using both these methods. First, you'll return column A to its default width of 8.43 characters, using the Standard Width command as follows:

1 **Click cell A1 to make it current and to deselect the cell selection A3:A6.**

2 **Click the Format menu; then move the mouse pointer down to highlight the Column command.**

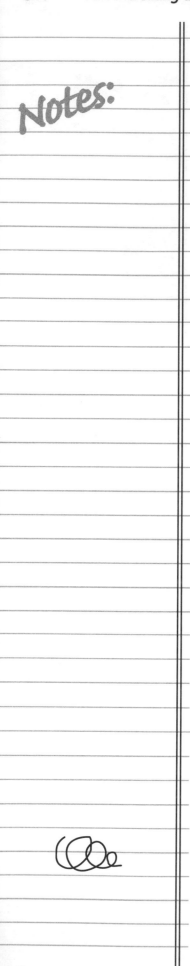

3 **Click <u>S</u>tandard Width on the Column continuation menu to open the Standard Width dialog box.**

Note that the standard width of 8.43 is automatically displayed in the <u>S</u>tandard Column Width text box. All you have to do to return column A to this width is select the OK button. You could, however, use this dialog box to set column A to whatever width you wanted by typing a new value in this text box.

4 **Click OK or press Enter to reset column A to the standard column width of 8.43 characters.**

Now that column A is back to standard width, you're ready to try manually widening column A with the mouse pointer.

5 **Position the mouse pointer on the frame at the border between column A and column B.**

6 **When the mouse pointer changes to a double-headed arrow, drag to the right until the column is wide enough for you to see all the company names listed in cells A3:A9 (at about 30.00 charac-ters in the cell address indicator); then release the mouse button.**

When you release the mouse button, Excel widens column A to the position where the dividing line extending from the double-headed arrow appears in the worksheet. If you released the mouse button too soon and column A still isn't wide enough to display all the company names, repeat this procedure of dragging the border between column A and column B to the right.

In the final steps of this exercise, set the width of column A to 34 characters using the Width command.

7 **Click F<u>o</u>rmat on the menu bar, move the mouse pointer down to highlight <u>C</u>olumn on the pull-down menu, and click <u>W</u>idth on the Column continuation menu to open the Column Width dialog box.**

The Column Width text box in this dialog box shows you the current width of the column (this value will vary, depending upon how far you dragged the border between columns A and B to the right).

8 **Type *34* in the <u>C</u>olumn Width text box; then click the OK button or press Enter.**

When you click OK or press Enter, Excel sets the width of column A to this new value. To check that column A is really 34 characters wide, position the mouse pointer on the border between columns A and B and hold down the mouse button until you can read the Width setting that appears in the cell address indicator on the formula bar.

Exercise 2-6: Adjusting the row height

Excel automatically adjusts the height of the rows in the worksheet to fit the largest-size text entered in their cells (a kind of automatic AutoFit, if you will). You can, however, manually adjust the row height either by dragging the double-headed mouse pointer up and down the row's lower border or by using the <u>H</u>eight command that appears when you select the <u>R</u>ow command on the <u>F</u>ormat pull-down menu.

Note that you increase the vertical space *between rows of data* in a table by strategically increasing the height of some of its rows. This handy feature gives you an option for making the information in the table read better without having to resort to inserting blank spacer rows in the worksheet.

Try this exercise to get an idea of the impact that increasing certain row heights can have on the appearance of your sales table:

1 **Position the mouse pointer on the frame at the border between rows 1 and 2; then drag the double-headed mouse pointer downward. Release the mouse button when the cell address indicator reads Height: 18.75.**

If you go too far and increase the height of row 1 too much, drag back upward until the cell address indicator says Height: 18.75.

Next, you'll use the mouse pointer to increase the height of row 2 to 21 points.

2 **Position the mouse pointer on the frame at the border between rows 2 and 3; then drag the double-headed mouse pointer down until the cell address indicator reads Height: 21:00.**

Instead of using the mouse pointer to manually adjust the height of rows, you can use the Row Height dialog box to set the row by entering its new height in points. Try using this method to increase the height of rows 3 and 10 in your sales table to 18 points.

3 **Click cell A3 to make it current. Then click Format on the menu bar, highlight Row on the Format pull-down menu, and click Height on the Row continuation menu to open the Row Height dialog box.**

4 **Type *18* in the Row Height text box and either click OK or press Enter.**

Next, repeat this procedure to increase the height of row 10 (with the monthly and quarterly totals) to 18 points.

5 **Click cell A10 and then repeat steps 3 and 4 to set the height of row 10 to 18 points.**

At this point, your Mother Goose 1st Quarter Sales table should look like the one shown in Figure 2-1.

Now, you need to save your work before going on to the lesson on formatting cells by using the Formatting toolbar. However, you'll need to save this version of the sales tables with the modified column and rows as a new workbook in your personal folder. Whenever you need to save a copy of a workbook either with a new name or in a new location, you need to use the Save As command on the File menu as follows.

6 **Click File on the menu bar; then click Save As on the File menu to open the Save As dialog box.**

When the Save As dialog box opens, you'll notice that the name of your personal folder appears in the Save in drop-down list box and the current filename is highlighted in the File name list box (with a flashing cursor at the end of the current File name).

7 **Click the arrowhead mouse pointer to the immediate right of the filename to deselect it and position the I-beam mouse pointer right after the *s* in *Sales*.**

8 **Press the spacebar and then type *(fmt)* for "formatted" version to rename this copy of the MGE Quarterly Sales to MGE Quarterly Sales (fmt).**

9 **Check that the name of your personal folder is displayed in the Save in drop-down list box; then, if this is the case (and it should be), either click Save or press Enter to save the modified workbook under its new name.**

By saving your modified version of the MGE Quarterly Sales as MGE Quarterly Sales (fmt), you preserve the original unchanged version of the sales table on your hard disk (for future exercises in this unit).

☑ Progress Check

If you can do the following, you've mastered this lesson:

❑ Use AutoFit to adjust a column width or row height to the best fit.

❑ Widen columns and rows with the double-headed-arrow mouse pointer.

❑ Widen columns and rows by using the Format pull-down menu.

Figure 2-1: The MGE
Quarterly Sales table
after adjusting the
width of column A and
the height of various
rows.

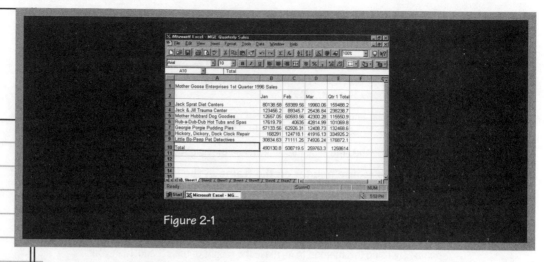

Figure 2-1

Lesson 2-3

Formatting Cells from the Formatting Toolbar

In Excel for Windows 95, you apply the formatting that you want your data entries to use to the cells that contain them. Although you will usually format the cells after you've entered data in them, you can just as well format empty cells beforehand so that any data entered into them takes on that formatting.

In formatting cells, you can change any of the following attributes:

- Fonts, which can include not only the font to be applied to the cell entries (such as Courier or Times New Roman) but also the font size, the style (such as bold, italic, strikethrough, and so on), and the color

- Alignment, which can include the horizontal and vertical alignment of the entries in their cells (given their column widths and row heights), whether or not overflow characters wrap to new lines in the cells, and their orientation

- Number format, which can include such things as how many decimal places and what special characters (such as dollar signs, percent signs, and such) are to be displayed by the values in the cells

- Borders, which can include where to apply the borderline and what thickness and type of line (as well as what color of line) to use

- Patterns, which can include the type of pattern as well as the color to use

- Protection, which indicates whether cells are locked or unlocked, which determines whether you can make changes to them when you turn on the protection feature in their particular worksheet or workbook

You can apply many of the most common of these formatting changes with the buttons on the Formatting toolbar (the second toolbar from the top; the toolbar right above the formula bar). In the next four exercises, you'll get practice using these various buttons to apply different types of formatting to the Mother Goose 1996 Sales table in your MGE Quarterly Sales workbook.

Exercise 2-7: Changing the font and font size of the table headings

In this first exercise, you'll use the Font, Font Size, Bold, Italic, and Underline buttons on the Formatting toolbar to spruce up the Mother Goose 1996 Sales table in your MGE Quarterly Sales (fmt) workbook. Before you begin this exercise, be sure that you have MGE Quarterly Sales (fmt) open (this is the workbook that contains the column width and row height adjustments that you made in Exercises 2-3 to 2-6 of this unit).

1 **Position the cell pointer in cell A1 with the spreadsheet title; click the Bold button and then the Italic button on the Formatting toolbar.**

When you click the Bold button, the long spreadsheet title in cell A1 appears in boldface type. When you click the Italic button, this title now appears in boldface, italic type.

Unfortunately, Arial (a Microsoft Helvetica knockoff) doesn't look very good in italics, so go ahead and remove this type style from cell A1.

2 **Click the Italic button on the Formatting toolbar a second time to remove the italic style from the spreadsheet title.**

Attribute buttons such as the Bold, Italic, and Underline buttons on the Formatting toolbar are *toggles*. You click once to depress the button and apply the attribute to the selected cells. Click a second time to "un-depress" the button and remove the attribute from the selected cells.

Next, you'll apply a new font and font size to the table's row and column headings.

3 **Click cell A3 (the cell with Jack Sprat Diet Centers in it); then hold the Shift key and click cell A10 (the cell with Total in it) to select the cell range A3:A10.**

4 **Click the drop-down button to the immediate right of the Font drop-down list box; then scroll down the list until you can click Times New Roman to select it as the new font for cells A3:A10.**

5 **Click the drop-down button to the immediate right of the Font Size drop-down list box; then scroll down the list until you can select 12 points as the new font size for cells A3:A10.**

Next, you're going to format the column headings in cells B2, C2, D2, and E2 with the same font and font size. Instead of selecting these cells and then repeating Steps 4 and 5, you'll do this with the Format Painter button on the Standard toolbar. You can use this Format Painter button to copy formatting from the current cell to any of the cells that you select after clicking the Format Painter button.

6 **Click cell A3 to make it current and deselect the range A3:A10.**

Now that cell A3 is current, Excel will pick up its formatting when you click the Format Painter button.

7 **Click the Format Painter button on the Standard toolbar.**

The mouse pointer changes to a white cross with a paintbrush beside it. You'll use this mouse pointer to drag through the cell range B2:E2 to apply the formatting picked in cell A3 to these four cells that contain the column headings.

8 **Click cell B2 (the cell with Jan in it) and, without releasing the mouse button, drag to the right. After you've selected all the way to cell E2, release the mouse button.**

As soon as you release the mouse button, Excel changes the font and font size of the column headings in cells B2:E2 to 12-point, Times New Roman type.

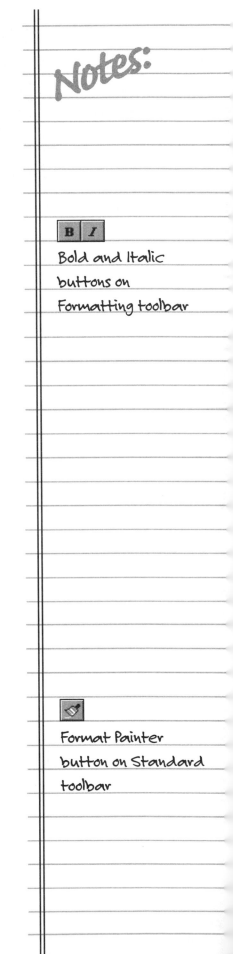

Notes:

Bold and Italic buttons on Formatting toolbar

Format Painter button on Standard toolbar

use the Format
Painter button to
apply multiple
formatting in one
cell to other blocks
of cells in the
spreadsheet.

Note that when you're using the Format Painter, its button stays depressed on the Standard toolbar only until you release the mouse button after clicking your first cell or dragging through your first cell range. If you want to be able to continue to format other cells by painting them with the white-cross-plus-paintbrush mouse pointer, you need to double-click the Format Painter button instead of just clicking it. When you double-click the Format Painter button, it remains depressed and active until you click this button again or press Esc. During the time that this button is active, you can continue to apply whatever formatting you've loaded onto it to other cells by either clicking them or dragging through them.

Exercise 2-8: Changing the alignment of the table headings

In this exercise, you get some practice at modifying the alignment of the column and row headings in MGE Quarterly Sales table using the alignment buttons on the Formatting toolbar.

The first of these alignment buttons that you will use is the Center Across Columns button. You'll use this button to center the spreadsheet title in cell A1 over columns A through E of the worksheet.

1 **Click cell A1 to make it current; then hold down the Shift key as you click cell E1 to select the cell range A1:E1.**

After you select the cells in the columns over which the cell entry in the active cell is to be centered, you are ready to click the Center Across Columns button to make it happen.

Center Across
Columns button

2 **Click the Center Across Columns button on the Formatting toolbar to center the spreadsheet title in cell A1 across columns A through E.**

When you click this button, Excel centers the spreadsheet title over columns A through E in row 1 of the worksheet.

Next, you'll right-align the row headings in cells A3 through A10 with the Align Right button on the Formatting toolbar.

3 **Click cell A3 to make it active and deselect the range A1:E1; then hold down Shift as you click cell A10 to select the range A3:A10.**

Align Right button

4 **Click the Align Right button on the Formatting toolbar to align all these text entries (A3:A10) with the right edges of their cells.**

Finally, you're ready to center the column headings in their cells in the cell range B2:E2.

5 **Click cell B2 to make it current and then hold down the Shift key as you click cell E2 to select the cell range B2:E2.**

Center button

6 **Click the Center button on the Formatting toolbar to center the column headings in their cells.**

Excel centers the headings in their cells (although it's hard to tell that *Qtr 1 Total* is centered in cell E2 because its column currently isn't any wider than the formatted text — you'll take care of this in Exercise 2-9, coming right up).

7 **Press the ↓ key to make cell B3 (with 80138.58) active and deselect the cell range B2:E2.**

At this point, your spreadsheet should look like the one shown in Figure 2-2.

8 **Save your changes up to now in the MGE Quarterly Sales (fmt) workbook by clicking the Save button on the Standard toolbar or pressing Ctrl+S.**

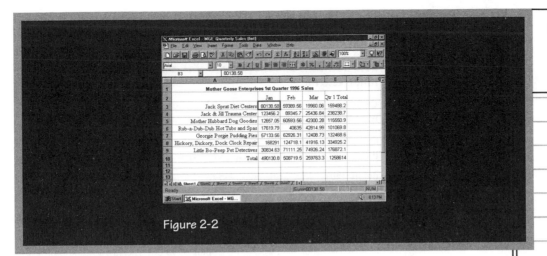

Figure 2-2

Figure 2-2: Mother Goose
1st Quarter Sales table
after formatting the
headings.

Exercise 2-9: Applying number formats to the sales figures

on the test

In this exercise, you will get some practice at applying two of the most common number formats (Comma Style and Currency Style) to the values in the sales table. The Comma Style format adds two decimal places along with commas to separate thousands, hundred thousands, millions, and so on. The Currency Style format adds the two decimal places and the comma(s) plus a dollar sign.

First, you will apply the Comma Style number format to the monthly sales figures in the cell range B3:D9. Then you will apply the Currency Style number format to the totals in the cell ranges B10:E10 and the E3:E9.

1 **With the cell pointer still in cell B3, hold down the Shift key as you click cell D9 (with 74926.24 in it) to select the range B3:D9.**

2 **Click the Comma Style button on the Formatting toolbar.**

As soon as you click the Comma Style button to apply the Comma number format to the cells in the range B3:D9, Excels displays ###### in each of these cells. Remember that this merely indicates that the widths of the columns containing these cells is currently too narrow to display these values with Comma Style number formatting.

3 **Click Format on the menu bar, highlight Column on the pull-down menu, and then click AutoFit Selection on the continuation menu.**

4 **Click cell B10 to make it current and deselect the cell range B3:D9; then hold the Shift key down as you click cell E10 to select the range B10:E10.**

5 **Click the Currency Style button on the Formatting toolbar.**

As you can see, applying the Currency Style format has caused #######s to appear in cell range B10:E10.

6 **Click cell E3 to make it current and deselect the cell range B10:E10. Then hold the Shift key down as you click cell E9 to select the range E3:E9.**

7 **Click the Currency Style button on the Formatting toolbar to apply the Currency number format to the cell range E3:E9.**

Now you can get rid of those ridiculous looking #######s in the totals by widening columns B through E. To do this, select the entire range of cells containing the sales figures and totals (cell range B3:E10) and then apply the AutoFit Selection command to this block of cells.

Notes:

Comma Style button

Currency Style button

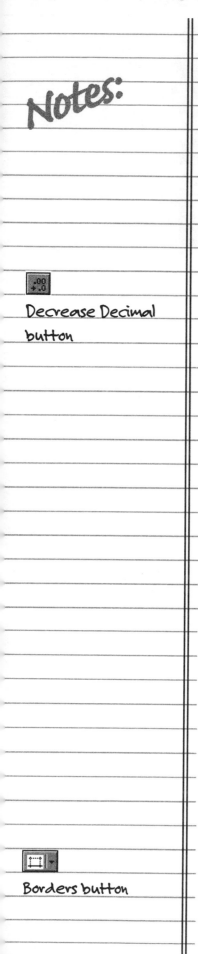

Notes:

Decrease Decimal button

Borders button

8 Click cell E3 to make it active and deselect the range E3:E9; then hold down the Shift key as you click cell B10 to select the cell range E3:B10.

9 Click F̲ormat on the menu bar, highlight C̲olumn on the pull-down menu, and then click A̲utoFit Selection on the continuation menu.

As soon as you select the A̲utoFit Selection command, Excel widens columns B through E sufficiently to display all the totals in your table.

Before saving your work, you need to make one more change to the formatting of the sales figures and totals by getting rid of the two decimal places normally displayed by both the Comma and Currency number formats (whole dollar amounts are just fine for this table). To make this change, you can use the Decrease Decimal button on the Formatting toolbar. Clicking this button removes decimal places from the display of values; clicking its counterpart (the Increase Decimal button beside it) adds decimal places.

10 Click the Decrease Decimal button twice to display only whole dollar amounts in all the values in the cell range B3:E10; then click cell A1 to make this cell current and deselect range B3:E10.

Now, check your work against the table shown in Figure 2-3. If everything checks out, go ahead and save your work as outlined in step 10.

11 Click the Save button on the Standard toolbar or press Ctrl+S to save your changes in this workbook.

Exercise 2-10: Using borders and color in the sales table

In this last exercise of this lesson on formatting cells from the Formatting toolbar, you'll be adding borders and changing the colors of some of the cells and cell entries. To make these formatting changes, you'll be using the Border, Color, and Font Color pop-up palettes. These palettes appear individually when you click on one's drop-down button. The cell or cell range you wish to format must be selected before using these pop-up palettes.

Before you begin formatting the sales table with the Border, Color, and Font Color palettes on the Formatting toolbar, I'm going to have you remove the display of the worksheet gridlines. With these gridlines removed, you'll be able to really see the effect of adding border lines to different parts of the table.

1 Click T̲ools on the menu bar; then click O̲ptions on the pull-down menu.

2 If necessary, click the View tab in the Options dialog box and click the G̲ridlines check box to remove its check mark before clicking OK or pressing the Enter key.

Now that you've gotten rid of the worksheet gridlines, you're ready to use your Border, Color, and Font Color palettes on the Formatting toolbar.

3 Click cell A2 to make it current; then hold down the Shift key as you click cell E10 to select the range A2:E10.

4 Click the drop-down button attached to the Borders button on the Formatting toolbar.

Your worksheet should now resemble the one shown in Figure 2-4, with the cell range A2:E10 selected, the Border palette displayed, and the worksheet gridlines hidden.

Now you're ready to add borders to the cell range A2:E10.

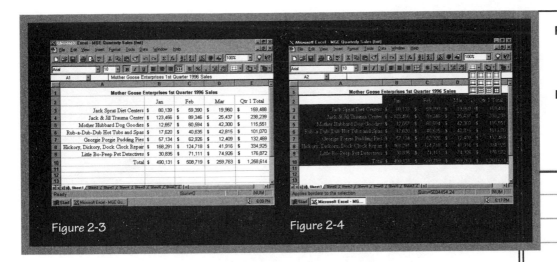

Figure 2-3

Figure 2-4

Figure 2-3: Mother Goose 1st Quarter Sales table after formatting the sales figures and totals.

Figure 2-4: Mother Goose 1st Quarter Sales worksheet with the pop-up Border palette and no gridlines.

5 **Click the second button from the left in the last row of the Borders palette (the button with the square divided into four panes) to add borders to all four sides of the cells that are selected.**

Okay. That takes care of the borders for this table. Next, you'll make the cells in the cell range A1:E1 bright blue and then switch the font color for the spreadsheet title from black to white.

6 **Click cell A1 and hold down the Shift key as you click cell E1 to select the range A1:E1.**

7 **Click the drop-down button attached to the Color button on the Formatting toolbar.**

Color button

8 **Click the bright blue button in the first row of the Color palette (the button that is fifth in from the left) to switch the cell color from white to blue.**

9 **Click the drop-down button attached to the Font Color button on the Formatting toolbar; then click the white button in the first row of Font Color (the button that is second from the left) to switch the text color from black to white.**

Font Color button

Because the entire range A1:E1 is still selected, the bright blue cell background with white text appears only in cell A1 until you deselect the range in the next step.

Next, you'll make the cells with the row and column headings bright yellow, the cells with the sales figures light yellow, and (finally) the cells with the totals light green.

10 **Click cell A2 and then hold down the Shift key as you click cell A9 to select the range A2:A9. Next, click the drop-down button attached to the Color button on the Formatting toolbar and then click the bright yellow button in the fourth row of the Color palette (the third button from the left) to make these cells bright yellow.**

11 **Click cell B2; then hold down the Shift key while you click cell D2 to select the range B2:D2. Next, click the Color button on the Formatting toolbar to switch the cells in this range from white to bright yellow.**

Next, you'll make the cell range B3:D9 light yellow.

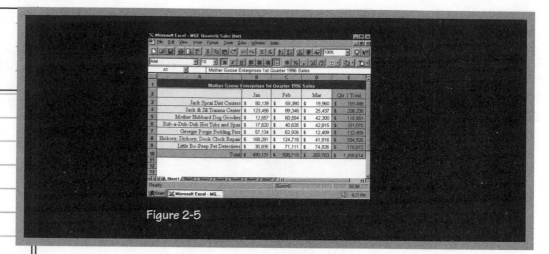

Figure 2-5: Mother Goose 1st Quarter Sales table after adding borders and color to some cells.

Figure 2-5

☑ Progress Check

If you can do the following, you've mastered this lesson:

❑ Select a new font, font size, and type style for your text from the Formatting toolbar.

❑ Change the alignment of your cell entries by using the Formatting toolbar.

❑ Format values in your worksheet with the Comma Style and Currency Style number formats.

❑ Add borders and change the cell and text color by using the Formatting toolbar.

12 Click cell B3 and then hold down the Shift key as you click cell D9 to select the range B3:D9. Next, click the drop-down button attached to the Color button on the Formatting toolbar and then click the light yellow button in the third row of the Color palette (the third button from the left) to switch the cells in this range from white to yellow.

Finally, you need to select the cell ranges with the totals and make them light green.

13 Click cell E2; then hold down the Shift key as you click cell E10 to select the range E2:E10. Next, click the drop-down button attached to the Color button on the Formatting toolbar and then click the light green button in the fifth row of the Color palette (the third button from the left) to switch the cells in this range from white to light green.

14 Click cell D10; then hold down the Shift key as you click cell A10 to select the range A10:D10. Next, click the Color button on the Formatting toolbar to switch the cells in this range from white to light green.

15 Click cell A1 to make this cell current and deselect the range A10:D10.

At this point, your sales table should look like the one shown in Figure 2-5 (except that yours, hopefully, will be shown in color, not in black and white).

16 Save your changes up to now in the MGE Quarterly Sales workbook by clicking the Save button on the Standard toolbar or pressing Ctrl+S.

Lesson 2-4

Formatting Cells from the Format Cells Dialog Box

on the test

Most of the time when formatting your spreadsheet, you can get away with just using the buttons on the Formatting toolbar. There are, however, some times when you need to bring out the heavy artillery in the form of the Format Cells dialog box to make a particular formatting change. Excel has made it easy to display this dialog box by assigning it the shortcut key combination Ctrl+1 (by the way, that's Ctrl plus the *number* 1, not Ctrl plus the *function key* F1).

Notes:

The Format Cells dialog box contains the following tabs: Number, Alignment, Font, Border, Patterns, and Protection. With the exception of the Protection tab, each of these tabs brings together all the options for a particular type of formatting such as number formatting, alignment in cells, font changes, and so on.

Of particular interest at this early point in your study of Excel are the options on the Number and Alignment tabs. The Number tab contains every category of number format known to Excel. In addition, you can also use the Number tab's formatting codes to create custom number formats of your own. On the Alignment tab, in addition to the regular Left, Center, Right, and Center across selection options (which are also available with the Left Align, Center, Right Align, and Center Across Columns buttons on the Formatting toolbar), you find very special options for aligning cell entries vertically in their cells, wrapping the text, and changing the text orientation.

The exercises in this lesson are designed to give you experience with some of the options available only on the Alignment and Number tabs of the Format Cells dialog box.

Exercise 2-11: Changing the text wrap, vertical alignment, and orientation of cell entries

In this exercise, you will practice changing the alignment of some of your sales table headings by using special options such as Wrap Text, centered vertical alignment, and a text orientation that displays the heading turned 90 degrees counterclockwise.

First, you'll start by centering the spreadsheet title in cell A1 vertically in row 1.

1 **With the cell pointer still in cell A1 of Sheet1 of the MGE Quarterly Sales (fmt) workbook, press Ctrl+1 to open the Format Cells dialog box; then click the Alignment tab.**

To center the title vertically in its cells (*cells* because the title is currently centered horizontally across columns A through E), you need to select the Center radio button in the Vertical section of the Format Cells dialog box.

2 **Click the Center radio button under Vertical in the Format Cells dialog box; then click OK or press Enter.**

Excel centers the spreadsheet title vertically in row 1 so that its text is no longer sitting on the very bottom of the cell range.

Next, you'll apply the Wrap Text option to the row headings in column A.

3 **Click cell A3 to make it current; then hold down both the Shift and Ctrl keys as you press the ↓ key to select down to cell A10.**

Now that the cell range A3:A10 is selected, you can apply the Wrap Text option to these cells.

4 **Press Ctrl+1 to open the Format Cells dialog box. Click the Wrap Text check box below the Vertical section to put a check mark in this check box; then click the Left radio button in the Horizontal options before you click OK or press Enter.**

At this point, the row headings in the cell range A3:A10 are once again left-aligned; however, you will see the effect of the Wrap Text option if you now narrow column A somewhat, forcing some of the text to be wrapped to new lines in their cells and forcing Excel to increase their row height to accommodate the new lines.

5 **Position the mouse pointer on the border between columns A and B, drag the double-headed-arrow pointer to the left until the cell address indicator reads Width: 21:00, and release the mouse pointer.**

All you can tell at this point is that column A is narrower and not all of the company names are displayed completely. To see the magic, you need to take one more step and apply AutoFit to these "incomplete" rows.

6 **Click F̲ormat on the menu bar, R̲ow on the pull-down menu, and A̲utoFit on the continuation menu.**

That's the ticket! Now, you can see the effect of the Wrap Text option on the cell entries in the range A3:A10. Note how the Mother Goose companies now appear on two lines in their cells and how Excel has increased the height of their rows to accommodate this new formatting.

Finally, you're going to change the orientation of the column headings in the cell range B2:E2.

7 **Click cell B2 to make it active and hold down the Shift and Ctrl keys while you press the → key to select to the end of the table (cell range B2:E2).**

8 **Press Ctrl+1 to open the Format Cells dialog box; then click the Text option in the Orie̲ntation section of this dialog box that has the text running up 90 degrees counterclockwise (this is the middle one, below the normal Text example, sandwiched between two other Text options) and click OK or press Enter.**

You can tell that the text for the months has been reoriented and is now running up the cells. To increase the row height sufficiently to see The Qtr 1 Total column heading, you need to apply AutoFit to this row.

9 **Double-click the frame at the border between row 2 and row 3 to apply AutoFit to row 2 and press the ← key to select cell A2 and deselect the range B2:E2.**

Now you should be able to see your reoriented headings. Take a second and check your sales table against the one shown in Figure 2-6. If everything checks out, go ahead and save your changes.

10 **Save your changes in the MGE Quarterly Sales (fmt) workbook by clicking the Save button on the Standard toolbar or by pressing Ctrl+S.**

11 **Click F̲ile on the menu bar and click C̲lose on the pull-down menu to close the MGE Quarterly Sales workbook.**

Creating custom number formats

When you first take a look at the Number tab in the Format Cells dialog box, you see a long list of formatting options in the Category list box. When you click on any category (with the exception of the General and Text categories) in the Category list box, various list and option check boxes appear that allow you to select different codes that define how a number will be formatted.

The best way to get a handle on these format codes is to activate a cell containing a representative value that needs formatting and then open the Format Cells dialog box and select a category for it on the Number tab. Because each category has its own formatting options, just click different options in the various list boxes. Excel shows how the value in the active cell would appear with that format in the Sample area of the Format Cells dialog box. When you find the format that you want to use, you can then apply it to the active cell (as well as to any other cells in the range that are also selected) by clicking OK or pressing Enter.

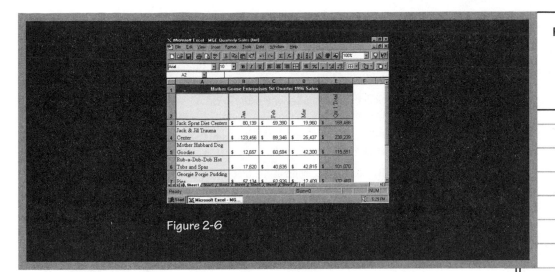

Figure 2-6: Mother Goose 1st Quarter Sales worksheet showing off some pretty specialized alignment features.

Figure 2-6

To create a custom number format, you have to select Custom (in the Category list box) and then enter the format codes that the new format is to use (in the Type text box). This is not as hard as it may seem initially because you can put together the codes for the custom format by selecting the closest existing format in the Type list box and then editing those codes in the Type text box above.

The last three exercises in this lesson give you practice in creating custom formats as well as in using the Special formatting category that is a new feature in Excel for Windows 95. By doing these exercises, you'll not only learn how to create custom formats but also start to understand the coding system that Excel uses in the existing number formats.

Exercise 2-12: Applying the Special number format

In this exercise, you'll use a new Excel for Windows 95 formatting category called Special that includes a zip-codes-plus-four format (which enters a hyphen between the first five and the last four numbers of the zip code), a telephone number format (which automatically encloses the first three digits of the value in parentheses for the area code, separates the next three digits in the value from the area code by a space, and inserts a hyphen in between these three digits and the last four to separate the prefix from the rest of the telephone number), and a social security number format that inserts hyphens to group numbers in the appropriate places.

You'll start this exercise by opening a new workbook to hold this and the rest of the custom formats that you'll be creating.

1 **Open a new workbook by clicking the New Workbook button on the Standard toolbar or pressing Ctrl+N.**

Next, you'll enter sample values that you can use to apply the Special category formats.

2 **Make cell A2 active, type *8005552121*, and click the Enter button on the formula bar.**

Because there are so many digits in your sample value, Excel has to convert it to scientific notation (that's what the 8.01E+09 is). You'll need to widen the column with AutoFit to display all of its numbers in cell A2.

3 **Double-click the double-headed-arrow mouse pointer on the frame at the border between columns A and B to use AutoFit to widen column A.**

Now that you can see your entry in cell A2, you're ready to open the Format Cells dialog box.

4 **Press Ctrl+1 to open the Format Cells dialog box, and, if necessary, click the Number tab.**

The Number tab contains a Category list box for selecting existing formats; the General category is highlighted. General is one of the few number formats that don't offer any formatting options. This is kind of a non-formatting number format that doesn't add much to the values that you add. The message "General format cells have no specific number format" bears this out. Above this message you see the Sample area containing the value 8005552121 that you entered in the active cell.

5 **Click Special in the Category list box.**

When you select Special in the Category list box, the Type list box appears to the right with new number formats for Zip Code, Zip Code + 4, Phone Number, and Social Security Number.

6 **Click Phone Number in the Type List Box.**

When you select Phone Number in the Type list box, Excel automatically formats your value and displays the result in the Sample box above. The result should read (800)555-2121.

7 **Click OK or press Enter to apply the Phone Number format to the value in cell A2.**

As you might have expected, your new telephone number format requires a wider column A to be displayed in cell A2. You'll need to widen the column with AutoFit to display all of its numbers in cell A2.

8 **Double-click the double-headed-arrow mouse pointer on the frame at the border between columns A and B to use AutoFit to widen column A.**

If all goes well, the value in cell A2 should now appear as (800)555-2121 in the worksheet. You are now ready to move on to the next exercise and learn to create your own custom number format in Excel for Windows 95.

Exercise 2-13: Creating a custom date format

In this next exercise, you'll be creating a custom date format that will show the date, spell out the name of the month, and show all four digits of the year, separated by hyphens. So, for example, you could enter 11-30-94 in a cell and have Excel display the date as

> 30-November-1994

after applying your custom date format to it.

To create this custom date format, you'll start by entering a sample date in cell A4 of the worksheet that already contains the telephone number (800)555-2121 in cell A2.

1 **Click cell A4, type *1-11-96*, and click the Enter button to complete the entry without moving the cell pointer.**

Note how Excel automatically converts your date entry to 1/11/96 in cell A4.

2 **Press Ctrl+1 to open the Format Cells dialog box, and then, if necessary, click the Number tab.**

Note that Excel recognized your entry and selected Date in the Category list box.

The closest date format codes are the 4-Mar-95, fifth down from the top in the Type list box. Choose different codes to see how they affect the 1/11/96 date shown in the Sample area.

3 **Click 4-Mar-95 in the Type list box.**

Note how the 1/11/96 in the Sample area has changed to 11-Jan-96.

Now that you have selected the closest existing format option, you will go to the Custom category so you can edit its code to achieve your desired result.

4 **Click Custom in the Category list box.**

The format codes d-mmm-yy (for the date format you just selected) appear in the Type text box (where the actual editing takes place and is highlighted) as well in the list box below.

5 **Position the arrowhead mouse pointer after *yy* in the Type text box to position the insertion point at the end of the existing date codes.**

To get Excel to spell out the word *January*, you need to add a fourth *m* to the code *mmm* to make it *mmmm*.

To get Excel to display all four digits of the year, you have to add *yy* to the *yy* codes already in the existing format (giving you *yyyy*).

6 **Press the ← key three times to move the insertion point before the last hyphen.**

7 **Type *m* and press the → key once.**

The Type text box should now read d-mmmm-yy, and your change is reflected in the sample window above that now reads 11-January-96. Next you're ready to change the year codes as follows.

8 **Type *yy* so that there are four y codes in a row.**

The Type text box now contains d-mmmm-yyyy, and the Sample area contains 11-January-1996.

9 **Click OK or press Enter to create the custom date number format and apply it to the date entered in cell A4.**

As you might have expected, your new custom date format requires a wider column A to be displayed in cell A4.

10 **Double-click the double-headed-arrow mouse pointer on the frame at the border between columns A and B to use AutoFit to widen column A.**

If all went well, you should now see 11-January-1996 displayed in cell A4. Before you move on to the final number format exercise, open the Format Cells dialog box to see where your new custom format has been added.

11 **Press Ctrl+1 to open the Format Cells dialog box again.**

Note how Excel has added the format codes for your custom date format to the bottom of the Custom format codes shown in the Type list box.

12 **Click the Cancel button or press the Esc key to close the Format Cells dialog box.**

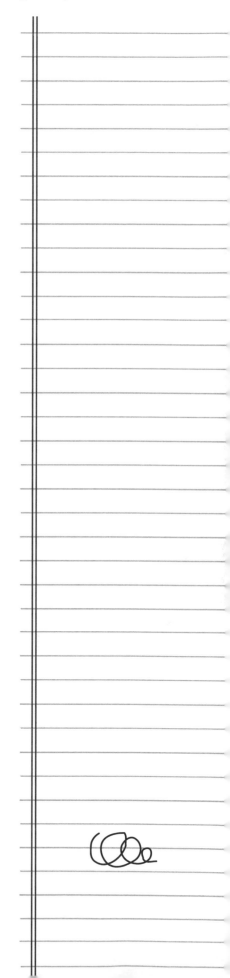

Coding hidden formats

In creating hidden formats, you can have the format hide only the values in the cells (while still displaying text entries), have it hide zeros in the cells (while displaying any other positive or negative values), or have it hide any and all entries in the cells.

To understand how you'd create these variations on the "hidden" theme, you have to understand that there can be up to four different sections in a number format and that each section is separated by a semicolon (;). The first section of the format tells Excel how to treat positive values. The second section tells Excel how to treat negative values. The third (optional) section tells Excel how to treat zero values. The fourth (optional) section tells Excel how to treat text entries.

If you create a format with only one section, all values (positive, negative, and zero) use the formatting codes in that section, although they have no effect on text. If you create a custom format with two sections, positive and zero values use the codes in the first section, negative values use the codes in the second section, and text ignores the whole thing. If you create a custom format with three sections, positive values use the codes in the first section, negative values use the codes in the second section, zeros use the codes in the third section, and text isn't affected at all. And if you create a custom format with four sections, positive values use the codes in the first section, negative values use the codes in the second section, zeros use the codes in the third section, and text uses the codes in the fourth section.

To hide any or all of these different types of entries, you can create a custom code that doesn't enter anything (by leaving it blank) in the pertinent sections. To create a hidden format that hides all types of values (positive, negative, and zero) and text, you create four empty sections by entering three semicolons in a row like this

```
;;;
```

(The first section is in front of the first semicolon, the second section is between the first and second semicolons, the third section is between the second and third semicolons, and the fourth section is after the third, last semicolon.)

To create a hidden format that hides all types of values but displays text, you create a format with three empty sections by entering two semicolons in a row, as in

```
;;
```

(The first section is in front of the first semicolon, the second section is between the first and second semicolons, and the third section is after the second, last semicolon.)

To create a custom format that hides only zeros in the cells (while it continues to display positive and negative values as well as text), you need to create a format with three sections and select format codes for the positive and negative values in the first two sections followed by an empty section entered with just a semicolon, as in

```
#,##0_);(#,##0);
```

The codes in the first section tell Excel to add commas between thousands and a space at the end that is as wide as the close parenthesis (this is the meaning of the strange _) codes right before the first semicolon) to all positive values. The codes in the second section tell Excel to put negative values in a closed pair of parentheses as well as add commas to separate thousands. The lack of anything in the third section (after the last semicolon) tells Excel to blank out the display of zeros.

Exercise 2-14: Creating custom hidden formats

In this last exercise on number formats, you'll create three slightly different hidden formats. The first custom hidden format will hide the display of whatever is entered in the cells where you apply it (positive values, negative values, zeros, or text). The second custom hidden format will hide the display of all values while continuing to display text entries in the cells where you apply it. The last custom hidden format will hide only zeros while continuing to display all positive and negative values as well as all text in the cells where you apply it.

Before you create these custom hidden formats, you need to enter some data entries in your worksheet that can act as guinea pigs for testing out the new formats.

1 **Enter the word *peanut* in cell A6, the number *0* in cell A7 (be sure that you enter a zero and not a capital O), the number *2500* in cell A8, and the negative number *-500* in cell A9.**

2 **Click cell A6, hold down the Shift key as you click cell A9 to select the range A6:A9, and press Ctrl+1 to open the Format Cells dialog box.**

Because no close formats appear in the available categories, select the Custom category.

3 **If necessary, click the Number tab and then click Custom in the Category list box.**

In the Type list box, you should now see the General category highlighted. Now you're ready to replace the General category in the Type text box with your three semicolons.

4 **Double-click somewhere in the Type text box; then type ;;; (three semicolons in a row with no spaces in between).**

You should now see only three little semicolons, all in a row, in the Type text box.

5 **Click OK or press Enter to create this hidden format and apply it to the cell selection A6:A9 with your guinea pig entries.**

Everything should now be hidden in the cell selection A6:A9. Note, however, that the word *peanut* continues to appear on the formula bar after the address A6.

6 **Press Ctrl+1 to open the Format Cells dialog box, position the mouse pointer somewhere after the three semicolons, and click the Type text box.**

The insertion point should be flashing after the last semicolon in the Type text box.

7 **Press the Backspace key to delete the third semicolon; then click OK or press Enter to create this second hidden format and apply it to the selected cell range A6:A9.**

Notes:

Notes:

☑ **Progress Check**

If you can do the following, you've mastered this lesson:

❑ Align cell entries vertically.

❑ Wrap cell entries onto more than one line.

❑ Apply a number format from the Format Cells dialog box.

❑ Create a custom style number using the codes from an existing style.

This second hidden format blanks out the 0, 2500, and -500 values in cells A7, A8, and A9, while continuing to display the *peanut* text in cell A6.

8 Press Ctrl+1 to open the Format Cells dialog box, scroll to the top of the Type list box, and click the eighth line of the format codes (not including *General* at the very top) that reads #,##0.00_);(Red)(#,##0.00) in the Type list box.

Now all you have to do is add a semicolon to these codes that tell Excel how to treat positive and negative values.

9 Click the Type text box somewhere after its number format codes so that the insertion point is positioned after the last close parenthesis and then press ; (a single semicolon).

Now your code text box should contain the codes #,##0.00_);(Red)(#,##0.00); in it.

10 Click OK or press Enter to create this final hidden format and apply it to the cell selection A6:A9.

Now you should see *peanut* in cell A6, 2,500.00 in cell A8, and (500.00) in cell A9. The 0 in cell A7 continues to remain hidden.

11 Click cell A7 to make this cell current and deselect the cell range A6:A9.

Look at the formula bar and verify that cell A7 still contains 0. Also, notice that (500.00) now appears in red (assuming, of course, that you're using a color monitor). The codes for the negative values in this custom format include Red, which changes the color of all negative numbers from black to red.

12 Type *5200* in cell A7; then press the ↑ key to complete this entry and move the cell pointer up to cell A6.

Note that as soon as you replace the 0 value with this positive number, Excel not only reveals the entry but also applies the formatting called for by the codes in the first section of your custom format.

13 Click cell A7 to make it current and then press 0 (zero) and press Enter to return this value to the cell.

Before you go on to the next lesson, you need to save your styles as part of a new workbook file.

14 Click the Save button on the Standard toolbar (or press Ctrl+S) to open the Save As dialog box.

15 Make sure that the name of your personal folder appears in the Save in drop-down list box. If necessary, double-click your personal folder to open it.

16 Double-click somewhere in the File name text box; then type *Custom Formats* as the new filename.

17 Click OK (or press Enter) to save your file in your personal folder and close the Save As dialog box.

Formatting Cells with Styles

The only trouble with custom number formats is that they become part of only that workbook for which you create them (when you save the workbook). If you want to reuse certain custom formats, you have to either re-create them from scratch in the new workbook or attach these custom formats to styles and then merge the styles into the new workbook.

In Excel for Windows 95, a style can dictate the number, font, alignment, border, patterns, and protection settings for the cells to which it is applied. Excel contains a number of predefined styles that you can use or modify. However, you can easily add to these existing styles by creating new ones. The easiest way to create a new style in Excel is to select a cell or cell range that already uses all the formatting you want included in the style. When you give a name to your new style, Excel will then create the style by example from the selected cell range.

Exercise 2-15: Creating a Telephone and Full Date style

In this exercise, you'll use the sample telephone number formatted with your special telephone number format in cell A2 and the sample date formatted with your custom date format in cell A4 in Sheet1 of the Custom Formats workbook to create two new styles by example.

1 **Click cell A2 containing (800)555-2121 to make it current; then click Format on the menu bar and click Style on the pull-down menu.**

Excel opens the Style dialog box with Normal entered as the name of the current style in the Style Name text box.

2 **Type *Telephone* as the name for the new style in the Style Name text box.**

As soon as you type the new style name, the Style Includes (By example) section of the Style dialog box changes to show you the codes for the custom telephone number format next to the Number check box.

3 **Click OK or press Enter to create the Telephone style.**

Next, you'll use the sample date in cell A4 to create a Full Date style by example.

4 **Click cell A4 containing 11-January-1996 to make it current; then click Format on the menu bar and click Style on the pull-down menu.**

5 **Type *Full Date* as the name for the new style in the Style Name text box and click OK or press Enter to create this new style.**

6 **Click the Save button on the Standard toolbar (or press Ctrl+S) to save your Telephone and Full Date styles as part of the Custom Formats workbook.**

Exercise 2-16: Creating styles for the hidden formats

In this exercise, you'll create styles for the three different hidden formats that you created in Exercise 2-14. The first style will be called *Hide Zeros*. This style will use the custom hidden format that hides only zeros in a cell range. The second style will be called *Hide Values*. This style will use the custom hidden format that hides all values but continues to display text entries. The third style will be called *Hide All*. This style will use the custom hidden format that hides anything entered into the cell range to which it's applied.

1 **Click cell A6 and then hold down the Shift key as you click cell A9 to select the range A6:A9.**

Currently, this range is formatted with the custom hidden format that displays everything but zeros in the cells.

2 **Click Format on the menu bar; then click Style on the pull-down menu.**

This first style will be called Hide Zeros.

3 **Type *Hide Zeros* in the Style Name text box; then click OK or press Enter.**

Next, you'll need to apply the hidden format that hides everything but text. This style will use the custom format with the two semicolon codes (;;).

4 **Press Ctrl+1 to open the Format Cells dialog box; then (if necessary) click Custom in the Category list box on the Number tab and double-click the ;; codes in the Format Codes list box.**

When you double-click these codes, Excel closes the Format Codes dialog box and applies their format to the selected cells in the range A6:A9 (hiding all the values in the selected cell range while continuing to display *peanut* in cell A6).

5 **Click Format on the menu bar and click Style on the pull-down menu.**

This second style will be called Hide Values.

6 **Type *Hide Values* in the Style Name text box; then click OK or press Enter.**

Next, you'll need to apply the hidden format that hides everything, including text. This style will use the custom format with the three semicolon codes (;;;).

7 **Press Ctrl+1 to open the Format Cells dialog box, and double-click the ;;; codes in the Format Codes list box.**

Excel hides all the entries in the selected cell range.

8 **Click Format on the menu bar; then click Style on the pull-down menu.**

This third style will be called Hide All.

9 **Type *Hide All* in the Style Name text box and click OK or press Enter.**

Before you go on to Exercise 2-17 to learn how to merge the styles in your Custom Formats file into another workbook, you should apply your Hide Zeros style to the current cell selection so that you can see every entry in the range A6:A9 except for the zero entered in cell A7.

10 **Click Format on the menu bar; then click Style on the pull-down menu to open the Style dialog box.**

11 Click the Style Name drop-down list button. Then click Hide Zeros in the list to insert its name in the text box before you click OK or press Enter to close the Style dialog box and to apply this style to the selected cell range A6:A9.

When you apply this style to the range A6:A9, the text and two value entries are redisplayed, with only cell A7 with the zero in it still blanked out.

12 Click cell A1 to make it current. Then click the Save button on the Standard toolbar (or press Ctrl+S) to save your Hide Zeros, Hide Values, and Hide All styles as part of the Custom Formats workbook.

Exercise 2-17: Merging styles into a new workbook

Currently, the styles (as well as the custom formats from which they're created) are all saved in your Custom Formats workbook file. In this exercise, you'll learn how to go about merging the styles in your Custom Formats workbook into a new workbook so that you can make use of their custom formatting.

1 Click the New Workbook button on the Standard toolbar to open a new workbook.

2 In cell A2, enter the date of your birth in cell A2 (following the format 2-15-49).

3 In cell A3, enter the word *Yes!*

4 In cell A4, enter *0* (zero).

5 In cell A5, enter *10000*.

6 Click cell A2; then hold down the Shift key as you click cell A5 to select the cell range A2:A5.

7 Click Format on the menu bar; then click Style on the pull-down menu to open the Style dialog box.

8 Click the Merge button to open the Merge Styles dialog box.

The Merge Styles From list box shows the names of all the other workbook files that you have open, including the name of the file with the styles that you want to merge into the current workbook.

9 Click Custom Formats.xls in the Merge Styles From list box to select it; then click OK or press Enter to add the styles to your new workbook.

When you choose OK or press Enter, Excel closes the Merge Styles dialog box and returns you to the Style dialog box. Here, you'll want to make sure that the custom styles in the Custom Formats workbook are successfully merged.

10 Click the Style Name drop-down button. Then click the Hide Values style before clicking OK (or pressing Enter) to apply this style to the cell selection A2:A5.

As soon as you choose OK or press Enter, all of the values in the cell range A2:A5 disappear, leaving only the text *Yes!* displayed in this range.

Mission accomplished! You now know how to merge the styles you created in the Custom Formats workbook into any other workbook you might be working on. You can now close both your Book2 and Custom Formats workbooks.

☑ Progress Check

If you can do the following, you've mastered this lesson:

❑ Create a style by example.

❑ Merge styles from one workbook to another.

11 Click **F**ile on the menu bar; then click **C**lose on the pull-down menu. Click the **N**o button in the alert box that asks you about saving your changes.

As soon as you close Book2, your Custom Formats workbook becomes active. Go ahead and close this workbook as well before you complete the last little lesson in this unit on formatting a table of data with AutoFormat.

12 Click **F**ile on the menu bar. Then click **C**lose on the pull-down menu to close the Custom Formats workbook.

Lesson 2-6 | # Using AutoFormat on a Table of Data

---

on the test

The last lesson in this unit on formatting the spreadsheet is actually the simplest. You can use the AutoFormat feature to apply a whole bunch of predefined formatting to a table of data in just one single operation.

The only catch to using this feature is that, prior to selecting the AutoFormat command on the Format pull-down menu, you must have the cell pointer positioned in one of the cells of the table (any one of the cells will do). If you don't and you select the AutoFormat command, you'll get an alert box indicating that AutoFormat cannot detect a table around the active cell, and you'll have to try the command again after repositioning the cell pointer.

Assuming that the cell pointer is surrounded by a table of data, Excel automatically selects all the cells in that table and opens the AutoFormat dialog box where you can choose among 16 different predefined table formats to be used.

Exercise 2-18: Using AutoFormat on the MGE 1996 1st Quarter Sales table

In this exercise, you'll get some experience using AutoFormat to format your original Mother Goose Enterprises 1st Quarter 1996 Sales table in your MGE Quarterly Sales workbook — not the "fmt" version, MGE Quarterly Sales (fmt), which you created for doing the earlier formatting exercises.

1 Click the Open button on the Standard toolbar or press Ctrl+O.

2 Double-click the MGE Quarterly Sales file icon in the Look **i**n list box to open this workbook.

The cell pointer should be in cell A1 (its position when you last saved this workbook). As long as the cell pointer is anywhere within the cell range A1:E10, you can use the AutoFormat feature.

3 Click F**o**rmat on the menu bar; then click **A**utoFormat on the pull-down menu to open the AutoFormat dialog box.

Note that Excel has automatically selected all the cells of your sales table (A1:E10) as it opened the AutoFormat dialog box. By default, the first table format (called Simple) is selected in the **T**able Format list box. (You can see a sample of its formatting in the Sample section of the AutoFormat dialog box.) Go ahead and see how your sales table looks in this table format.

4 **Click OK (or press Enter) to apply the Simple table format to your Mother Goose 1st Quarter 1996 Sales table.**

After formatting with the Simple table format, your table should like the one shown in Figure 2-7. The big problem with this table format is that it doesn't use a number format that aligns all the sales figures and totals. You'd better try another table format.

5 **Click F̲ormat on the menu bar and then click A̲utoFormat on the pull-down menu to open the AutoFormat dialog box.**

6 **Double-click Accounting 1 in the Table Format list box to apply this table format.**

Whoops! This table format is no good because it applies AutoFit to all the table columns, and the first column has been widened way too much to accommodate the spreadsheet title. You'd better try something else.

7 **Click F̲ormat on the menu bar. Then click A̲utoFormat on the pull-down menu to open the AutoFormat dialog box.**

8 **Double-click List 3 in the Table Format list box to apply this table format.**

There's the ticket! After formatting with the List 3 table format, your sales table should look like the one shown in Figure 2-8, with its sales figures and totals all formatted properly and its title nicely centered over the entire table.

You should save this version of the sales table under a new name.

9 **Click F̲ile on the menu bar; then click Save A̲s on the pull-down menu.**

10 **Position the mouse pointer at the end of the current filename in the File n̲ame text box; then click to put the insertion point at the end of that filename. Press the spacebar and type *(afmt)* to make the new filename MGE Quarterly Sales (afmt) ("afmt" for AutoFormat). Then click the Save button or press Enter.**

When you click Save or press Enter, Excel saves a copy of the workbook with your formatted Mother Goose 1996 Sales table formatted under the filename MGE Quarterly Sales (afmt).

Recess

Congratulations! You've now made it through your second unit (and you have to admit that it was a lot easier this time around, now that you have more experience in using both these course materials and, more to the point, Excel). At this point, you'll probably want to quit Excel (by clicking F̲ile on the menu bar and E̲xit on the pull-down menu) and give yourself and your computer a much-deserved rest before going on to Unit 3, where you'll learn how to print your work.

Notes:

☑ **Progress Check**

If you can do the following, you've mastered this lesson:

❑ Apply a bunch of predefined formatting to a table of data in one operation.

Figure 2-7: Here's how your sales table looks in the Simple table format.

Figure 2-8: Here's how your sales table looks in the List 3 table format.

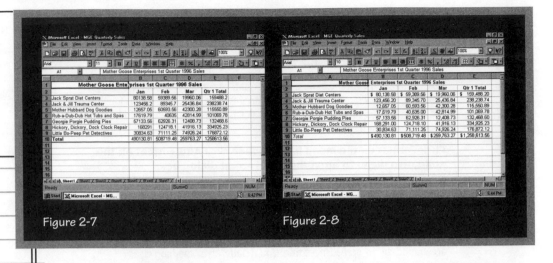

Figure 2-7   Figure 2-8

Unit 2 Quiz

Test your knowledge by answering the following questions about formatting the worksheet by using the knowledge that you just gained in Unit 2. For each of the following questions, select the letter of the correct response (and remember, I'm not above asking questions where more than one response is correct).

1. **All of the following statements about changing the default file location in Excel are true except:**

   A. The folder designated as the default file location is the one automatically selected whenever you open the Open dialog box.

   B. The folder designated as the default file location is the one automatically selected whenever you open the Save As dialog box.

   C. To change the default file location, you use the Default File Location option on the Edit tab of the Options dialog box.

   D. You need to change the default file location each time that you start Excel; otherwise the program goes back to using the Excel folder default file location.

2. **All of the following statements about using AutoFit to adjust the width of a column are true except:**

   A. When you use AutoFit to adjust a column in one worksheet, Excel adjusts all of the corresponding columns in all of the other worksheets in that workbook.

   B. You can use AutoFit on all the columns in a worksheet.

   C. AutoFit widens or narrows a column just enough to display its widest cell entry.

   D. To use AutoFit to adjust the width of a column, you click its right column border with the double-headed-arrow mouse pointer. To use AutoFit to adjust the height of a row, you click its lower border with the double-headed-arrow mouse pointer.

3. **All of the following statements regarding aligning spreadsheet entries in their cells are true except:**

   A. You can change the default right-alignment of values to left or center.

   B. You can't center entries with values in them across columns, only those with text entries.

   C. You can rotate cell entries 180 degrees so that their text appears upside-down.

   D. You can force text entries to wrap to new lines in their cells when their characters exceed the current width of their columns.

4. **All of the following statements about applying number formats to cells are true except:**

   A. Number formats have no effect on cells containing text entries.

   B. Applying a number format to a cell containing a value actually changes the number entered or calculated in that cell according to the particular requirements of that number format.

   C. The default number format that's applied to all values when they're first entered or calculated in the worksheet is called General.

   D. The number formats available on the Formatting toolbar include Currency, Comma, and Percentage.

5. **All of the following statements regarding the styles in Excel are true except:**

   A. In Excel, you can create a new style by example.

   B. In order for your custom styles to be available when you begin working in a new workbook, the styles must be merged into the new workbook from an existing workbook that's currently open.

   C. Styles cover all types of formatting except for changing the color of the cells and the color of their fonts.

   D. A style can be applied to the range of cells currently selected by choosing the style's name on the Style drop-down box on the Formatting toolbar.

Unit 2 Further Exercises

In these exercises, you get a chance to apply what you learned about formatting in Unit 2 to the Mother Goose 1st Quarter 1997 Projected Sales table that you created in the Further Exercises for Unit 1. Remember that this sales table is located on the second worksheet (Sheet2) in your MGE Quarterly Sales workbook.

Exercise 2-19: Formatting the Mother Goose 1997 Projected Sales table in the MGE Quarterly Sales (fmt) workbook

In this exercise, you'll apply a variety of different kinds of formatting to the Mother Goose 1996 Sales table in the MGE Quarterly Sales (fmt) workbook.

1. Open your MGE Quarterly Sales (fmt) workbook in your personal folder within the Excel 101 folder.

2. Click the Sheet2 sheet tab to make the second worksheet with the unformatted Mother Goose 1st Quarter 1997 Projected Sales table active.

3. Change the font of the spreadsheet title in cell A1 to 10-point Times New Roman Bold. Then center this text over columns A1:E1.

4. Widen column A to 28 characters.

5. Change the font of the table's row and column headings to 10-point Times New Roman Bold.

6. Right-align the table's row headings in their cells.

7. Center the table's column headings in their cells.

8. Format the sales figures in the cell range B3:D9 with the Comma Style number format with two decimal places.

9. Format the totals in the cell ranges B10:E10 and E3:E9 with the Currency Style number format with two decimal places.

10. Use AutoFit Selection to widen the table's columns so that you can see all the formatted data.

11. Make cell A1 of Sheet2 current before you make Sheet1 with the Mother Goose 1st Quarter 1996 Sales table active; then save your work and close your MGE Quarterly Sales (fmt) workbook.

Exercise 2-20: Formatting the Mother Goose 1997 Projected Sales table in the MGE Quarterly Sales (afmt) workbook

In this exercise, you'll use the AutoFormat feature to format the Mother Goose 1st Quarter 1997 Projected Sales table in the MGE Quarterly Sales workbook.

1. Open your MGE Quarterly Sales (afmt) workbook in your personal folder inside the Excel 101 folder.

2. Click the Sheet2 sheet tab to make the second worksheet with the unformatted Mother Goose 1st Quarter 1997 Projected Sales table active.

3. Use the AutoFormat command to apply the Colorful 2 format to the Mother Goose 1st Quarter 1997 Projected Sales table.

4. Format the sales figures in the cell range B3:D9 with the Comma Style format without any decimal places.

5. Format the totals in the cell ranges B10:E10 and E3:E9 with the Currency Style format without any decimal places.

6. Make cell A1 in Sheet2 current before you make Sheet1 with the Mother Goose 1st Quarter 1996 Sales table active and then save your changes to the MGE Quarterly Sales (afmt) workbook and exit Excel.

Printing the Spreadsheet

Objectives for This Unit

✓ Using Print Preview to catch layout problems before you print

✓ Printing all or any part of your workbook

✓ Adding a header, a footer, and print titles to a report

✓ Changing the default print settings, including the orientation of the printing, paper size, and page margins

✓ Inserting manual page breaks when necessary into a report

Prerequisites

◗ Practice folder in your Excel 101 folder with the sample files provided on the floppy disk that came with this book

◗ All lessons and exercises in Unit 2 completed

◗ Unit 2 Quiz and Unit 2 Further Exercises successfully completed

Welcome to Unit 3, on printing the spreadsheet. Being able to print the spreadsheets you create in Excel for Windows 95 is a basic skill on par with being able to enter the spreadsheet data in a workbook and then being able to save the workbook on disk. All the work that you do in entering and formatting your workbook is for naught if you don't know how to get its information down on paper.

The goal for this unit is to make you comfortable with all aspects of printing your spreadsheets. As a result of studying this unit, you should be able to open any workbook and print any or all of its information. In printing the necessary information, you should be able to control the page layout and add any necessary page enhancements (such as headers and footers with page numbers or titles to repeat column or row headings on each page) as required for the report.

Printing Spreadsheet Data

Lesson 3-1

on the test

The only trick to printing the information in your spreadsheet is getting used to Excel's page-layout scheme. Unlike when printing a word-processed document with a program like Word (where the paragraphs are normally no wider than the paper that you're using), the columns of information often are much wider than your paper when printing worksheets with Excel. Whereas Word normally pages the document vertically by determining how many lines

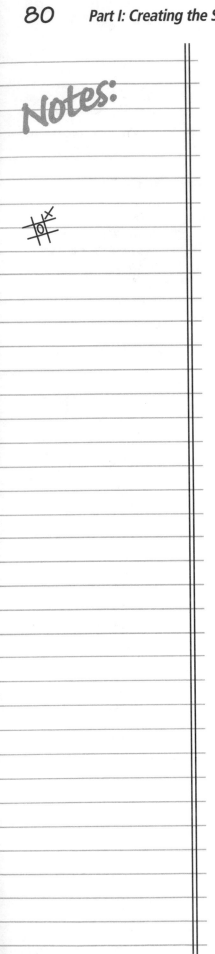

Notes:

of text will fit on each page, Excel must page the worksheet many times both vertically (by determining how many rows of information will fit) and horizontally (by determining how many columns of information will fit).

When paging a worksheet for a printed report, Excel first pages down the rows of the first columns to be printed before moving to the right to page down the rows for all the remaining columns to be printed. Also, keep in mind that, when paging, Excel does not break up the data in a column or row. If all the data in a row will not fit at the bottom of the page, Excel will move that entire row to the next page. Likewise, if all the data in a column will not fit at the right edge of the page, Excel will move the entire column of information to another page.

When you print, Excel prints (by default) all the information in whatever worksheets are selected. If you have only the current worksheet active (meaning that only the sheet tab of the current worksheet is selected), Excel only prints all the information in that worksheet. You can, of course, change this printing default whenever you need to so that you can print a particular part of a single worksheet, a particular group of worksheets in your workbook, or even the entire workbook.

In the exercises in this lesson, you'll get practice with printing the different parts of your workbook, all the way from a particular range of cells to the entire workbook. But before you start madly printing your little heart out (and potentially wasting a whole bunch of paper), your first exercise will be with using the Print Preview feature to preview the page layout before you actually start the printing.

Exercise 3-1: Previewing the page layout

The Print Preview feature opens a special Print Preview window that lets you see how many pages will be required to print the selected spreadsheet data and lets you see where page breaks will occur. In the Print Preview window, you can also make last-minute changes to the page layout of the report by using the Setup and Margins buttons at the top of the window before you send the job to the printer by using the Print button. Keep in mind that you can't make changes to the spreadsheet data displayed in the Print Preview window. If you happen to catch a mistake in the Print Preview window, you have to use the Close button to return to the normal worksheet window and take care of the error there.

To start this exercise, you will need to start Excel and open one of the sample workbooks provided in the Practice folder on the floppy disk that came with your *Dummies 101* book. By now, these sample files should be copied on the hard disk in your Excel 101 folder.

1 **Start Excel from Windows 95; then click the Open button on the Standard toolbar (or press Ctrl+O) to open the Open dialog box.**

You're going to start by opening the Bo-Peep Client List workbook in the Practice folder. This folder is located within the Excel 101 folder on your hard disk.

2 **Double-click the Practice folder icon in the Open dialog list box to open this folder. Then locate and double-click the Bo-Peep Client List file.**

The Bo-Peep Client List workbook contains a copy of the Little Bo-Peep Pet Detectives clients database that you'll be using when you learn about database management in Unit 7. For now, you'll use this clients database with the Print Preview feature to see how many pages it would take to print this database.

3 **Click the Print Preview button on the Standard toolbar or click the File menu bar and then click Print Preview on the pull-down menu.**

Doing this opens the Print Preview window, as shown in Figure 3-1. This window shows the first page of the database as it would print. Note that, at the bottom of the window, Excel tells you that you're currently looking at Page 1 of 4. At the top of the Print Preview window, you'll notice a series of buttons from Next to Help.

Before you explore these pages in Print Preview, you'll first want to add the row and column headings to the printed report so that you can see which columns and rows are included on each page.

4 **Click the Setup button at the top of the Print Preview window to open the Page Setup dialog box. Click the Sheet tab if necessary; then click the Row and Column Headings check box before you click OK or Press Enter.**

Excel adds the column and row headings from the worksheet frame to the preview pages (although you probably feel like you're at the eye doctor's trying to read the bottom line of one of his crazy eye charts).

5 **Position the mouse pointer in the upper-left corner of the Preview: Page 1 of 4 area in the Print Preview window. When the pointer changes to a magnifying glass icon, click the mouse button to zoom in on the page.**

You can use the magnifying glass pointer to zoom in on a particular part of the page and then use the arrowhead mouse pointer to zoom back out; or you can use the Zoom button at the top of the window to both zoom in and zoom out and then scroll to the part of the page that you want to see.

Having zoomed in on the upper-left corner of the page, you should now be able to read the first four columns (A through D) and the first few rows (1 through 16 or so) of data.

6 **Press the ↓ key until you can see the last row on this page (row 42). Then click the → key (until you've scrolled to the last column) and the ↑ key (until you see the column letters showing the letters B through F). Then click anywhere on the page with the arrowhead pointer to zoom out to full-page view.**

Page 1 of the report contains the first six columns (A through F) of the first 42 rows of data in this database.

While you're in the Print Preview window, you can use the Next and Previous buttons to step through the pages of the report, or you can use the PgUp or PgDn key on the cursor pad to do the same thing. You can also use the vertical scroll bar to scroll back and forth through the pages.

7 **Click the Next button at the top to display Page 2 of the report. Click the Zoom button to zoom in on the second page and click the left-arrow button on the horizontal scroll bar until you can see the row headings (43 through 50). Then click the mouse button once to zoom back out to full-page view.**

Page 2 of the report contains the first six columns (A through F) of the last eight rows (row 43 through 50) of data.

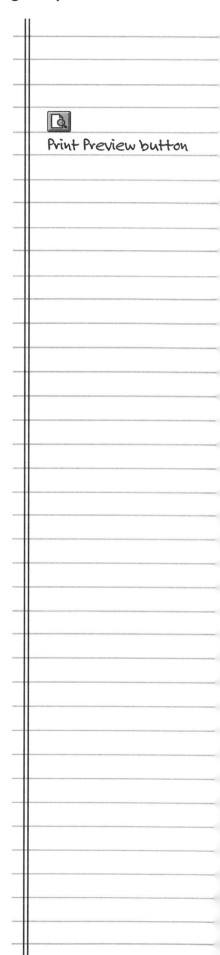

Print Preview button

Figure 3-1: When you open the Print Preview window, Excel shows you how the first page of the report will print.

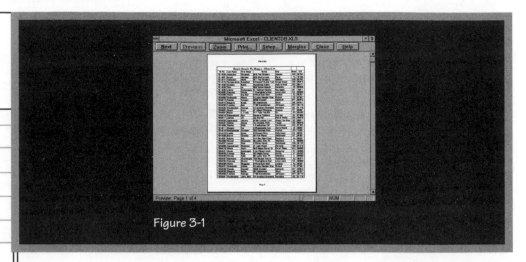

Figure 3-1

Notes:

8 **Press the PgDn key once to advance to page 3 of 4 in the Print Preview window.**

Page 3 of the report contains the last five columns of data (columns G through K) of the first 42 rows of data.

9 **Press the PgDn key once more to advance to page 4 of 4 in the Print Preview window.**

Page 4 of the report contains the last five columns of data (columns G through K) and the last eight rows (43 through 50) of data.

Having now seen how Excel pages this database report, moving down the rows and then across the columns, you are going to use the Setup button to change this paging arrangement to across the columns and then down the rows.

10 **First, press the PgUp key three times to return to Preview: Page 1 of 4. Next, Click the Setup button in the Print Preview window. Then click the Across, then Down radio button on the Sheet tab of the Page Setup dialog box before you click OK or press Enter.**

After changing this setting, Excel will repage the report.

11 **Press the PgDn key to move through all four pages of the repaged report.**

Using this arrangement, the first and second pages of the report now contain the first and last sets of columns for the first 42 rows of data, while the third and fourth pages contain the first and last sets of columns for the last eight rows of data.

12 **Click the Setup button. Then click the Row and Column Headings check box to deselect it and click the Down, then Across radio button to select it in the Sheet tab of the Page Setup dialog box before you click OK or press Enter.**

Excel removes the column and row headings from the report and repages it down the rows and then across the remaining columns of data.

13 **Click the Close button to close the Print Preview window and return to the worksheet containing the clients database.**

Exercise 3-2: Printing the worksheet with the Print button

In this exercise, you'll use the Print button to print a copy of the clients database. When you click the Print button on the Standard toolbar, Excel prints one copy of all the data in the current worksheet by using all of the program's default print settings on the Windows default printer.

1 **Make sure that your printer is turned on and has paper (at least four sheets are needed for printing this report).**

2 **Click the Print button on the Standard toolbar to begin printing the report.**

After you click the Print button, Windows briefly displays a Printing box with a message indicating which page is being sent to the printer. When all four pages have been sent to the printer, this Printing box disappears, and you can resume work in Excel.

When all four pages of the report have been printed, examine each page. Notice how Excel has automatically added a header (with the name of the worksheet, which has been changed from Sheet1 to Client List in this example) and a footer (with the page numbers) to each page of the report.

Exercise 3-3: Printing the worksheet with the Print command

In this next exercise, you'll use the Print command to change a few settings before you reprint the clients database. When you select the Print command on the File menu (or press Ctrl+P), Excel displays the Print dialog box where you can modify any of the print settings, including what printer to use, what part of the worksheet to print, which pages to print, and how many copies to print. The Print dialog box also contains a Properties button that enables you to change various printer settings and a Preview button that takes you back to the Print Preview window so that you can preview the effects of your changes before you print the report.

1 **Click File on the menu bar and click Print on the pull-down menu or press Ctrl+P.**

When you do this step, Excel opens the Print dialog box (like the one shown in Figure 3-2). Note that, by default, the Selected Sheet(s) radio button is selected in the Print What section, 1 is listed in the Number of copies text box, and the All radio button is selected in the Page Range section.

2 **Click the Preview button in the Print dialog box to open the Print Preview window; then click the Setup button to open the Page Setup dialog box.**

Next, you'll add the worksheet gridlines to the printout by selecting the Gridlines check box on the Page Setup dialog box.

3 **Click the Sheet tab in the Page Setup dialog box; then click the Gridlines check box to place a check mark in its check box.**

Next, you'll adjust the orientation of the printing (from its normal portrait mode to landscape mode) on the Page tab.

Print button

Figure 3-2: The Print dialog box enables you to change a whole bunch of settings before you print.

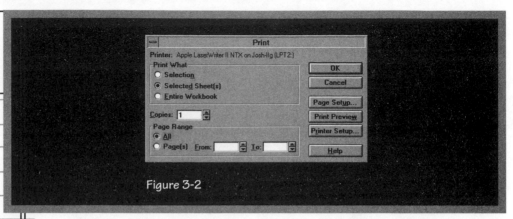

Figure 3-2

4 **Click the Page tab. Then click the Landscape radio button in the Orientation section before you click OK or press Enter.**

Excel returns to the Print Preview window and changes the print orientation to landscape mode so that you can see this change's effect on the printing of the clients database. Notice that, in the landscape orientation, the first page (which is still Page 1 of 4) contains many more columns of data. You can sometimes use landscape printing to good effect when the worksheet data that you're printing is much wider than it is tall.

5 **Press the PgDn key to page through all four pages of the report in landscape mode.**

Notice how Page 3 and Page 4 of the report just contain the Receivable and Credit columns. To get the report down from four to two pages total, you can either change the margin settings or use the Fit to Scaling option to force Excel to scale the data so that it fits onto two pages.

For this exercise, you'll use the Fit to Scaling option to get the report down to two pages.

6 **Click the Setup button in the Print Preview window to open the Page Setup dialog box. Then click the Fit to radio button on the Page tab. Press Tab to select the tall text box. Click the up scroll arrow once or type *2* (so that you see "Fit to: 1 page(s) wide by 2 tall" in the Scaling area) before you click OK or press Enter.**

You can use the Scaling options to adjust the size of the printing, or set a percentage with the Adjust to option, or let Excel figure out how much to scale the printing to fit a set number of pages with the Fit to option.

7 **Click the Print button in the Print Preview window to print the clients database on two pages in landscape mode with gridlines.**

Exercise 3-4: Printing the entire workbook

In this exercise, you'll get a chance to print an entire workbook. You'll start this exercise by closing the Bo-Peep Client List workbook and opening the MGE 1996 Qtr 1 Sales workbook located in the Practice folder.

1 **Click File on the menu bar and then click Close on the pull-down menu. Click the No button when asked to save the changes in this workbook.**

2 Click the Open button on the Standard toolbar or press Ctrl+O. Then open the MGE 1996 Qtr 1 Sales workbook in the Practice folder by double-clicking MGE 1996 Qtr 1 Sales in the Open list box.

This workbook contains four worksheets with their sheet tabs named Sprat Diet Ctr., Sprat Diet Chart, J&J Trauma Ctr., and J&J Trauma Chart respectively. The first and third sheets contain sales tables with first quarter income for the Jack Sprat Diet Centers and Jack and Jill Trauma Centers. The second and fourth sheets contain 3-D column charts representing these sales.

3 Click File on the menu bar and then click Print (or press Ctrl+P) to open the Print dialog box.

4 Click the Entire Workbook radio button in the Print What area of the Print dialog box; then click the Print Preview button.

5 Press the PgDn key to page through the four pages in this report; then click the Print button at the top of the Print Preview window to print these pages.

Exercise 3-5: Printing selected worksheets

In this exercise, you'll learn how to print only selected worksheets in a workbook. For this exercise, you'll continue to use the MGE 1996 Qtr 1 Sales workbook from the Practice folder that you opened in Exercise 3-4. You'll start by printing the Sprat Diet Chart and J&J Trauma Chart.

1 Click the Sprat Diet Chart sheet tab to select it.

This is the first sheet that you want to print.

2 Hold down the Ctrl key as you click the J&J Trauma Chart sheet tab.

Now both sheet tabs should be selected (indicated by white tabs instead of gray), although the Sprat Diet Chart tab should remain active.

When you hold down the Ctrl key as you click, Excel lets you select the sheet tab of the second sheet to be printed (the J&J Trauma Chart sheet tab) without deselecting the sheet tab of the first sheet to be printed (the Sprat Diet Chart sheet tab).

3 Click File on the menu bar and then click Print (or press Ctrl+P) to open the Print dialog box.

Note that the Selected Sheet(s) radio button is automatically selected in the Print What section of the Print dialog box.

4 Click the Preview button to open the Print Preview window. Then press the PgDn and PgUp keys to move back and forth between the two pages previewed in this report.

Because you already have a printout of these two 3-D column charts from the previous printing exercise, you can close Print Preview without sending this two-page report to the printer.

5 Click the Close button to close the Print Preview window and return to the Sprat Diet Chart worksheet.

Now you need to deselect the Sprat Diet Chart and J&J Trauma Chart sheets.

Notes:

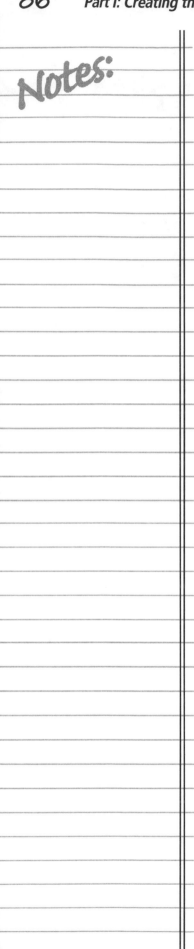

6 Click the Sprat Diet Ctr. sheet tab (the first one) to select this worksheet and to deselect the Sprat Diet Chart and J&J Trauma Chart worksheets.

You can always deselect a group of selected worksheets by clicking any other sheet tab in the workbook that's *not* currently selected.

Exercise 3-6: Printing a range of cells in a worksheet

In this last printing exercise in this lesson, you'll print a specific range of cells in a single worksheet. To start this exercise, you'll close the MGE 1996 Qtr1 Sales workbook and open the MGE Annual Sales workbook in the Practice folder.

1 Press Ctrl+F4 (function key F4) to close the MGE 1996 Qtr 1 Sales workbook. Answer <u>N</u>o when asked whether you want to save changes.

2 Click the Open button on the Standard toolbar or press Ctrl+O and then open the MGE Annual Sales workbook in your Practice folder by double-clicking MGE Annual Sales in the Open dialog list box.

This workbook contains four very wide and short worksheets showing Mother Goose Enterprises Sales and Projections for the years 1994 – 1997. You will start by printing only the first quarter sales of 1994 totaled for all nine Mother Goose Enterprises companies.

3 With the cell pointer in cell A1 of the Mother Goose 1994 Sales worksheet, hold down the Shift key while you click cell E12 with the Quarter 1 total to select the cell range A1:E12.

After selecting the cells to be printed in the worksheet, you still need to tell Excel to print just this selection in the Print dialog box.

4 Click <u>F</u>ile on the menu bar. Then click <u>P</u>rint on the pull-down menu (or press Ctrl+P) and click the Selectio<u>n</u> radio button in the Print What section of the Print dialog box.

5 Click the P<u>r</u>eview button to open the Print Preview window with Page 1 of 1.

6 Click the Prin<u>t</u> button to print the first quarter 1994 Sales table with the totals for all Mother Goose companies.

Next, you will print the first quarter sales tables for 1994 and 1995 as well as the projected sales for 1996 and 1997.

7 Click cell A1 in the 1994 Sales worksheet to deselect the cell range A1:E12 that you just printed; then click the 1997 Projected sheet tab to select this worksheet and make it active.

8 With the cell pointer in cell A1 of the 1997 Projected worksheet, hold down the Shift key while you click cell E12 to select the cell range A1:E12. Then hold down the Shift key while you click the 1994 Sales sheet tab.

When you hold down the Shift key as you click sheet tabs, Excel selects all the sheets between the active one and the tab you last clicked. Currently, the cell range A1:E12 is selected in all the selected sheets (1994 Sales, 1995 Sales, 1996 Projected, and 1997 Projected).

9 Click <u>F</u>ile on the menu bar. Then click <u>P</u>rint on the pull-down menu (or press Ctrl+P) and click the Selectio<u>n</u> radio button in the Print What section of the Print dialog box.

10 Click the P<u>r</u>eview button to open the Print Preview window. Then click the <u>Z</u>oom button and the <u>N</u>ext button three times to page through the rest of pages in this report.

After previewing the pages of this report, you can return to the MGE Annual Sales workbook without actually printing these four pages.

11 Zoom to full-page view before you click the <u>C</u>lose button to close the Print Preview window and return to the 1997 Projected worksheet. Then click cell A1 to deselect the cell range A1:E12 in the four selected worksheets. Click the 1994 Sales sheet tab to deselect the 1995 Sales, 1996 Projected, and 1997 Projected worksheets.

Now you can close this workbook before going on to Lesson 3-2.

12 Press Ctrl+F4 to close the MGE Annual Sales workbook.

Congratulations! You're well on your way to becoming a whiz at printing in Excel. All you need now is a little more experience with varying the printing options, and you'll be an expert.

☑ **Progress Check**

If you can do the following, you've mastered this lesson:

❑ Preview the page layout of a report before you print it.

❑ Print your worksheet with the Print button on the Standard toolbar.

❑ Print a report in landscape mode with gridlines.

❑ Print all the data in the entire workbook.

❑ Print specific ranges of cells in a worksheet.

Adding Headers, Footers, and Print Titles to a Report

Lesson 3-2

on the test

As you saw in the exercises in Lesson 3-1, Excel automatically adds a header and footer to the reports that you print. The header centers the name of the worksheet at the top of the page, while the footer centers the page number at the bottom. In the exercises in this lesson, you'll learn how to customize this standard header and footer.

In addition to headers and footers, you can also add another kind of repeated heading to your reports called *print titles*. Print titles use data entered in particular rows and columns of the worksheet (such as those with the row or column headings) and reprints this information at either the top or the left of each page in the report. Print titles using the top row of column headings are useful for reports with lots of rows of data so that the reader can identify the data in each column on every page of the report. Print titles using the first column of row headings are useful for reports with lots of columns of data so that the reader can identify the data in each row on every page of the report.

Exercise 3-7: Modifying the default header and footer

In this first exercise, you will make changes to the default header and footer used by Excel in all new reports that you print. You'll start this exercise by opening the Bo-Peep Client List workbook that you first used in Exercise 3-1.

Notes:

1 Click the Open button on the Standard toolbar or press Ctrl+O. Then open the Bo-Peep Client List workbook in the Practice folder by double-clicking the folder and then double-clicking the Bo-Peep Client List file icon in the Open dialog list box.

Now, you'll open the Page Setup dialog box from the File pull-down menu.

2 Click File on the menu bar and click Page Setup on the pull-down menu to open the Page Setup dialog box. Then click the Header/ Footer tab.

The Header/Footer tab in the Page Setup dialog box contains two drop-down list boxes: one called Header, and the other called Footer. You can use these drop-down list boxes to select a new piece of information to be used as the header or footer for the report.

3 Click the drop-down button to the right of the Header text box to open its drop-down list. Click the filename, Bo-Peep Client List, in this list to insert this filename into the Header text box.

You should see Bo-Peep Client List centered in the sample area right above the Header drop-down list box.

The header in the printout will now display the name of the workbook file (rather than the name of the worksheet) centered at the top of the page.

4 Click the drop-down button to the right of the Footer text box to open its drop-down list. Use the vertical scroll bar to scroll the list up until you see the Page 1 of ?; then click Page 1 of ? to insert it into the Footer text box.

Page 1 of 1 should now appear centered in the sample footer area right below the Footer drop-down list box. When you select Page 1 of ? in a header or footer, Excel replaces the question mark with the total number of pages in the report as Page 1 of 4, Page 2 of 4, and so on.

5 Click the Print Preview button in the Page Setup dialog box to open the Print Preview window.

First check your new header by zooming in on it in Page 1 of 4 in the Print Preview window.

6 Position the magnifying glass mouse pointer on the header at the top of the page; then click the mouse to zoom in.

You should now be able to read the filename, Bo-Peep Client List, in the header on this page. Now check out the footer.

7 Click the arrowhead mouse pointer anywhere on the screen to zoom out. Then position the magnifying glass mouse pointer somewhere on the footer text to zoom in on the footer text.

You should now be able to read the footer text, Page 1 of 4, at the bottom of the previewed page.

8 Click the Next button to page through all four pages of the report.

Each time that you click the Next button to advance the page, the footer is incremented by one page number, as in Page 2 of 4, Page 3 of 4, on up to Page 4 of 4.

9 Click the screen with the arrowhead pointer to zoom out on Page 4 of 4 and then click the Close button at the top of the Print Preview window to return to the Bo-Peep Client List workbook.

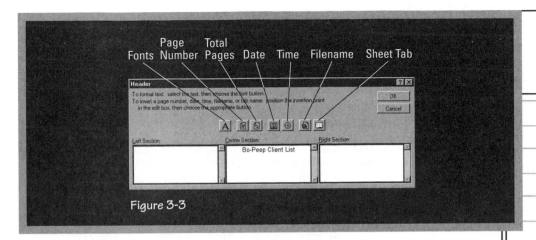

Exercise 3-8: Adding a custom header and footer to a report

In addition to the predefined headers and footers that you can select right on the Header/Footer tab of the Page Setup dialog box with the Header and Footer drop-down list boxes, you can also create custom headers and footers with the Custom Header and Custom Footer buttons.

When you select these buttons, Excel opens a Header or Footer dialog box that divides the custom header or footer into three sections: a Left Section (where the text is left justified at the top or bottom of the page), a Center Section (where the text is centered between page margins), and a Right Section (where the text is right justified). The Header Footer dialog boxes also contain special buttons for changing the font of the header or footer text and for inserting items like the current page number, total pages, current date or time, filename, and sheet tab (see Figure 3-3).

In this exercise, you will create a custom header and footer for a report printed from the Bo-Peep Client List.

1 **Click File on the menu bar and click Page Setup on the pull-down menu to open the Page Setup dialog box; then (if necessary) click the Header/Footer tab.**

Currently, the header for this report prints the filename centered at the top of the page.

2 **Click the Custom Header button to open the Header dialog box.**

The Left Section of the Header will contain the company name, Little Bo-Peep Pet Detectives.

3 **Type *Little Bo-Peep Pet Detectives* in the Left Section list box. Then press the Tab key to advance to the Center Section.**

In the Center Section, you will replace Bo-Peep Client List with the words Client List.

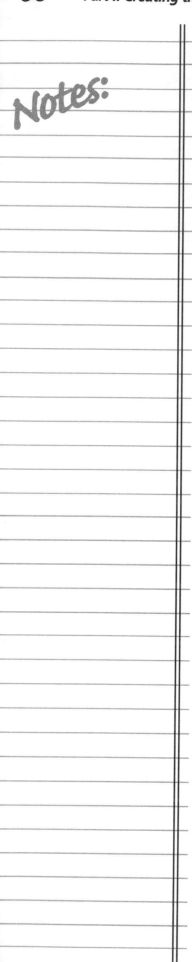

Notes:

4 **Type *Client List* in the <u>C</u>enter Section; then press Tab to advance to the <u>R</u>ight Section.**

In the Right Section, you will insert the current date.

5 **Click the Date button (the fourth one from the right; the button with the calendar icon).**

Excel inserts the code &[Date] in the Right Section. (The program will replace this code with the current date in the actual report header.)

Check the contents of your Header dialog box against those of the one shown in Figure 3-4. If everything checks out, proceed to the next step.

6 **Click the OK button to close the Header dialog box and return to the Header/Footer tab of the Page Setup dialog box.**

You can get an idea of how your custom header will appear in the report from the sample area and the contents of the Header drop-down list box.

Next, you'll use the Custom Footer button to customize the footer for the Clients database report.

7 **Click the <u>C</u>ustom Footer button to open the Footer dialog box.**

In the Left Section of the custom footer, you will insert the filename, Bo-Peep Client List.

8 **Click the Filename button (the second one from the right; the button with the XL workbook icon). Then press Tab to advance to the <u>C</u>enter Section.**

Excel inserts the &[File] code in the Left Section; this code will display the name of the workbook file. Next, in the Center Section, you'll replace the Page &[Page] of &[Pages] codes with the message *Confidential!* in boldface type.

9 **Type *Confidential!* in the <u>C</u>enter Section; then position the mouse pointer in front of the *C* in *Confidential* and hold down the Shift key as you click the mouse button to select the entire <u>C</u>enter Section and all of its characters.**

To format a section of a custom footer or header, you use the Font button to open the Font dialog box.

10 **Click the Font button (the very first button; the button with the letter A on it) to open the Font dialog box. Then click Bold in the F<u>o</u>nt Style list box before you click OK or press Enter.**

In the Right Section, you will reinsert the codes Page &[Page] of &[Pages] that enter the current page number with the total number of pages in the form Page 1 of 4.

11 **Press Tab to advance to the Right Section. Type *Page* and press the spacebar, click the Page Number button (the second button from the left), and press the spacebar again. Type *of* and press the spacebar a third time before you click the Total Pages button (the third button from the left).**

Excel inserts the text and codes Page &[Page] of &[Pages] in the Right Section of the custom footer.

Check the contents of your Footer dialog box against those of the one shown in Figure 3-5. If everything checks out, proceed to the next step.

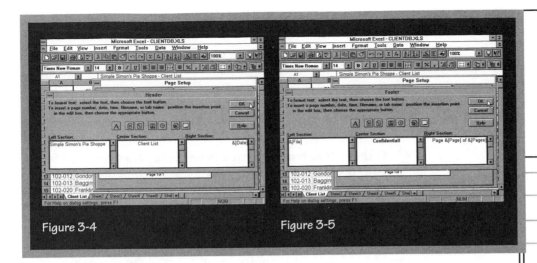

Figure 3-4

Figure 3-5

Figure 3-4: The Header dialog box with the custom header for the Bo-Peep Client List database report.

Figure 3-5: The Footer dialog box with the custom footer for the Bo-Peep Client List database report.

12 **Click the OK button to close the Footer dialog box and return to the Header/Footer tab of the Page Setup dialog box.**

You can get an idea of how your custom footer will appear in the report from the contents of the Footer drop-down list box and the sample area below it.

13 **Click the Print Preview button and then preview your custom header and footer by zooming in and out on each section of the preview page.**

After you've finished previewing the report, you'll want to leave the Preview window in full-page view before returning to the Bo-Peep Client List worksheet.

14 **Click the Zoom button if necessary to display the full page and then click the Close button to return to the Bo-Peep Client List worksheet.**

Exercise 3-9: Adding column headings as print titles

In this exercise, you get an opportunity to see how you can use the column headings in row 2 of the Bo-Peep Client List worksheet as print titles that identify the data in each column on every page of the report.

1 **Click File on the menu bar. Then click Page Setup on the pull-down menu to open the Page Setup dialog box.**

To specify the column headings in row 2 as the print titles, you need to select the Rows to Repeat at Top text box on the Sheet tab.

2 **Click the Sheet tab in the Page Setup dialog box and then click somewhere in the Rows to Repeat at Top text box to position the insertion point in this text box.**

To designate row 2 with the column headings for the Client List worksheet, you only need to select one cell in this row.

3 Click cell A2 in the Client List worksheet to the left of, and in back of, the Page Setup dialog box.

When you select cell A2, Excel inserts the absolute row address for row 2 ($2:$2) in the Rows to Repeat at Top text box in the Page Setup dialog box and, at the same time, puts a marquee (the marching ants) around the cells in row 2 in the worksheet itself.

4 Click the Print Preview button to see (in the Print Preview window) the effect of designating row 2 as the print title for this report.

5 Position the magnifying-glass mouse pointer somewhere on row 2 in the full-size page. Then click the mouse to zoom in on the first few rows at the top of Page 1 of 4.

6 Click the Next button at the top of the Print Preview window to examine the top few rows of Page 2 of 4.

Note how designating row 2 as the print title has caused Excel to repeat the column headings, ID No and so on, at the top of the last few rows of data on this page.

7 Click the Next button again to examine the top few rows of Page 3 of 4.

Here you see the column headings Anniversary through Credit at the top of the last few columns of data on this page.

8 Click the Next button one last time to examine the top few rows of Page 4 of 4.

Note how row 2 print title has caused Excel to repeat the column headings Anniversary through Credit at the top of the last few rows of data.

9 Click the Zoom button to zoom out on Page 4 of 4; then click the Close button to close the Print Preview window and to return to the Client List worksheet.

Exercise 3-10: Adding row headings as print titles

In this exercise, you'll add the row headings in columns A, B, and C of the Bo-Peep Client List worksheet (with the ID numbers and clients' first and last names) as print titles in the report; these headings will then identify the data in each row of every page.

1 Click File on the menu bar; then click Page Setup on the pull-down menu to open the Page Setup dialog box.

To specify the row headings in columns A, B, and C as the print titles, you need to select the Columns to Repeat at Left text box on the Sheet tab.

2 Click somewhere in the <u>C</u>olumns to Repeat at Left text box on the Sheet tab to position the insertion point in this text box.

To designate columns A through C with the row headings for the Client List worksheet, you need to drag through three cells in these columns in the worksheet.

3 Click the title bar of the Page Setup dialog box and then use the title bar to drag this dialog box down until you can see cells A1, B1, and C1 in the Client List worksheet.

Now you can designate columns A through C as the row print titles by dragging through and selecting cells A1:C1.

4 Click cell A1 in the Client List worksheet and then drag to the right until $A:$C appears in the <u>C</u>olumns to Repeat at Left text box in the Page Setup dialog box and you see the marching ants marching down the borderline between columns C and D in the worksheet.

When you select the cell range A1:C1, Excel inserts the absolute column range address $A:$C in the Columns to Repeat at Left text box in the Page Setup dialog box, while at the same time putting a marquee (the marching ants) at the borderline between columns C and D in the worksheet itself.

5 Click the Print Previe<u>w</u> button to see (in the Print Preview window) the effect of designating columns A through C as the row print titles for this report.

6 Click the magnifying-glass mouse pointer somewhere in the upper-left corner of the full-size page. Then click the right-arrow scroll button on the horizontal scroll bar to zoom in on the five columns of the first several rows at the top of Page 1 of 4.

7 Click the <u>N</u>ext button at the top of the Print Preview window twice to examine the first columns and rows of Page 3 of 4.

Note how designating columns A through C as the row print titles has caused Excel to repeat the data in these columns so that the ID No, Last Name, and First Name columns are now juxtaposed against the columns with data in the Anniversary, Years, Receivable, and so on.

8 Click the <u>Z</u>oom button to zoom out on Page 3 of 4. Then click the <u>C</u>lose button to close the Print Preview window and return to the Bo-Peep Client List worksheet.

☑ **Progress Check**

If you can do the following, you've mastered this lesson:

❏ Modify the default report header and footer.

❏ Create a custom header and footer.

❏ Designate rows and columns of a worksheet as print titles.

Changing the Print Settings for a Report

Lesson 3-3

In performing the exercises in Lesson 3-1, you gained experience with changing a few of the default print settings, such as changing the orientation of the printing, adding the gridlines to the printout, and changing Excel's page scheme in the report to across the columns and then down the rows. As you've undoubtedly noticed, the tabs on the Page Setup dialog box contain quite a few printing options.

Particularly noteworthy are the Paper Size option on the Page tab and the margin and centering options on the Margins tab. The Paper Size option enables you to change the size of paper that is being used in printing your report. To change the paper size, click the Paper Size drop-down button and select the appropriate paper size in the drop-down list (the choices found here depend upon the type of printer that is currently selected). The margin options on the Margins tab not only enable you to change the size of the four page margins (top, bottom, left, and right) but also enable you to adjust the distance of the header and footer text from the edge of the page and to center the printing horizontally or vertically on the page. In addition to being able to change the page margins from the Margins tab of the Page Setup dialog box, you can also adjust the margins directly in the Print Preview window.

In the next exercise in this lesson, you practice changing the page margins and centering the printing on the page. In the last exercise in this lesson, you'll get practice adjusting the automatic paging of a report by inserting a manual page break.

Exercise 3-11: Centering the printing and changing the margins

In this exercise, you'll center the printing of the report using the Bo-Peep Client List worksheet between the left and right margins before modifying these margins in the Print Preview window.

1 **With the Bo-Peep Client List workbook still open in Excel, click File on the menu bar; then click Page Setup on the pull-down menu to open the Page Setup dialog box.**

To center the printing horizontally between the left and right margins, you first need to select the Margins tab.

2 **Click the Margins tab in the Page Setup dialog box.**

Note that two check boxes are in the Center on Page section of the Margins tab. To center the printing between the left and right margins, you select the Horizontally check box.

3 **Click the Horizontally check box in the Center on Page section near the bottom of the Margins tab to put a check mark in this check box.**

Notice that, after you select the Horizontally check box, the little worksheet grid in the Preview section of the Margins tab is now centered on the page between the left and right margins.

4 **Click the Print Preview button to see the effect of centering the printing horizontally in the Print Preview window.**

Page 1 of 4 is now centered between the left and right margins on the page.

Next, you'll use the Margins button in the Print Preview window to display the top, bottom, left, and right page margins along with the header and footer margins and column width indicators.

5 **Click the Margins button at the top of the Print Preview window.**

When the margin, header, footer, and column width indicators are displayed in the Print Preview window, you can adjust any of them by dragging them with the double-headed-arrow mouse pointer.

Before you start manipulating the left and right margin settings with the mouse, get some practice with positioning the mouse pointer on the right spots.

6 Position the mouse pointer anywhere on the left margin indicator (the dotted vertical line that extends from the top to the bottom of the page at the immediate left of the first column of data). When the pointer changes to a double-headed arrow, click and hold for a second before releasing the mouse button (without doing any dragging).

Note that, when you hold down the mouse button, the Preview: Page 1 of 4 indicator on the status bar at the bottom of the window changes to Left Margin: 0.74.

7 Position the mouse pointer anywhere on the right margin indicator to the immediate right of the last column of data on this page and then hold down the mouse button until you can read its current size on the status bar.

The right margin size can read anywhere from 0.74 to 0.76 on the status bar, depending upon the type of monitor that you're using.

Now, you'll increase the left margin from 0.75 to 1 inch (or about as close to 1 inch as you can get when dragging the left margin, which is 0.99 inch with my monitor).

8 Position the mouse pointer anywhere on the left margin indicator, drag to the right until its current size on the status bar is 1.00 inch (or as close as you can get to 1.00), and then release the mouse button.

By now, you've probably gotten the idea that changing the margin settings with the mouse is a pretty imprecise business. If you want to set the margins exactly, you'll usually have to enter the measurements in the Margins tab of the Page Setup dialog box.

9 Click the <u>S</u>etup button at the top of the Print Preview window to open the Page Setup dialog box.

10 In the Margins tab, press the Tab key three times to select the <u>L</u>eft text box and type *1*.

11 Press Tab again to select the <u>R</u>ight text box, type *1*, and click OK to return to the Print Preview window.

In the Page 1 of 4 preview, you can see that Excel has increased both the left and right margins to as close to 1 inch as your monitor can display.

12 Click the <u>M</u>argins button to hide the margin and column width indicators in the Print Preview window. Then click the Close button to return to the Bo-Peep Client List worksheet

Now you need to save all the print settings you've changed in a new workbook called Little Bo-Peep Client List (Print) before you close this workbook and go on to Exercise 3-12.

13 Click Save <u>A</u>s on the <u>F</u>ile menu to open the Save As dialog box. Click the Up One Level button to open the Excel 101 folder in the Save <u>i</u>n list box and then double-click the icon for your personal folder. Click in the File <u>n</u>ame text box to place the insertion point at the end of Bo-Peep Client List, press the spacebar, and type *(Print)* before you click <u>S</u>ave or press Enter to create a new file: Bo-Peep Client List (Print).

14 Press Ctrl+F4 to close this workbook.

Notes:

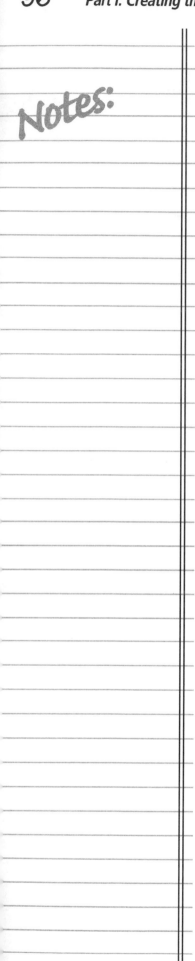

Notes:

Exercise 3-12: Adding manual page breaks to a report

As you know, Excel automatically inserts page breaks, depending upon many factors, such as the number of complete columns and rows of data that will fit on the page (given the paper size), the size of the margins, the orientation of the printing on the page, and the like. Sometimes, however, you find that you need to insert your own page breaks in the worksheet to rectify bad page breaks inserted by the program.

To insert a page break into your report, position the cell pointer in the cell at the column and row in the worksheet where the page break is to occur before you choose the Page Break command on the Insert pull-down menu. Excel indicates the page break in the worksheet by displaying a dotted line along the column and row border involved.

To remove a page break that you've inserted in a worksheet, position the cell pointer in a cell along the page break border before you choose the Remove Page Break command (which replaces the Page Break command) on the Insert pull-down menu.

To see how this works, you'll insert page breaks in the 1994 Sales worksheet in the MGE Annual Sales workbook to make this report page look better.

1 **Click the Open button on the Standard toolbar or press Ctrl+O. Then click the Up One Level button, double-click the Practice folder icon, and open the MGE Annual Sales workbook in the Practice folder by double-clicking its file icon in the Open dialog list box.**

You'll start by turning on the display of the automatic page breaks so that you can see all your page breaks in the worksheet. (This display is normally turned off.)

2 **Click Tools on the menu bar; then click Options on the pull-down menu to open the Options dialog box, where you click the Automatic Page Breaks check box on the View tab to put a check mark in this check box. Then click OK or press Enter to close the Options dialog box.**

Next, you need to designate column A with the Mother Goose Enterprises company names as the row print titles for this report.

3 **Click File on the menu bar and click Page Setup on the pull-down menu. Click the Sheet tab and then click the Columns to Repeat at Left text box before you click cell A1 in the 1994 Sales worksheet.**

When you click cell A1 in the worksheet, Excel inserts the absolute column range address $A:$A in the Columns to Repeat at Left.

4 **Click the Page tab, locate the down spinner button to the right of the Adjust to radio button in the Scaling section, and click it twice to change the percentage from 100 to 90.**

Before you can tell where you need to insert a page break in the 1994 Sales worksheet, you have to use Print Preview to see how Excel will page this report.

5 Click the Print Preview button in the Page Setup dialog box to open the Print Preview window. Then position the magnifying-glass mouse pointer about in the middle of the data shown at the top of the Page 1 of 4 preview to zoom in on the page.

6 Press the → and ← keys until you've scrolled back and forth through all the columns of data in the zoomed-in Page 1 of 4 preview.

Note how the April column of sales data appears all by its lonesome on this page and is split off from the May, June, and Qtr 2 Total data (which appear on Page 2 of 4).

7 Click the Close button to return to the 1994 Sales worksheet.

Now you'll insert a page break between columns E and F that will force the column of April sales data onto the second page with the May, June, and Qtr 2 Total data.

8 Click cell F1 to make it current. Then click Insert on the menu bar and click Page Break on the pull-down menu.

When you select the Page Break command, Excel inserts a vertical dotted line down the border between columns E and F, indicating the location of this page break.

9 Click the Print Preview button on the Standard toolbar to open the Print Preview window again.

That's better. Now the reader can see just the first quarter sales info on the first page. You'd better see how page 2 turned out.

10 Click the Next button to view Page 2 of 4. Then use the ← and → keys to scroll back and forth through the columns of information on this page.

Whoops! Now the July sales data is split off from the other third quarter data on page 3. You'll have to insert a page break between columns I and J to push the July sales data to page 3. And while you're at it, you should probably anticipate how this will orphan the October sales data, and insert yet another page break between columns M and N.

11 Click the Close button to return to the 1994 Sales worksheet; then press the → key until the cell pointer is in cell J1. Click Insert on the menu bar. Then click Page Break on the pull-down menu to insert a page break between columns I and J.

You should now see a dotted line running down the border of columns I and J, indicating this page break.

12 Press the → key until the cell pointer is in cell N1, click Insert on the menu bar, and click Page Break on the pull-down menu to insert a page break between columns M and N.

You should now see a dotted line running down the border of columns M and N, indicating this page break. Return to Print Preview one more time and check out the pages with all of your page breaks.

13 Click the Print Preview button and click the Next button to examine the page breaks in all four pages of the report. When you're finished, click the arrowhead pointer somewhere on the page to zoom out. Then click the Close button to close Print Preview and return to cell N1 in the 1994 Sales worksheet.

Now you can remove the display of the page breaks in the 1994 Sales worksheet before you close the MGE Annual Sales workbook.

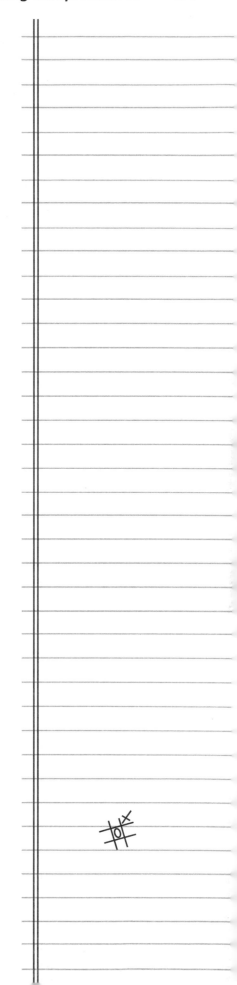

☑ **Progress Check**

If you can do the following, you've mastered this lesson:

❑ Select a new page size and change the page margins.

❑ Center the printing of a page, both horizontally and vertically.

❑ Add and remove manual pages breaks.

14 Click **T**ools on the menu bar; then click **O**ptions on the pull-down menu to open the Options dialog box. Click the **A**utomatic Page Breaks check box on the View tab again, this time to remove the check mark from its check box. After you've done this, click the OK button or press Enter to close the Options dialog box.

Save a copy of this workbook in your personal folder.

15 Press Ctrl+Home to make cell A1 current, click **F**ile on the menu bar, and click Save **A**s on the pull-down menu. Click the Up One Level button to open the Excel 101 folder in the Save **i**n list box. Then double-click the icon for your personal folder. Click in the File **n**ame text box to place the insertion point at the end of MGE Annual Sales. Then press the spacebar and type *(pg)* for page breaks, before you click **S**ave or press Enter.

You have saved a copy of this workbook (with the page breaks) titled MGE 1996 Sales(pg) in your personal folder, and you're now ready to quit Excel.

16 Press Alt+F4 to close your copy of the MGE Annual Sales (pg) workbook and quit Excel.

Recess

Good going! You've not only made it through your third unit but also have reached a significant milestone by completing the first part of your course on Excel for Windows 95.

After you've rested up a bit, you'll have plenty to do because, following the normal quiz and further exercises for Unit 3, you'll find a Part I review, test, and lab assignment covering all the material in these first three units. Be sure to complete both the Unit 3 Quiz and Further Exercises (as well as the Part I Test and Lab Assignment) before you go on to Unit 4 in Part II to learn all about working with cell ranges.

Unit 3 Quiz

Test your knowledge by answering the following questions about formatting the worksheet by using the information that you learned in Unit 3. For each of the following questions, select the letter of the correct response (and remember, I'm not above asking questions where more than one response is correct).

1. **All of the following statements about the printing defaults in Excel are true except:**

   A. Excel automatically prints one copy of the report.

   B. Excel automatically prints whatever cells happen to be selected when you choose the Print command.

   C. Excel automatically prints the filename centered in the header and the page number in the footer.

   D. Excel automatically prints the cells' column and row gridlines in the report.

2. **All of the following statements about using Print Preview in Excel are true except:**

   A. You can zoom in and out on each previewed page to examine the data in detail.

   B. You can adjust the page and header and footer margins for the report in either full-page view or after zooming in on the page.

   C. You can make changes to the data provided that you've zoomed in on the page.

   D. You move back and forth between pages by pressing the PgUp and PgDn keys, after zooming in on the page.

3. **All of the following statements about using print titles in a report are true except:**

   A. You define which columns and rows to use as print titles by selecting some of their cells in Print Preview.

   B. Print titles can include rows of column headings that are printed at the top of each page in the report.

   C. Print titles can include columns of row headings that are printed at the left edge of each page in the report.

   D. Excel includes the print titles that you've defined for the report in the pages when displayed in the Print Preview window.

4. **Suppose that you need to print a worksheet with just a couple more columns of data than will fit on a single page. Which of the following methods is the easiest way to print this report on a single page?**

   A. Decrease the left and right margin settings.

   B. Assign a smaller font to the data and then resize all the column widths.

   C. Use the Adjust to Scaling option in the Page Setup dialog box and set the percentage to 80 percent of normal size.

   D. Use the Fit to Scaling option in the Page Setup dialog box to set the printing to one page wide by one page tall.

Unit 3 Further Exercises

In these two further exercises, you get a chance to apply what you learned about printing in Unit 3 by printing reports using your MGE Quarterly Sales (fmt) workbook. Remember that this workbook contains two worksheets: Sheet1 (with the Mother Goose Enterprises 1st Quarter 1996 Sales) and Sheet 2 (with the Mother Goose Enterprises 1st Quarter 1997 Projected Sales).

Exercise 3-13: Printing the MGE Quarterly Sales (fmt) workbook

In this first exercise, you'll print the entire workbook, using Excel's other default print settings.

1. Start Excel and open the MGE Quarterly Sales (fmt) workbook that's saved in your personal folder.

2. Print one copy of the entire workbook.

Exercise 3-14: Printing the Mother Goose Enterprises 1st Quarter 1996 Sales worksheet

In this second exercise, you'll print a report using the Mother Goose Enterprises 1st Quarter 1996 Sales data in Sheet1.

1. Print one copy of the Mother Goose Enterprises 1st Quarter 1996 Sales worksheet in landscape mode, centered both horizontally and vertically on the page, without worksheet gridlines, and with the filename centered in the header at the top and the page number centered in the footer at the bottom.

2. Exit Excel without saving your changes to the Mother Goose Quarterly Sales workbook.

Part I Review

Unit 1 Summary

- **To start Excel from the Windows 95 Taskbar:** Click the Start button and move the mouse pointer up to the Programs icon on the Start menu and then click the Microsoft Excel icon on the Programs continuation menu.

- **To open a new workbook in Excel:** Click the New Workbook button on the Standard toolbar.

- **To switch between the open workbooks:** Select the workbook's name on the Window pull-down menu.

- **To close the open workbooks:** Press Ctrl+F4 or choose Close on the File menu.

- **To make a new worksheet cell current with the mouse:** Click it.

- **To Use the Go To feature to move the cell pointer directly to a cell:** Enter its cell address.

- **To move back and forth between the sheets of your workbook:** Click their sheet tabs.

- **To enter text or a value in a cell and move to the next cell that requires data entry:** Press the appropriate arrow key.

- **To enter text or a value in a cell without moving the cell pointer:** Click the Enter box on the formula bar.

- **To create SUM formulas that total columns or rows of values:** Use the AutoSum button.

- **To copy a formula to cells to the right in a row or to rows down the column:** Drag the fill handle.

- **To fill out a series in columns to the right in a row or in rows down the column:** Drag the fill handle.

Unit 2 Summary

- **To change the default file location:** Use the Default File Location text box on the General tab of the Options dialog box.

- **To open your Excel workbook file:** Click the Open button on the Standard toolbar and then select the folder and file in the Open dialog box.

- **To adjust a column width or row height to the best fit:** Use AutoFit.

- **To adjust a column's width or height:** Drag the double-headed arrow mouse pointer on a column or row border.

- **To select a new font for the text in the selected cells:** Use the Font button on the Formatting toolbar.

- **To select a new point size for the text:** Use the Font Size button on the Formatting toolbar.

- **To add or remove Bold, Italic, or Underline type styles from the text:** Use the Bold, Italic, and Underline buttons on the Formatting toolbar.

- **To change the alignment of entries in your selected cells:** Use the Align Left, Center, and Align Right buttons on the Formatting toolbar.

- **To center a cell entry across all the columns in the cell selection:** Use the Center Across Columns button on the Formatting toolbar.

- **To add two decimal places and commas to separate the thousands in the values in the cells currently selected:** Use the Comma Style button on the Formatting toolbar.

- **To add Currency style formatting plus a dollar sign to the values:** Use the Currency Style button on the Formatting toolbar.

- **To add or remove borders around the cells selected:** Use the Borders button on the Formatting toolbar.

- **To change the color of the cells that are selected:** Use the Color button on the Formatting toolbar.

- **To change the color of the text in the cells that are selected:** Use the Font Color button on the Formatting toolbar.

Part I Review

Unit 3 Summary

▶ **To preview the page layout of a report before you print it:** Use the Print Preview button on the Standard toolbar.

▶ **To print one copy of the currently selected worksheet(s):** Use the Print button on the Standard toolbar.

▶ **To print all the data in the entire workbook:** Open the Print dialog box (Ctrl+P) and select the Entire Workbook radio button in the Print What area.

▶ **To print selected sheets of the workbook:** Select their sheet tabs; then click the Print button on the Standard toolbar or open the Print dialog box (Ctrl+P) and just choose OK or press Enter (because the Selected Sheet(s) radio button is the default in the Print What area).

▶ **To print a specific range of cells in a worksheet:** Select the range and then open the Print dialog box (Ctrl+P) and select the Selection radio button in the Print What area.

▶ **To modify the default report header or footer:** Open the Page Setup dialog box and select the new header or footer in the Header or Footer drop-down list boxes on the Header/ Footer tab.

▶ **To create a custom header or footer:** Use the Custom Header or Custom Footer button and then insert the necessary text and format codes in the appropriate section of the Header or Footer dialog box.

▶ **To designate column headings in rows of a worksheet as print titles for the report:** Select the Rows to Repeat at Top text box on the Sheet tab of the Page Setup dialog box; then select the cell range in the rows of the worksheet to be used.

▶ **To designate row headings in columns of the worksheet as print titles:** Select the Columns to Repeat at Left text in the Sheet tab; then select a cell range in the columns to be used.

▶ **To change the page margins by dragging the margin indicators on the previewed page:** Use the Margins button in the Print Preview window.

▶ **To change the page margins by entering new measurements:** Use the various margin options on the Margins tab of the Page Setup dialog box.

▶ **To add your own page breaks to a report:** Position the cell pointer along the row and column in the worksheet where the break is to occur; then choose Page Break on the Insert menu.

Part I Test

The questions on this test cover all of the material presented in Part I, Units 1-3. The first section is True/False, the second section is Multiple Choice, and the last section is Matching.

True False

Circle the letter of the answer (*T* for True and *F* for False) that best answers the question.

T F 1. To start Excel for Windows 95 from the Taskbar, you click the Microsoft Excel program icon on the Programs continuation menu.

T F 2. To open a blank workbook in Excel, you can click the Open button on the Standard toolbar.

T F 3. When you first go to save a workbook, Excel automatically wants to save the workbook in whatever folder is listed as the default file location.

T F 4. To enter text or value in a cell, the program must be in Enter mode.

T F 5. To move the cell pointer with the Go To feature, you type in its cell address.

T F 6. To widen a column of data to fit the longest entry in that column, you click on the frame at the column's right border.

T F 7. To use AutoFormat to format a table of data, you must select all the cells in that table before you choose AutoFormat on the Format menu.

T F 8. The fastest way to print the entire worksheet is by clicking the Print button on the Standard toolbar.

T F 9. In the Print Preview window, Excel maintains a "look but don't touch" policy that lets you zoom in any of the data but does not allow you to make changes to it.

T F 10. To set exact page margins for a report, you are better off entering measurements in the appropriate text boxes on the Margins tab of the Page Setup dialog box.

Multiple Choice

For each of the following questions, circle the correct answer. Remember that there may be more than one right answer to a question.

11. All of the following statements about moving the cell pointer with the keyboard are true except:

A. Pressing PgUp and PgDn moves the cell pointer one screenful to the left and right in the worksheet.

B. Pressing the ↑ and ↓ keys with the Ctrl key depressed moves the cell pointer up and down one screenful.

C. Pressing the Tab and Shift+Tab keys to move the cell pointer is the same as pressing the → and ← keys, respectively.

D. Pressing PgUp and PgDn with the Ctrl key depressed moves the cell pointer to the next and previous worksheet of the workbook.

12. All of the following statements about entering data in a worksheet are true except:

A. All formulas must begin with an equal sign (=).

B. All text entries are left-aligned in their cells.

C. All dates are entered as text in their cells.

D. All values are right-aligned in their cells.

Part I Test

13. **All of the following statements about formatting a worksheet are true except:**

    A. Number formats apply only to values in the cells to which they're applied.

    B. Font changes apply only to characters in text entries.

    C. AutoFormat only works on cell ranges that Excel can recognize as a table of data.

    D. Styles in Excel can apply font, number format, borders, color, and font color changes to the cells to which they're applied.

14. **All of the following statements about saving a workbook are true except:**

    A. When you first save a workbook, Excel automatically wants to save a new workbook file in the Excel folder on your hard disk.

    B. When you first save a workbook, Excel automatically suggests the temporary filename (Book1, Book2, and so on) as the filenames to use.

    C. When you save changes to a workbook, Excel saves the current position of the cell pointer in each worksheet in the workbook.

    D. When you use the Save As command on the File menu to save a workbook, you can both rename and relocate the file.

15. **All of the following statements about opening a workbook file are true except:**

    A. When you open a workbook, Excel automatically looks for all the Excel files in the Excel folder on your hard disk.

    B. You can open a workbook from the File pull-down menu provided it was one of the last four files opened in the program.

    C. Pressing Ctrl+O to open the Open dialog box is the same thing as clicking the Open button on the Standard toolbar.

    D. When you first open a workbook, Excel automatically positions the cell pointer in the first cell (A1) of the first worksheet.

Matching

In each of the following questions, match the items in the first column with the appropriate items in the second column by drawing a line from the item in the column on the left that connects to its counterpart in the column on the right.

16. **Match up each of the following Header and Footer icons with the correct function:**

    A.   1. Inserts code that prints the worksheet name.

    B.   2. Inserts code that prints the total number of pages in the report.

    C.   3. Inserts code that prints the filename of the workbook.

    D.   4. Inserts code that prints the current page number.

Part I Test

17. **Match up each of the following Standard toolbar icons with the correct function:**

    A. ⬜ 1. Opens existing Excel workbook file.

    B. 📂 2. Opens new Excel workbook file.

    C. 🔍 3. Totals values in a column or row.

    D. Σ 4. Displays first page of a report as it will be printed.

18. **Match up each of the following mouse pointer shapes with the correct function:**

    A. ⊕ 1. Used to copy a cell or fill out a series.

    B. ⊕🖌 2. Used to select cells in the worksheet.

    C. ✛ 3. Used to copy formatting from one cell to another.

    D. ↔ 4. Used to adjust the width of columns by dragging the column border.

19. **Match up each of the following Formatting toolbar icons with the correct function:**

    A. ≣ 1. Centers cell entries in their cells.

    B. ≣ 2. Left aligns entries in their cells.

    C. ⊞ 3. Right aligns entries in their cells.

    D. ≣ 4. Centers cell entries across all columns in the current cell selection.

20. **Match up each of the following Formatting toolbar icons with the correct function:**

    A. ⊡ 1. Removes decimal places from number formatting assigned to cells.

    B. ⬜ 2. Changes the color of the selected cells.

    C. .00 3. Changes the color of the text in the selected cells.

    D. 🖍 4. Adds or removes borders around the selected cells.

Part I Lab Assignment

This is the first of several lab problems that appear at the end of each part throughout this book. These lab problems are designed to allow you to apply the skills you learned in semi-realistic situations (I was going to say "real-life" situations, but what are the odds of you going to work for one of the Mother Goose Enterprises companies anyway?).

The lab assignments are a whole lot less step-directed than the other exercises that you've performed. The lab assignments merely lay out a general task to be done, and it's up to you to figure out what steps to take in Excel to get the job done. (Hey, that's realistic, isn't it?) In this first lab assignment, you are going to create, format, and print a new Mother Goose Enterprises projected sales worksheet for the first quarter of 1998.

Step 1: Creating the MGE 1st Quarter Projected 1998 sales worksheet

Open the MGE Quarterly Sales (fmt) workbook in your personal folder. Then enter the sales data in the third worksheet (Sheet 3) of the workbook, according to the layout and contents of following table:

	A	B	C	D	E
1	Mother Goose Enterprises 1st Quarter 1998 Sales (Projected)				
2		Jan	Feb	Mar	Qtr 1 Total
3	Jack Sprat Diet Centers	98670.63	73123.40	24575.82	
4	Jack and Jill Trauma Centers	152005.45	110006.89	31319.11	
5	Mother Hubbard Dog Goodies	15583.99	74605.82	52082.22	
6	Rub-a-Dub-Dub Hot Tubs and Spas	21694.37	50031.84	52715.96	
7	Georgie Porgie Pudding Pies	70345.70	77478.02	15278.25	
8	Hickory, Dickory, Dock Clock Repair	207208.29	153559.16	51609.24	
9	Little Bo-Beep Pet Detectives	37965.14	87555.73	92252.93	
10	Total				

After you've entered the data, create SUM formulas that total the monthly sales in cells B10:D10 and create SUM formulas in cells E3:E10 that total the quarterly sales.

Step 2: Formatting the MGE 1st Quarter 1998 projected sales worksheet

Format the MGE 1st Quarter 1998 projected sales worksheet by centering the spreadsheet title in cell A1 across cells A through E, centering and bolding the column headings in cells B2:E2, and right-aligning the row headings in cells A3:A10. Format the values in the cell range B3:D9 with the Comma Style number format with zero decimal places and format the totals in the cell ranges B10:E10 and E3:E9 with the Currency Style number format with zero decimal places. Widen all the columns in the sales table sufficiently to display all of their data.

Step 3: Printing the MGE 1st Quarter 1998 sales worksheet

Print a report with all the worksheets in the MGE Quarterly Sales (fmt) workbook and the name of the workbook file in the left section of the header, the page number and total pages in the Page 1 of ? format in the right section of the header, the name of each worksheet in the left section of the footer, the date in the center section of the footer, and the time in the right section of the footer.

After printing the report, save the workbook with Sheet1 active and the cell pointer in cell A1 of all three worksheets.

Modifying the Spreadsheet

Part II

In this part . . .

Part II completes the Excel for Windows 95 course on the spreadsheet. This part is made up of two units that expand your knowledge of manipulating and modifying spreadsheet data. Unit 4 teaches you the basics of working with cell ranges. Unit 5 teaches you the basics of editing the spreadsheet. Taken together, they complete your basic training on the Excel spreadsheet and get you ready to experience Excel's other non-spreadsheet-related features.

Working with Cell Ranges

Objectives for This Unit

✓ Selecting cell ranges with the mouse or keyboard

✓ Selecting nonadjacent cell ranges with the mouse or keyboard

✓ Selecting cell ranges with the Go To feature

✓ Getting running totals with AutoCalculate

✓ Naming cell ranges with Insert⇨Name⇨Define

✓ Creating names for cells from existing labels with Insert⇨Name⇨Create

✓ Selecting named ranges from the formula bar and with Go To

✓ Replacing cell addresses in formulas with column and row names

✓ Moving or copying cell ranges with drag and drop

✓ Moving or copying cell ranges with cut and paste

✓ Replacing formulas with their calculated values with Edit⇨Paste Special

Prerequisites

▸ All lessons and exercises in Unit 3 completed

▸ Unit 3 Quiz and Unit 3 Further Exercises successfully completed

Welcome to Unit 4, where you will learn all about selecting, naming, copying, and moving cell ranges. As a result of studying this unit, you should be able to efficiently select cell ranges with either the mouse or keyboard, name cell ranges, use those range names to select cell ranges and apply them to formulas, and copy or move cell ranges to new locations on their worksheets as well as between the sheets of a workbook.

Lesson 4-1

Selecting Cell Ranges

on the test

Up to now, most of the cell ranges that you've needed in the course of completing a particular exercise have been selected with the old Shift+click mouse method, whereby you click the first cell in the range and then hold down the Shift key as you click the last cell. Now it's time to learn some of the other mouse and keyboard methods for selecting ranges of cells in the worksheet.

Before you do, however, be sure that you're clear on the concept of a cell range. A *cell range* (or *cell selection*) in Excel is just another term for the block of cells that is currently selected. The smallest possible range in a worksheet is a single cell (that is, what you know as the active or current cell), whereas the largest possible cell range is all the cells in the worksheet. Most cell ranges that you will work with will be somewhere in between these two extremes: the blocks of cells that you work with will be made up of so many rows by so many columns.

In Excel, you can select more than one cell range at a time. Selecting more than one cell range at a time is known as selecting a *nonadjacent cell range* (or *nonadjacent selection*). Selecting a nonadjacent cell range is a really cool way to apply formatting to lots of different cell ranges in one operation. But some operations, such as copying and moving data in the worksheet, can't be done via nonadjacent cell selection.

Making cell selections with the mouse

To select a cell range with the mouse, you can either Shift+click the cells in the range or drag through them. To Shift+click them, you click the first cell in the range to make it active; then you hold down the Shift key as you click the last cell. To drag through the cells, you click the first cell to make it active and then hold down the mouse button as you move through the cells to select them.

To select more than one range for a nonadjacent selection, select the first range (either with Shift+click or by dragging through its cells) and hold down the Ctrl key as you click the first cell of the second range. Because you are holding down Ctrl, clicking the first cell of the second cell range does not deselect the first cell range. You then can select the second cell range with either the Shift+click or drag method. (Just don't let up on the Ctrl key until you've finished adding this second range to the nonadjacent cell range.)

When selecting a block of data for formatting or editing with the mouse, you can use a technique called AutoSelect. To select a block of cells with AutoSelect, you select a cell in the table, position the arrowhead mouse pointer on the side of the selected cell where you want the range expanded, and then hold down the Shift key (that good old Shift key!) as you double-click. Excel then selects all the cells in the table in the directions of that side.

You can also select larger cell ranges with the mouse. Table 4-1 recaps the techniques for selecting an entire column or row (as well as all the cells in the worksheet). If you need to select multiple neighboring columns and rows (as you might when using AutoFit), drag through their column letters or row numbers on the frame. To make a nonadjacent selection of entire columns and rows, simply hold down the Ctrl key as you drag through additional column letters or row numbers on the frame.

Table 4-1	Selecting Larger Cell Ranges with the Mouse
To Select	**Click**
The entire row	The row's number on the frame
The entire column	The column's letter on the frame
The entire worksheet	The worksheet button in the upper-left corner of the frame at the intersection of the column letters and row numbers (left of A and above 1)

Making cell selections with the keyboard

To select cell ranges with the keyboard, you can combine the keystrokes for moving the cell pointer with the Shift key (see "Moving the cell pointer with the keyboard" in Lesson 1-2). For example, holding down Shift when you press the → key selects cells in the columns to the right as you move the cell pointer. Excel continues to select cells for as long as you hold down the Shift key. Should you press a keystroke to move the cell pointer without holding down the Shift key when a cell range is selected, the cell selection immediately collapses as soon as Excel moves the cell pointer.

Instead of having to keep the Shift key depressed while extending a cell selection with the keyboard, you can place Excel in Extend mode (indicated by the display of EXT on the status bar) by pressing function key F8. While the program is in Extend mode, Excel will select all the cells between the active cell and the cell that you move to with the keyboard. (You can also make a cell selection with the mouse by clicking the last cell in the range — just as though you were doing the Shift+click thing.) After you've finished extending the cell range with the keyboard, you can then get out of Extend mode by pressing F8 again.

To make nonadjacent cell selections from the keyboard, you need to switch the program from Extend mode to Add mode by pressing Shift+F8. While the program is in Add mode, Excel lets you move the cell pointer to the first cell of the new range to be added to the nonadjacent selection without deselecting the first cell range. After you've positioned the cell pointer in the first cell of the new range, you have to switch the program from Add mode to Extend mode by pressing F8 again. This change makes it possible to once again select cells in the new range as you move the cell pointer. By alternating between Extend mode (F8) and Add mode (Shift+F8), you can add as many cell ranges as you like to the nonadjacent selection. Of course, once you've finished doing whatever it is you wanted to do to the nonadjacent cell range, you can collapse it by getting out of Extend mode (by pressing F8) or Add mode (by pressing Shift+F8) and then moving the cell pointer one more time.

Table 4-2 shows you the keystrokes for selecting entire columns and rows as well as for selecting the entire worksheet. Prior to selecting an entire row or column with Shift+spacebar or Ctrl+spacebar, you must remember to first position the cell pointer into one of the cells in the row or column that you wish to select. You can select multiple neighboring columns and rows by putting Excel in Extend mode and then pressing the → or ← key to add more columns or the ↑ or ↓ key to add more rows. You can make a nonadjacent selection of entire rows or columns by alternating between Extend mode and Add mode.

Table 4-2	Selecting Larger Cell Ranges with the Keyboard
To Select	*Press*
The entire row	Shift+spacebar
The entire column	Ctrl+spacebar
The entire worksheet	Ctrl+A or Ctrl+Shift+spacebar
From the active cell to the beginning of the row	Shift+Home

Exercise 4-1: Selecting cell ranges with the mouse

In this first selection exercise, you'll get practice selecting different-size cell ranges with the mouse. First you'll select some empty cells in a blank worksheet. Then you'll get practice selecting occupied cells in your MGE Quarterly Sales (afmt) workbook.

1   Start Excel and open MGE Quarterly Sales (afmt) (the AutoFormatted version of your Mother Goose Enterprises sales worksheets) that's in your personal folder.

Next, you'll practice selecting different ranges in Sheet3.

2   Click the Sheet3 tab to make this empty worksheet active.

Start by selecting the cell range B3:D11 by dragging through the cells.

3   Click cell B3 to make it active, drag down to row 11, and then drag right to column D and release the mouse button.

Now you'll create a nonadjacent cell selection by selecting a second cell range: G7:H16. To do this, you *must* hold down the Ctrl key as you drag through this second cell selection.

4   Hold down the Ctrl key as you click cell G7, drag down to row 16, and then drag over to column H. When the cell range G7:H16 is highlighted, release the mouse button.

At this point, both cell ranges (the larger, B3:D11, and the smaller, G7:H16) should be selected in Sheet3. Note, however, that cell G7 (the first cell of the second cell range) is the active cell in this nonadjacent cell selection.

Next, you'll try selecting an entire column of the worksheet.

5   Position the white-cross mouse pointer over the letter C on the column part of the worksheet frame and click the mouse button.

Because you didn't hold down the Ctrl key, as soon as you click C on the frame, Excel deselects the nonadjacent cell selection, while at the same time selecting all the cells in column C.

Go ahead and undo this change to restore your nonadjacent selection in Sheet3.

Notes:

6 **Reselect your nonadjacent selection as described in Steps 3 and 4. Then, this time, hold down the Ctrl key while you click the letter C on the column part of the worksheet frame.**

This time, Excel adds all the cells in column C to the nonadjacent selection made up of cell ranges B3:D11 and G7:H16.

Next, you'll select a range of rows in Sheet3.

7 **Click the number 3 in the row part of the worksheet frame and then drag down through the frame until you've selected the range of rows 3:13; then release the mouse button.**

How about selecting column ranges A:C, E, and G:I as a nonadjacent cell selection this time?

8 **Click the letter A in the column part of the worksheet frame; then drag to the right until columns B and C are both selected. Hold down the Ctrl key as you click the letter E on the frame; then click the letter G and drag to the right until columns H and I are both selected.**

Enough of selecting empty cells already. Next, you'll practice selecting the cells of your Mother Goose Enterprises 1st Quarter 1996 sales table with the AutoSelect feature.

9 **Click cell A1 to make this cell current and deselect the nonadjacent cell selection. Then click the Sheet1 sheet tab to make your worksheet with the Mother Goose Enterprises 1st Quarter 1996 sales table current.**

To use AutoSelect, you need to double-click the edges of the active cell on the side that you want to extend while you hold down the Shift key.

In order for this little AutoSelect technique to work, you need to move the cell pointer to cell A2 in the table.

10 **Click cell A2. Then position the arrowhead mouse pointer somewhere along the bottom edge of the cell pointer and hold down the Shift key as you double-click this edge.**

As soon as you double-click the bottom edge, Excel extends the selection down to A10 so that the range A2:A10 is now selected. Next, you'll extend the cell range to the right to column E.

11 **Position the arrowhead mouse pointer somewhere along the right edge of the selected cell range A2:A10 and hold down the Shift key as you double-click this edge.**

As soon as you double-click the right edge of the selected cell range A2:A10, Excel extends the selection to the right so that the range A2:E10 is now selected. The way to add the spreadsheet title in cell A1 to this selected range (A2:E10) is by Shift+clicking the top edge of the cell selection.

12 **Position the mouse pointer somewhere along the top edge of the cell selection A2:E10 and hold down the Shift key as you double-click with the arrowhead mouse pointer.**

Excel extends the cell selection up to select the cell range A1:E10.

13 **Click cell A1 to make it active and deselect the cell range A1:E10.**

Notes:

Exercise 4-2: Selecting cell ranges with the keyboard

In this second selection exercise, you'll get practice making variously sized cell selections with the keyboard. You'll use the same MGE Quarterly Sales (afmt) workbook that you opened for Exercise 4-1.

1 **Click the Sheet3 tab to make this empty worksheet active.**

First, you'll use Extend mode to select the cell range C4:F10 in Sheet3.

2 **Use the arrow keys to move the cell pointer to cell C4. Then press function key F8 to put Excel into Extend mode.**

When you press F8, EXT appears on the status bar to let you know that the program will now add cells to the cell selection as you move through them.

3 **Press the → key until cell F4 is highlighted; then press the ↓ key until the cell range extends down to row 10 and cell range C4:F10 is selected.**

Reduce the cell range from C4:F10 to C4:E9.

4 **Press the ↑ key once. Then press the ← key once.**

As long as the program is in Extend mode, you can keep changing the size and shape of the cell selection.

5 **Press the → key twice to extend the cell selection to the right to column G so that the cell range C4:G9 is highlighted.**

To make another cell selection in the worksheet and add it as part of a nonadjacent selection, you must switch to Add mode before you switch back to Extend mode.

6 **Press Shift+F8 to switch to Add mode. Then press the ↓ key until the cell pointer is in cell C12.**

When you press Shift+F8, ADD appears on the status bar. When the program is in Add mode, you can move the cell pointer with the keyboard or mouse without deselecting whatever cells are selected in the worksheet.

7 **Press F8 to switch back to Extend mode, press the ← key twice to select to cell A12, and press the ↑ key once to select up to cell A11.**

Now, both cell range C4:G9 and cell range A11:C12 are selected as a nonadjacent selection.

8 **Press F8 again to get out of Extend mode, press the ← key twice, and press the ↑ key until the cell pointer is in cell A1.**

As soon as you press the ← key the first time, Excel deselects both selected cell ranges in the nonadjacent cell selection.

Exercise 4-3: Selecting a cell range with Go To

In this exercise, you practice using the Go To feature to select all the cells between the current one and the one whose address you enter in the Go To dialog box. This technique comes in quite handy when you need to select a really large cell range in very different parts of the same worksheet.

1 **Click cell B2 to make it active.**

Now you'll open the Go To dialog box.

2 **Press function key F5 to open the Go To dialog box.**

Next, you'll enter (in the Reference text box) the address of the last cell in the range that you want to select.

3 **Type *f15* in the <u>R</u>eference text box.**

Before you click OK or press Enter in the Go To dialog box to send the cell pointer to this cell, you must remember to hold down the Shift key so that Excel will select all the cells between cell B2 and cell F15.

4 **Hold down the Shift key as you click OK (or press Enter).**

When the Go To dialog box disappears, the cell range B2:F15 is selected in Sheet3.

5 **Click cell A1 to deselect the cell range B2:F15 and make the first cell of Sheet3 active.**

6 **Click the Sheet1 sheet tab to make the worksheet with the Mother Goose Enterprises 1st Quarter 1996 sales table active.**

☑ Progress Check

If you can do the following, you've mastered this lesson:

❑ Select a cell range with the mouse or the keyboard.

❑ Make a nonadjacent cell selection with the mouse or the keyboard.

❑ Select a table of data with the AutoSelect feature.

❑ Select a range of data with the Go To feature.

Using AutoCalculate

Lesson 4-2

Excel for Windows 95 introduces a new calculation feature called AutoCalculate. With AutoCalculate, you can obtain totals on the fly simply by selecting the range of cells containing the values that you want summed. After the cells are selected, their totals appear in the AutoCalculate box on the status bar (following the text Sum=).

By default, the AutoCalculate feature will give you running totals using the SUM function for any values in the current cell selection. You can, however, also use AutoCalculate to obtain other simple statistical calculations on the fly such as the average, the maximum, the minimum, and the count of the values in the cell selection.

To obtain a calculation other than the total with AutoCalculate, click somewhere on the AutoCalculate box with the secondary mouse button and then select the desired calculation (Average, Count, Count Nums, Max, or Min) on the context menu.

Exercise 4-4: Calculating totals on the fly with AutoCalculate

In this exercise, you'll get some practice using AutoCalculate to obtain various statistics for different cell selections in the 1st Quarter 1996 sales table in Sheet1 of your MGE Quarterly Sales workbook.

Notes:

If you can do the following, you've mastered this lesson:

❑ Use AutoCalculate to get a running total of the values in a cell selection.

❑ Use AutoCalculate to obtain other statistics on the values in a cell range such as average, count of values, maximum value, and minimum value.

1 **With Sheet 1 of MGE Quarterly Sales workbook active, click B3 (containing $80,138.58) to make this cell active.**

Notice that, as soon as you select cell B3, the AutoCalculate box on the status bar changes to read Sum= $80,138.58.

2 **Hold down the Shift key as you click cell B9 to select the cell range B3:B9.**

As soon as you select this cell range, the AutoCalculate box on the status bar changes to read Sum= $490,130.81 (which just happens to jibe with the total calculated by the SUM(B3:B9) formula that's displayed in cell B10).

Next, you'll use AutoCalculate to find the average for the values in the cell selection B3:B9.

3 **Click the AutoCalculate box on the status bar with the secondary mouse button and highlight and click Average at the top of its context menu.**

When you do this, the AutoCalculate box on the status bar changes to read Average= $70,018.69.

Now check out the average for the cell range B3:D3 with the monthly sales for the Jack Sprat Diet Centers.

4 **Click cell B3 to deselect the cell range B3:B9 and then drag to the right until the cell range B3:D3 is selected.**

When you do this, the AutoCalculate box on the status bar changes to read Average= $53,162.73.

Next, you'll use AutoCalculate to find out the number of cells in the cell selection B2:D7.

5 **Click cell B2 to deselect the cell range B3:D3 and drag over and down until the cell range B2:D7 is selected.**

Now you need to change the AutoCalculate function from Average to Count.

6 **Click the AutoCalculate box on the status bar with the secondary mouse button. Then highlight and click Count near the top of the context menu.**

As soon as you select Count, the AutoCalculate box contents change to read Count=18.

Next, obtain the count of cells that contain values in the cell selection B2:D7 by selecting Count Nums rather than Count on the AutoCalculate context menu.

7 **Click the AutoCalculate box on the status bar with the secondary mouse button again, this time highlighting and clicking Count Nums on the context menu.**

As soon as you select Count Nums, the AutoCalculate box contents change to Count=15. According to AutoCalculate, 18 occupied cells are in the cell selection B2:D7 and 15 of these are values.

Go ahead and change AutoCalculate back to the default (totaling the values in the current cell) selection before you close the MGE Quarterly Sales (afmt) workbook.

8 **Click the AutoCalculate box on the status bar with the secondary mouse button and highlight and click Sum at the very bottom of the context menu.**

When you do this, the AutoCalculate box reads Sum=746816.21.

Now, close the MGE Quarterly Sales (afmt) workbook without bothering to save your changes.

9 Click File on the menu bar and Close on the pull-down menu to close the MGE Quarterly Sales (afmt) workbook. Click the No button if asked by an alert box if you want to Save changes in MGE Quarterly Sales (afmt).xls.

Naming Cell Ranges   Lesson 4-3

In Excel, you can give descriptive names to cells or cell ranges within your worksheet. There are two primary reasons for naming prominent (that is, often used) cells and cell ranges in your spreadsheet:

▶ You can select their cells for formatting, editing, or printing by selecting their range names either in the cell address drop-down list box on the formula bar or in the Go To dialog box.

▶ You can replace their cell addresses with their range names in formulas to help document the calculations that are being performed.

When assigning range names to cell ranges, you must begin the range name with a letter of the alphabet, you must not use spaces in the range name (use an underscore instead), and you must avoid assigning names that duplicate actual cell addresses in the worksheet. For example, you shouldn't name a range *X15* since there is a cell address X15 in the worksheet because, if you do, Excel will be confused as to whether you mean the cell range named *X15* or the cell whose address is *X15!*

As you will learn in completing Exercises 4-6 and 4-7 in this lesson, you can create a range name by selecting the cell (or range of cells in the worksheet) that is to be named and then entering the range name in the Define Name dialog box, or you can select the column and/or row heading(s) along with the cell or range of cells to be named and then have Excel create range names for the cell selection from those column and/or row heading(s).

Exercise 4-5: Creating the retail price table

For the exercises on defining and using range names, you'll start a new workbook and create (in its first worksheet) a simple table that computes the retail price of each kind of pie sold by the Georgie Porgie Pudding Pies company based on a healthy markup on the cost of the particular pie's ingredients.

1 Click the New Workbook button on the Standard toolbar to open a new workbook.

Next, enter the title for this worksheet in two cells, A1 and A2.

2 In cell A1, type *Georgie Porgie Pudding Pies* and press the ↓ key to move the cell pointer to cell A2.

3 In cell A2, type *Prices Per Unit* and press the → key.

Now you'll enter the column headings in cells B2 and C2.

4 In cell B2, type *Cost* and press the → key; in cell C2, type *Retail Price* and press Enter.

Next, you'll enter the row headings with the different types of pies in column A.

5 Press Ctrl+← key to move the cell pointer to cell A3. Then type *Pied Piper Pumpkin pie* and press Enter to move the cell pointer down to cell A4.

6 Type *King Cole Coconut Cream pie* and press Enter to move the cell pointer to cell A5. Then type *London Towne Lemon pie* and press Enter to move the cell pointer to cell A6. Finally, type *Mother Gooseberry pie* in cell A6 and click the Enter button on the formula bar to complete the row headings.

Now widen column A with AutoFit before you enter the costs of making each pie in the cell range B3:B6.

7 With the double-headed-arrow mouse pointer, double-click the border between columns A and B on the frame.

Now you're ready to enter the costs of each pie.

8 Select the cell range B3:B6, type *2.35* in cell B3, and press Enter. Type *1.85* in cell B4 and press Enter. Type *2.42* in cell B5 and press Enter. Finally, type *3* in cell B6 and press Enter one last time.

Next, you need to save your work so far on the retail price table.

9 Click cell C3 to make this cell active and deselect the cell range B3:B6.

10 Click the Save button on the Standard toolbar or press Ctrl+S. Then make sure that the name of your personal folder is listed in the Save in drop-down list box before you enter *Price Table* as the filename in the File name text box.

Exercise 4-6: Defining the markup constant for the retail price table

The retail price of each pie in your price table will be computed by formula based on a constant markup percentage of 150 percent of the cost of making each pie. Instead of entering this percentage in a cell in a worksheet, you will enter it as part of defining a cell range called *markup*.

1 With the cell pointer still in cell C3 of Sheet1 in the Price Table workbook, click Insert on the menu bar. Then move down to Name on the pull-down menu and click Define on the continuation menu to open the Define Name dialog box.

Because the cell pointer is in cell C3 with the column heading Retail Price above, Excel suggests the range name Retail_Price in the Names in Workbook text box for the absolute cell reference =Sheet1!$C$3 in the Refers to text box. Note that this cell reference is so absolute in this case that it includes the worksheet name (Sheet1) along with the absolute cell address ($C$3) separated by an exclamation point.

2 **Type *Markup* in the Names in Workbook text box.**

Next, you'll replace the absolute cell reference in the Refers to text box with the constant value of 150% (that's 1, 5, zero, and a percent sign).

3 **Press Tab twice to select the Refers to text box, type *150%*, and click OK or press Enter.**

Now that you've defined the Markup constant, you can use it to create a simple formula that calculates the retail price.

4 **Press = (equal sign). Then click cell B3 with the Pied Piper Pumpkin pie cost (2.35). Next, press * (asterisk).**

At this point, your formula appears as =B3* (both in the cell and on the formula bar). Now you must paste the range name, Markup, into your multiplication formula.

5 **Click Insert on the menu bar, move down to Name on the pull-down menu, and click Paste on the continuation menu to open the Paste Name dialog box.**

6 **Double-click Markup in the Paste Name list box or click it and then click OK or press Enter.**

Now your formula should appear as =B3*Markup (both in the cell and on the formula bar).

7 **Click the Enter box on the formula bar.**

The calculated result (3.525) appears in cell C3, while the formula (=B3*Markup) appears on the formula bar. Next, you need to use the fill handle to copy this formula down column C for the other pies.

8 **Drag the fill handle down until cell C6 is selected; then release the mouse button.**

Now all that's left to do in this exercise is to format the Cost and Retail Price values and then save your work.

9 **Hold down the Shift key as you press the ← key to extend the cell selection to column B. Then click the Currency style button on the Formatting toolbar.**

10 **Click cell A1 to make this cell active and deselect the range B3:C6; then click the Save button on the Standard toolbar (or press Ctrl+S) to save your changes.**

Exercise 4-7: Defining cell range names in the retail price table

In this exercise, you'll select all the cells in the retail price table and give your selection a range name. You can then use this range name to select these cells for formatting, editing, or printing quickly.

1 **With cell A1 active, hold down the Shift key as you click cell C6 to select the cell range A1:C6.**

Now that the entire table is selected, you must define its range name.

Notes:

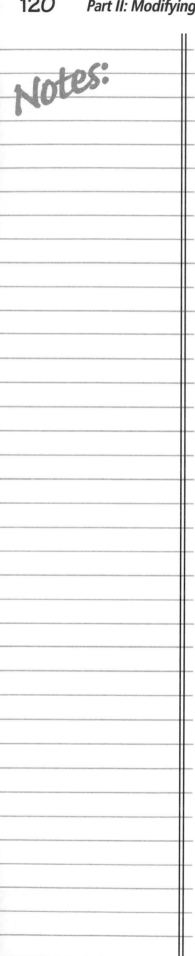

2 Click **I**nsert on the menu bar. Then move down to **N**ame on the pull-down menu and click **D**efine on the continuation menu to open the Define Name dialog box.

Because cell A1 is active, Excel suggests the name Georgie_Porgie_Pudding_Pies as the range name in the Names in Workbook text box. Go ahead and replace this name with Retail_Price_Tbl. When typing this new name, be sure to type an underscore (by holding down Shift as you type a hyphen) between each word. Note that Excel will assign this range name to the absolute cell addresses Sheet1!$A$1:$C$6.

3 Type *Retail_Price_Tbl* in the Names in **W**orkbook text box and click OK or press Enter.

Note how the name Retail_Price_... now appears in the current cell address indicator on the formula bar. This indicator always shows the range name if one is assigned to the active cell or the cell range that's currently selected.

Before moving on, you should use AutoFit Selection to adjust the width of the columns of this table before saving your changes.

4 With the cell selection A1:C6 still selected, click **F**ormat on the menu bar, highlight **C**olumn on the pull-down menu, and click **A**utoFit Selection on the continuation menu.

Now you need to save this workbook with the range name Retail_Price_Tbl assigned to the table cell range A1:C6 under a new filename.

5 Click cell A1 to deselect the cell range A1:C6, click **F**ile on the menu bar, and click Save **A**s on the pull-down menu to open the Save As dialog box.

Now you'll append (names) to the current filename.

6 Make sure that the name of your personal folder appears in the Save **i**n drop-down list box. Then click the insertion point after *e* in *Price Table* in the File **n**ame text box and press the spacebar before you type *(names)* and click the Save button or press Enter.

Exercise 4-8: Creating range names from column and row headings

In this exercise, you will use the column headings in cells A2 through C2 and the row headings in cells A3 through A6 to name the Cost and Retail Price cells in the cell range A2:C6.

1 Click cell A2 to make it current. Then drag the white-cross mouse pointer down to cell A6 and then over to cell C6 to select the cell range A2:C6.

This time, you'll select the Create command on the Name continuation menu to create range names from the headings in the top row and left column of the current cell selection.

2 Click **I**nsert on the menu bar, move down to **N**ame on the pull-down menu, and click **C**reate on the continuation menu to open the Create Names dialog box.

The Create Names dialog box contains four check boxes for indicating which rows and columns contain the text entries that you want used as the range names.

3 The Top Row and Left Column check boxes in the Create Names in section are checked by default. Click OK or press Enter to close the Create Names dialog box.

Before you try using the range names assigned with the Create Names dialog box to select different ranges in the retail price table, you need to save your changes to the Price Table workbook.

4 Click cell A1 to make it current and deselect the cell range A2:C6; then click the Save button or press Ctrl+S to save your changes to your Price Table (names) workbook.

Exercise 4-9: Selecting various named ranges in the price table

In this exercise, you'll use the current cell address indicator on the formula bar and the Go To dialog box to select the various named ranges in the retail price table.

1 Click the drop-down list button to the right of the current cell address on the formula bar in order to display the list of range names currently defined in your Price Table workbook.

The range names in this drop-down list appear in alphabetical order. All the names in this list except for Retail_Price_Tbl were defined by selecting the Top Row and Left Column check boxes in the Create Names dialog box.

Go ahead and find out which cells are referred to by the range name Cost.

2 Click Cost in the drop-down list.

Excel selects the cell range B3:B6. This column contains all the cost values for the different types of pies sold. This range name was created from the column heading (Cost) in cell B2.

Next, select the range name Retail_Price in the current cell address drop-down list.

3 Click the cell address drop-down list button on the formula bar and then click the range name Retail_Price in the list.

This time, Excel selects the cell range C3:C6 with the calculated retail prices. This range name was created from the column heading (Retail Price) in cell C2.

Now try selecting one of the range names created from the row headings with the pie names in column A.

4 Click the cell address drop-down list button on the formula bar and then click the range name Pied_Piper_Pumpkin_pie in the list.

Excel selects the cell range B3:C3 with the Cost and Retail Price for Pied Piper Pumpkin pie. This range name was created from the row heading (Pied Piper Pumpkin pie) in cell A3.

5 Click the cell address drop-down list button on the formula bar and then click the range name Mother_Gooseberry_pie in the list.

This time, Excel selects the cell range B6:C6 created from the row heading (Mother Gooseberry pie) in cell A6.

Next, select the range called Pie_Prices_Per_Unit with the Go To feature.

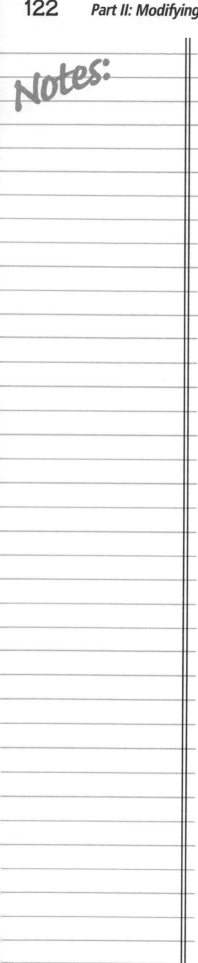

6 **Press function key F5 to open the Go To dialog box. Then double-click the range name Prices_Per_Unit in the Go to list box (or click this range name) and then click OK (or press Enter).**

Excel selects the cell range B3:C6, the cells with all the Cost and Retail Price values in this table. This range name was created using the table heading entered in cell A2.

Now try selecting the entire retail price table with the Go To dialog box.

7 **Press F5 to open the Go To dialog box. If necessary, use the scroll bar or scroll bar button to scroll down to the bottom of the Go to list box. Then double-click the range name Retail_Price_Tbl (or click this range name) and then click OK (or press Enter).**

Excel selects the cell range A1:C6 because this is the range that you assigned to this cell range by using the Define Name dialog box.

8 **Click cell A1 to make this cell active and deselect the cell range A1:C6.**

Exercise 4-10: Applying column and row names to formulas

In this exercise, you'll replace the cell references to the Cost column for each type of pie with the names created from the Cost column heading in B2 and pie row headings in the cell range A3:A6.

1 **Select the cell range C3:C6 that contains the formulas for computing the Retail Price.**

Next, open the Apply Name dialog box.

2 **Click Insert on the menu bar, move down to Name on the pull-down menu, and click Apply on the continuation menu to open the Apply Names dialog box.**

This dialog box contains a list of all the named ranges in the workbook. By default, all the names except Retail_Price_Tbl are selected. (Excel highlights them in blue on a color monitor.) You need to deselect Retail_Price and Prices_Per_Unit and leave just the names whose row and column names are to be used in replacing the cell references in the formulas.

3 **Click Retail_Price and Prices_Per_Unit in the Apply Names list box.**

When you click these names, Excel removes the blue highlights on a color monitor. Next, you need to expand the Apply Names dialog box by choosing the Options>> button.

4 **Click the Options>> button to expand the Apply Names dialog box to include the Omit Column Name if Same Column and Omit Row Name if Same Row check boxes along with the Row Column and Column Row radio buttons in the Name Order area.**

Normally, when replacing cell references in formulas with column and row names, Excel leaves out the column's range name if the cell reference is in the same column as the one used in the range name. Likewise, Excel leaves out the row's range name if the cell reference is in the same row as the one used in the range name.

In this case, you'll want both the column and the row range name to be displayed in the formula with the column name following the row name.

5 **Click the Omit <u>C</u>olumn Name if Same Column check box and click the Omit <u>R</u>ow Name if Same Row check box to remove the check mark from both these check boxes. Then click OK or press Enter.**

Note that the contents of the formula bar for the active cell C3 is now listed as

=Pied_Piper_Pumpkin_pie Cost*Markup.

Go ahead and check a couple of the other formulas in this column for calculating the Retail Price.

6 **Click cell C4 to make this cell active and deselect the cell range C3:C6.**

The contents of the formula bar for cell C4 now reads =King_Cole_Coconut_Cream_pie Cost*Markup.

7 **Press the ↓ key to make cell C5 current.**

The contents of the formula bar for cell C5 now reads =London_Towne_Lemon_pie Cost*Markup. And I'll bet it wouldn't surprise you too much to know that the contents of C6 for calculating the Retail Price for Mother Gooseberry pie is now =Mother_Gooseberry_pie Cost*Markup.

8 **Click cell A1 to make it current, click <u>F</u>ile on the menu bar, and click <u>C</u>lose on the pull-down menu. Click the <u>Y</u>es button or press Enter when asked to save the changes in the Price Table (names) workbook.**

☑ Progress Check

If you can do the following, you've mastered this lesson:

❏ Name a cell or cell range in the Define Name dialog box.

❏ Name cells with their column and row headings in the Create Names dialog box.

❏ Paste a range name into a new formula in the Paste Names dialog box.

❏ Apply range names to existing formulas in the Apply Names dialog box.

Copying and Moving Cell Ranges   Lesson 4-4

on the test

From time to time, you will find it necessary to move or copy cell ranges to different parts of a worksheet (or even another worksheet) in the same or a different workbook. Excel provides two methods for moving and copying cell ranges:

▶ The drag-and-drop method allows you to pick up the cell range and put it (or a copy of it) down in a new location in the same worksheet.

▶ The cut-and-paste method allows you to put the range (or a copy of it) in the Windows Clipboard and then paste it in a new location in the same worksheet or a different worksheet. You *must* use the cut-and-paste method when moving or copying a range from one worksheet to another or from one workbook to another.

When moving or copying a range with drag and drop, keep in mind that if any of the cell ranges that you're dropping stuff into overlap cells that are already occupied, Excel will display an alert box with the message

    Replace contents of destination cells?

Notes:

If you select the No button in this dialog box, Excel will abort the move or copy operation. If you select the Yes button, Excel will continue the operation and, in so doing, replace the existing cell entries in those cells that overlap the moved or copied cell range.

If you paste a range of cells that has been cut or copied to the Clipboard into a new location so that some or all of its cells overlap existing entries, Excel will just go ahead and, without warning, replace the existing entries with those in the moved or copied cell range. If this ever happens unintentionally, you need to click the Undo button on the Standard toolbar (or press Ctrl+Z) right away to restore the original entries to their cells and abort the move or copy operation.

Exercise 4-11: Copying and moving cell ranges with drag and drop

In this exercise, you'll get a chance to play around with moving and copying cell ranges with drag and drop. You'll practice the drag-and-drop technique on the data in the MGE Annual Sales workbook located in the Practice folder within your Excel 101 folder.

1 **Bring up the Open dialog box by clicking the Open button on the Standard toolbar or pressing Ctrl+O. If you don't see the Practice folder icon in the Open dialog list box, click the Up One Level button to open the Excel 101 folder in the Look in list box; then double-click the Practice folder icon in the Open dialog list box to open this folder before you double-click the MGE Annual Sales file icon in the list box to open this workbook file.**

This workbook contains annual and projected annual sales worksheets for the Mother Goose Enterprises companies. You'll start by dragging the second quarter total sales table in the cell range F2:I12 in the 1994 Sales worksheet down below the first quarter total sales table in this worksheet.

2 **Click the right scroll arrow on the horizontal scroll bar until you can see columns F through I on the screen.**

3 **Click cell F2, drag down to row 12, and then drag over to column I so that the cell range F2:I12 is selected.**

To drag a cell selection to a new location in the worksheet, you need to position the arrowhead mouse pointer on an edge of the selection before you start dragging it.

4 **Position the arrowhead cell pointer somewhere on the lower edge of the selected cell range and drag the outline of this cell range down so that its top edge is in line with the top of row 15.**

Now that you've dragged the cell range outline down to the correct row, you can begin dragging it to the left to the correct column.

5 **Drag the cell range outline to the left until the worksheet scrolls left so that you can see columns A through F on your screen. (To get the worksheet to scroll, you'll have to drag the cell range outline all the way to column A.)**

Now all that remains to do is to drag the cell outline slightly to the right to position it over the cell range B15:E25.

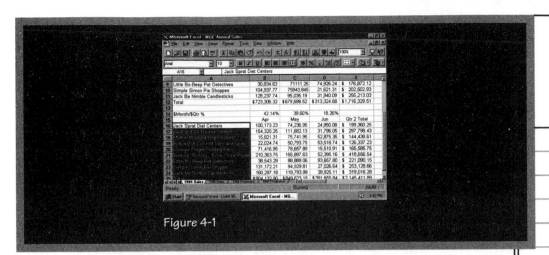

Figure 4-1

Figure 4-1: You can use drag and drop both to move and to copy cells, as shown by the new layout of this MGE Annual Sales worksheet.

6 **Drag the outline of the cell range to the right until it encloses the empty cell range B15:E25 in the worksheet. Then release the mouse button to move the cell entries.**

When you release the mouse button, Excel moves the cell range with the second quarter sales and totals from the cell range F2:I12 to B15:E25.

Now you need to copy the row headings in the cell range A3:A12 above down to the second quarter sales and totals table that you just moved to the cell range B15:E25.

7 **Scroll the worksheet up until you can see row 1 on-screen. Then click cell A3 (with Jack Sprat Diet Centers) and hold down Shift as you click cell A12 (with Total) to select the cell range A3:A12.**

To copy a cell selection with drag and drop rather than just move it, you need to hold down the Ctrl key as you drag the cell range. When you position the mouse pointer on an edge of a cell selection when the Ctrl key is depressed, Excel adds a little plus sign to the arrowhead pointer, indicating that you will be copying the range rather than just moving it.

8 **Position the arrowhead mouse pointer on the bottom of the cell selection and hold down the Ctrl key as you drag the outline of the cell range A3:A12 down column A. When the outline of this cell range to be copied encloses the cell range A16:A25 in the worksheet, release the mouse button.**

If, when you release the mouse button, you find that Excel has moved the cell range A3:A12 rather than copied it, press Ctrl+Z right away to undo the move. Then repeat Step 8, this time making sure that you've got the Ctrl key depressed before you start dragging the cell range.

If all went well, your Store Totals worksheet should now look like the one shown in Figure 4-1.

9 **Click File on the menu bar, click Close on the pull-down menu, and click the No button when asked to save your changes in the MGE Annual Sales workbook.**

Exercise 4-12: Copying and moving cells with cut and paste

In this exercise, you get some practice using the Clipboard to cut and paste and copy and paste cell ranges. To get this practice, you'll use the retail price table saved in the Price Table (names) workbook that you created for the exercises in Lesson 4-3.

1 **Bring up the Open dialog box by clicking the Open button on the Standard toolbar or by pressing Ctrl+O. Click the Up One Level button to open the Excel 101 folder in the Look in list box. Double-click your personal folder in the Open dialog list box to open it before you double-click Price Table (names) in the File name text box to open this workbook file.**

Before you can copy the price table, you have to select its cells.

2 **Click the current cell address drop-down button and then click Retail_Price_Tbl in the drop-down list.**

Excel responds by selecting the entire table in the cell range A1:C6.

3 **Click the Copy button on the Standard toolbar or press Ctrl+C.**

When you cut or copy a cell range to the Clipboard, Excel responds by putting a marquee around the cell selection and displaying the message "Select destination and press ENTER or choose Paste" on the status bar.

In selecting the destination for the cell selection, you need designate only the first cell in the worksheet for the moved or copied cell range. In fact, should you designate more cells than just the first, you must make sure that the destination cell selection matches exactly that of the one that's being moved or copied. Otherwise, you get a message like "Copy (or Cut) and paste areas are different shapes," and you must then repeat the operation.

4 **Click the Sheet2 sheet tab to make this worksheet current. Then click the Paste button on the Standard toolbar (or press Ctrl+V) to paste a copy of the price table in the cell range A1:C6 of Sheet2.**

When you use the *Paste* command (rather than the Enter key) to paste a cut or copied cell range, Excel retains the cut or copied cells in the Clipboard so that you can paste them in other locations in the same or different worksheets. When you press *Enter* to do the pasting, it's a one-shot deal because Excel empties the Clipboard in the process of pasting the cut or copied cell entries.

Before going on, you need to compare the copy of the price table on Sheet2 with the original table on Sheet1.

5 **Click the Sheet1 sheet tab to make the first worksheet current.**

Note that the original table not only is still selected but also retains its marquee. Also, note that the column width adjustments in the original table were not transmitted to the copy of table in Sheet2 (its columns still need adjusting because only the cell entries and their formatting were copied).

In the next part of the process, you'll move the original retail price table to a new location in Sheet1 using cut and paste. First, however, you'll remove that distracting marquee from around the cell selection.

6 **Press the Esc key to remove the marquee from around the cell selection in Sheet1. Then click the Cut button on the Standard toolbar or press Ctrl+X.**

When you first cut a cell range to the Clipboard, Excel responds exactly as if you had copied the range to the Clipboard (same old marquee around the range and same old message on the status bar). Only when you complete the

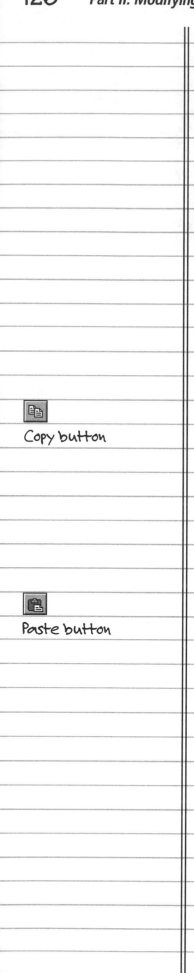

Copy button

Paste button

move by pressing Enter or pasting the range does Excel actually remove the cell selection from its original location.

Next, you'll select the destination cell, T1, with the Go To dialog box.

7 **Press function key F5, type the destination cell address *(t1)* in the Reference text box, and click OK or press Enter.**

Now you're ready to paste the original retail price table into the cell range T1:V6. This time, complete the paste operation by pressing Enter instead of clicking the Paste button or pressing Ctrl+V.

8 **Press the Enter key to paste the cells. Then press the → key three times to scroll the worksheet to the right so that all the columns in the moved retail price table are visible.**

Now you need to check the original cell range (A1:C6) to make sure that the retail price table was moved.

9 **Press Ctrl+Home to move the cell pointer directly to cell A1.**

As you can see, the retail price table is no longer in the cell range A1:C6. But what about all the range names that you gave to different parts of this table? You should try selecting the price table by selecting the Retail_Price_Tbl range name on the cell address drop-down list.

10 **Click the current cell address drop-down button and click Retail_Price_Tbl in the drop-down list.**

Excel responds by selecting the cell range T1:V6 in Sheet1, the very location to which you moved the original retail price table.

This brings up a very important point: When you move a named cell range, Excel automatically keeps track of the new cell location and reassigns the range name to it. You can test this by selecting the Pied Piper Pumpkin pie range name to make sure that this name has been reassigned to the cell range U3:V3, the cells to which the Pied Piper Pumpkin pie Cost and Retail Price entries have been moved.

11 **Click the current cell address drop-down button and click Pied_Piper_Pumpkin_pie in the drop-down list.**

Excel responds by selecting the cell range U3:V3. Before going on to the last exercise in this unit, move this table back to its original location.

12 **Click the current cell address drop-down button, click Retail_Price_Tbl in the drop-down list, and then press Ctrl+X, Ctrl+Home, and (finally) Ctrl+V.**

Exercise 4-13: Using Paste Special

In this exercise, you learn how to use the Paste Special dialog box to replace the formulas in the retail price table that you copied from Sheet1 to Sheet2 with values. As it stands now, the retail price formulas in the copy of the table in Sheet2 are linked to costs in the original table in Sheet1 rather than to the copied costs in Sheet2.

You can verify this by replacing the King Cole Coconut Cream pie cost of $1.85 in cell B4 of the original price table with $2.85 and then examining its effect on the copy of the price table in Sheet2.

1 **Click cell B4 in Sheet1, type *2.85,* and click the Enter box on the formula bar.**

Note that when you replace the King Cole Coconut Cream pie cost of $1.85 in cell B4 with $2.85, the Retail Price in cell C4 automatically increases to $4.28. Now check what effect this change has had on the copy of the table in Sheet2.

Cut button

Notes:

Notes:

2 **Click the Sheet2 sheet tab to make this worksheet active.**

Note that, although the King Cole Coconut Cream pie Retail Price in cell C4 of Sheet2 has increased to $4.28, the Cost remains $1.85. This is because the formula in C4 of Sheet2 is =King_Cole_Coconut_Cream_pie Cost*Markup, and Excel considers the cell at the intersection of the row heading (King Cole Coconut Cream pie) and the column heading (Cost) to be cell C4 in Sheet1, not cell C4 in Sheet2.

Many times, you will want to cut any links such as this between the original data and copies of it by pasting only the values into the copies without the formulas. By copying only values, you in essence "freeze" the data, making an historical copy that is never updated.

To see how this works, you'll now replace the copy of the price table in Sheet2 (with the formulas) with a copy that has only *values*.

3 **Click the Sheet1 sheet tab to make the worksheet with the original retail price table current.**

Now select the table and copy its cells to the Clipboard.

4 **Click the current cell address drop-down button, click Retail_Price_Tbl in the drop-down list, and click the Copy button on the Standard toolbar (or press Ctrl+C).**

5 **Click the Sheet2 sheet tab to make the worksheet with the copy of the table you're about to replace active, and, if necessary, click cell A1 in Sheet1 to make this first cell active.**

Next, you'll need to select the Paste Special command on the Edit pull-down menu to open the Paste Special dialog box, rather than click the regular Paste button or press Ctrl+V.

6 **Click Edit on the menu bar and click Paste Special on the pull-down menu to open the Paste Special dialog box.**

The Paste Special dialog box has all sorts of buttons and boxes. Right now, however, you're only interested in the Values radio button in the Paste section.

7 **Click the Values radio button and click OK or press Enter.**

Now you need to check out the contents of the cells in the Retail Price column of this price table copy.

8 **Click cell C3 to make it current.**

On the formula bar, note that the content of this cell is now 3.525 rather than the formula =Pied_Piper_Pumpkin_pie Cost*Markup.

9 **Press the ↓ key to go down through the other Retail Price cells in this column, examining the contents of each one on the formula bar.**

Next, check back with the original.

10 **Click the Sheet1 sheet tab to make Sheet1 current, press the Esc key to get rid of the marquee around the table, and (finally) click cell C3.**

The content of this cell on the formula bar is still =Pied_Piper_Pumpkin_pie Cost*Markup.

Go ahead and save this version of the workbook with the table containing values on Sheet2 under the filename Price Table (values) before you quit Excel.

☑ **Progress Check**

If you can do the following, you've mastered this lesson:

❑ Move or copy a cell range with drag and drop.

❑ Move or copy a cell range with cut and paste.

❑ Replace formulas in a cell range with their calculated values in the Paste Special dialog box.

11 Click Eile on the menu bar and then click Save As on the pull-down menu. Make sure that the name of your personal folder appears in the Save in drop-down list box. Then drag the I-beam mouse pointer through *names* in the filename *Price Table (names)* in the File name text box. After you have this text selected, replace it by typing *values* so that the new filename appears as *Price Table (values)* in this text box. Finally, click the Save button or press Enter to save this version of the workbook under this new filename.

Now go ahead and exit Excel.

12 Click Eile on the menu bar and click Exit on the pull-down menu to quit Excel.

Unit 4 Quiz

Test your knowledge by answering the following questions about working with cell ranges by using the information that you just gained in Unit 4. For each of the following questions, select the letter of the correct response (and remember that I'm not above asking questions where more than one response is correct).

1. **All of the following statements about making cell selections with the mouse are true except:**

    A. To select a rectangular cell range, you can drag through the cells.

    B. To select an entire column of cells, you click the column letter on the frame.

    C. To select a nonadjacent cell selection, after selecting the first cell range, you must hold down the Ctrl key when selecting the subsequent cell ranges.

    D. To AutoSelect a cell range of data in a worksheet, you can position the cell pointer in the first cell and then double-click it on the bottom and right edges.

2. **All of the following statements about making cell selections with the keyboard are true except:**

    A. You can select a rectangular cell range by holding down Shift as you press the appropriate arrow keys.

    B. You can select a table of data by positioning the cell pointer in the first cell and then holding down Shift as you press Ctrl+→ and Ctrl+↑.

    C. You can select an entire column of data by pressing Shift+spacebar.

    D. You can select all the cells in the entire worksheet by pressing Ctrl+A.

3. **All of the following statements about naming cells are true except:**

    A. Range names cannot have spaces in them.

    B. Range names cannot have numbers in them.

    C. Range names should not duplicate cell addresses in the worksheet.

    D. Range names must be no longer than eight characters long.

4. **All of the following statements about moving and copying cell ranges with drag and drop are true except:**

    A. To move a cell selection, you hold down Shift as you drag the selection to its new location in the worksheet.

    B. To copy a cell selection, you hold down the Ctrl key as you drag the selection to its new location in the worksheet.

    C. You can't use drag and drop to copy or move cell ranges to another worksheet or workbook.

    D. Excel warns you if you're about to replace some existing cell entries with the cell range that you've moved or copied.

5. **All of the following statements about moving and copying cell ranges with the Clipboard are true except:**

    A. To move a cell selection, you can cut it to the Clipboard with Ctrl+X; but to copy a cell, you copy it with Ctrl+C.

    B. To paste a cell selection that's been cut or copied to the Clipboard, you select all the cells where the range is to be moved or copied to and then paste the cell selection with Ctrl+V.

    C. You can use cut and paste to copy or move cell ranges to other worksheets and even to another workbook.

    D. Excel warns you if you're about to replace some existing cell entries with the cell range that you've moved or copied.

Unit 4 Further Exercise

In this further exercise, you get a chance to apply what you learned about working with cell ranges in Unit 4.

Exercise 4-14: Naming cell ranges in the MGE Quarterly Sales workbook

In this exercise, you assign names to some cell ranges in your MGE Quarterly Sales (afmt) workbook.

1. Start Excel. Then open the MGE Quarterly Sales (afmt) workbook in your personal folder.

2. Assign the range name MGE_Qtr1_Sales to the entire sales table (cell range A1:E10) in Sheet1.

3. Assign the column headings in cell range B2:E2 and the row headings in the cell range A3:A10 to the sales and total cells in the table.

4. Test out your range names by selecting them from the cell address drop-down list.

5. Click cell A1 to make it current and save the MGE Quarterly Sales (afmt) workbook and quit Excel.

Editing the Spreadsheet

Prerequisites

▶ All lessons and exercises in Unit 4 completed

▶ Unit 4 Quiz and Unit 4 Further Exercises successfully completed

Objectives for This Unit

✓ Editing a cell entry in its cell or on the formula bar

✓ Using Undo to recover from mistakes

✓ Zooming to zoom out or in on data

✓ Freezing columns and rows as worksheet titles

✓ Inserting new cells, columns, and rows in a worksheet

✓ Deleting cells, columns, and rows from a worksheet

✓ Adding notes to cells

✓ Finding and replacing data in a worksheet

✓ Spell-checking a worksheet

✓ Renaming and reordering sheets in a workbook

✓ Creating SUM formulas that total values in different worksheets in a workbook

Following the importance of entering, formatting, and printing spreadsheet data comes the importance of editing the spreadsheet's data and layout. The goal for Unit 5, then, is to make you comfortable with all aspects of changing the spreadsheet, from manually editing cell entries, through inserting cells in (and deleting cells from) the worksheet, all the way to finding and replacing as well as spell-checking the spreadsheet data.

Lesson 5-1

Editing Data Entries

You can always change the contents of your cells at any time after you enter them. In editing a cell entry, you have a choice: you can either replace the entry altogether, or you can change only the part of the entry that needs revision. To replace an entry, position the cell pointer in the cell and just enter the new entry on top of the old. To edit an entry, you can either edit the entry in its cell in the worksheet or edit its content on the formula bar.

To edit an entry in its cell, position the cell pointer in the cell and double-click the cell with the white-cross pointer or press function key F2. Doing this step places the insertion point within the cell entry. If you press F2, the insertion point is automatically positioned at the very end of the entry. If you double-click the cell, the insertion point is positioned at approximately the place in the entry where you positioned the white-cross pointer.

To edit an entry on the formula bar, position the cell pointer in the cell and then click the I-beam pointer at the place in the data entry where you want the insertion point positioned.

After the insertion point is inserted somewhere in a cell entry, Excel goes into Edit mode, and the Cancel, Enter, and Function Wizard buttons reappear on the formula bar. When the program is in Edit mode, the arrow keys that normally complete a cell entry when the program is in Enter mode now move the insertion point from character to character within the cell entry. So to complete your edit and enter your revised entry in the cell, you *must* either click the Enter box on the formula bar or press the Enter key (in fact, all keys that move the cell pointer are out, not just the arrow keys).

Sometimes, instead of revising or replacing a cell entry, you will need to delete the cell entry. In the parlance of Excel, this process is referred to as *clearing* the cell (as opposed to *deleting* the cell, which means to remove the cell with all its contents from the worksheet while at the same time shifting the remaining cells to fill in the gap).

The easiest way to clear a cell range is to select it and press the Delete key. When you do this step, Excel clears just the data entered in cells in the range (referred to as the *contents*), leaving behind any formatting or notes that may have been added. (You'll learn about notes in Lesson 5-3, coming up shortly.) If you want to clear a cell range of everything (contents, formulas, notes, you name it), you have to use the Clear command on the Edit menu and select All from its continuation menu. (This continuation menu also contains Contents, Formats, and Notes commands for removing any one of these things from the cell range).

Exercise 5-1: Revising data entries in their cells

In this first editing exercise, you'll open the Sprat Diet Centers 96 P&L workbook which contains an income statement for the Jack Sprat Diet Centers (one of the many Mother Goose Enterprises companies you've encountered before).

1   Start Excel. Then bring up the Open dialog box.

The workbook file that you want to work with is in the Practice folder within your Excel 101 folder.

2 **Double-click the Practice folder icon in the Open dialog list box to open it in the Look in list box. Then double-click the Sprat Diet Centers 96 P&L in the Open dialog list box to open this workbook.**

The first thing that you have to change in this spreadsheet is the title.

3 **With the cell pointer still in cell A1, press function key F2.**

Excel positions the insertion point at the very end of spreadsheet title text in cell A1 and puts the program into Edit mode as indicated by the reappearance of the Cancel, Enter, and Function Wizard buttons on the formula bar and the appearance of Edit on the status bar.

4 **Press the Home key, press Ctrl+→ once to position the insertion point in front of the *S* in Sprat, and press the Delete key until you've wiped out the characters *Sprat Diet*.**

In Edit mode, the Delete key removes characters to the immediate right of the insertion point, while the Backspace key removes characters to the immediate left of the insertion point.

5 **Type *& Jill Trauma* in the cell entry and press the Enter key to complete this edit and put the revised text entry into cell A1.**

When Excel is in Edit mode, you must either click the Enter button (the one with the check mark) on the formula bar or press the Enter key to complete your editing and put the revised entry in the current cell.

Before you make any more changes to this worksheet, you need to save its workbook under a new filename in your personal folder.

6 **Click File on the menu bar and click Save As on the pull-down menu.**

You'll name this workbook J&J Trauma Centers 96 P&L in your personal folder.

7 **Click the Up One Level button to open the Excel 101 folder in the Look in list box. Then double-click the icon for your personal folder in the Open dialog list box. Use the I-beam pointer to select the text *Sprat Diet* in the File name text box. Then replace this selected text by typing *J&J Trauma* (so that the new filename now reads J&J Trauma Centers 96 P&L) and click Save or press Enter.**

Now that you've renamed the workbook with File⇨Save As, you don't have to worry about inadvertently saving Jack & Jill Trauma Centers' income in the Jack Sprat Diet Centers' income statement.

Next, you'll revise the 1996 revenue for the Jack & Jill Trauma Centers in cell B3 from 4,550,000.00 to 5,750,000.00.

8 **Position the white-cross pointer in cell B3 so that it's in front of the *4* in 4,550,000.00. Then double-click the mouse.**

Excel positions the insertion point at the front of the value in cell B3 when it goes into Edit mode.

9 **Press the Delete key twice to get rid of the *45* in 4550000, type *57* to change this value to 5750000, and click the Enter button on the formula bar.**

Next, you'll revise the Equipment costs in cell B6 from 250,000.00 to 200,000.00.

10 **Position the white-cross pointer at the far right side of cell B6. Then double-click the mouse button to place the insertion point at the very end of the -250000 number entry in this cell. Move the I-beam mouse pointer out of the way before you press the ← four times to move the insertion point so that it's between the *5* and *0* of -250000.**

Notes:

Notes:

In the Edit mode, keys like Home, End, ←, →, ↑, and ↓ move the insertion point in the cell entry instead of moving the cell pointer in the worksheet (as is the case in the Ready and Enter modes).

11 **Press the Backspace key once to delete *5* from the value (20000). Then press *0* (so that 200000 now appears on the formula bar) and press the Enter key.**

You should now see (200,000.00) in cell B6. Save your changes in the J&J Trauma Centers 96 P&L workbook before going on to Exercise 5-2, where you'll learn how to make changes to a cell entry on the formula bar.

12 **Click the Save button on the Standard toolbar (or press Ctrl+S) to save your changes.**

Exercise 5-2: Revising data entries on the formula bar

In this second editing exercise, you'll get some practice in making edits to a cell entry on the formula bar instead of in the cell itself. This editing technique is most useful when the cell entry you need to edit is really, really long, because Excel automatically expands the formula bar to as many lines as are needed to display all the characters in the entry whenever the cell pointer is in its cell. This capability gives you immediate access to any part of the cell entry with the I-beam mouse pointer, thus making editing a lot simpler.

In your J&J Trauma Centers 96 P&L workbook, you'll start practicing editing on the formula bar by revising the Rent for Jack & Jill Trauma Centers in cell B7 from 512,300.00 to 500,000.00.

1 **Position the I-beam mouse pointer on the formula bar right after the *5* in the value 512300 and drag the mouse pointer to the right until you've selected the numbers *123*.**

2 **Type *000* and click the Enter button on the formula bar.**

Cell B7 should now appear as (500,000.00). Next, you'll replace the old Payroll expense (345,000.00) in cell B8 with a new Payroll expense (285,650.00). The easiest way to make this change is simply to replace the existing entry with the revised one.

3 **With the cell pointer in cell B8, type *-285650* in the cell and press Enter.**

The value (285,650.00) should now appear in cell B8. Now save your changes to the J&J Trauma Centers 96 P&L workbook before going on to the last editing exercise.

4 **Click the Save button on the Standard toolbar or press Ctrl+S.**

Exercise 5-3: Clearing cells of their data entries and using Undo/Redo

In this last exercise on editing cell entries, you get some practice in clearing cells of their entries rather than revising them. First, you'll begin by deleting the Real Lean Cuisine row heading in cell A17 as well as the value 185,000.00 in cell B17.

1 Use the vertical scroll bar to scroll the Jack & Jill Trauma Centers 1996 Income statement until you can see the Other Income section of the spreadsheet.

2 Select cells A17 (with the Real Lean Cuisine row heading) and B17 (with 185,000.00). Then press the Delete key.

As soon as you press Delete, Excel removes the contents of both cells. Keep in mind, however, that clearing a cell with the Delete key has no effect on the formatting assigned to the cell. For example, although cell B17 now appears empty, the Comma number format with two decimal places is still assigned to this cell. You can see this for yourself by entering a new value in cell B17.

3 Press the → key to make cell B17 active, type *1234*, and click the Enter button on the formula bar.

As soon as you click the Enter button, the formatted value 1,234.00 appears in cell B17. If you want to remove the formatting as well as the contents of a cell, you need to use the Edit⇨Clear⇨All command.

4 Click Edit on the menu bar, click Clear on the pull-down menu, and click All on the continuation menu.

Now test the effect of clearing everything from cell B17 by reentering 1234 there.

5 Type *1234* a second time and click the Enter button on the formula bar.

This time, just 1234 (using the default General format) appears in cell B17. Now, return the cell to its empty state by using the Undo feature.

6 Click the Undo button on the Standard toolbar or press Ctrl+Z.

The first time that you use Undo, Excel restores the spreadsheet to the state it was in before you took your last action (which, in this case, was entering 1234 in cell B17), thus clearing the cell. Excel also changes the Undo Entry command on the Edit menu to Redo (u) Entry.

If you then use the Undo command a second time without taking any other action in Excel, the Undo action is actually a Redo.

To see how this works, try selecting Undo again.

7 Click the Undo button on the Standard toolbar or press Ctrl+Z a second time.

This time, Excel undoes its Undo which makes it redo the 1234 entry in cell B17, which you just went and undid to clear cell B17! (Oh, well. You get the idea.) This technique of switching back and forth between Undo/Redo can be used for worksheets such as this one to do a really simple what-if analysis by switching between one entry and an alternate. (You'll see how this works when you do Exercise 5-6.) For now, you just need to return cell B17 to its empty state and save your workbook.

8 Click the Undo button on the Standard toolbar or press Ctrl+Z a third time.

Excel removes the 1234 entry from cell B17.

9 Press Ctrl+Home to move the cell pointer to cell A1. Click File on the menu bar, click Close on the pull-down menu, and click Yes or press Enter to save your changes.

Undo button

☑ Progress Check

If you can do the following, you've mastered this lesson:

❑ Edit a data entry in its cell.

❑ Edit a data entry on the formula bar.

❑ Clear data entries from their cells.

❑ Use Undo/Redo to undo and then redo your last action.

Locating the Areas that Need Editing

Notes:

A big part of editing a spreadsheet consists of locating the data that needs revising. Excel offers several methods for manipulating the worksheet display:

- The Zoom feature enables you to increase and decrease the magnification of the worksheet cells so that you can zoom in and zoom out on the data.

- The Freeze Panes enable you to designate the top rows with column headings and/or the leftmost columns with row headings that always remain displayed as you scroll new data in other parts of the worksheet into view.

- The Split feature enables you to divide the worksheet window into four different panes, each of which can display data from different parts of the worksheet.

In the next three exercises in this lesson, you'll get an opportunity to experience the usefulness of all three of these methods in keeping tabs on your information, thus making it easier to get your spreadsheet editing completed.

Exercise 5-4: Zooming in and out on a worksheet

In the first exercise, you'll get a chance to use the Zoom feature. Excel offers various Zoom options in the Zoom dialog box (opened by selecting Zoom on the View pull-down menu) as well as on the Zoom Control drop-down list box found on the Standard toolbar. Both the Zoom dialog box and the Zoom Control drop-down list box enable you to select specific percentages of normal (such as 75%, 100%, and 200%), which either increase or decrease the magnification of the cells. In addition to set percentages, you can also select a cell range and have Excel determine how much to increase or decrease the magnification to fit just the selection on the screen.

To perform this Zoom exercise, you'll need to open a new workbook called Fuzzy Wuzzy Media-Annual Sales that's in your practice folder.

1 **Bring up the Open dialog box, click the Up One Level button to open the Excel 101 folder icon in the Look in list box, and double-click the Practice folder icon in the Open dialog list box to open it. Locate the Fuzzy Wuzzy Media-Annual Sales file in the Open dialog list box and double-click its name to open this workbook.**

You should now see the Consolidated Sales worksheet that consolidates the projected sales for the years 1996 through 1998 for Fuzzy Wuzzy Media (a soft and warm multimedia company with such interactive hits as *Fuzzy's Silly Songs* and *Fuzzy Freaks Out*).

Start by using the Zoom feature to zoom out on the data so that you can see just how wide the Consolidated Sales spreadsheet is.

2 **Click the drop-down button to the right of the Zoom Control drop-down list box and click 75% in the drop-down list.**

At 75% of normal, you can see the projected sales from January through August in columns B through K. Next, try zooming out more.

3 **Click the drop-down button to the right of the Zoom Control drop-down list box and click 50% in the drop-down list.**

At 50% of normal, you can see the projected sales from January through December in columns B through P, and you can also see a partial column of data to the right of the column P. Now, try zooming out to 25% of normal to see if you can get a fix on all of the worksheet's data.

4 **Click the drop-down button to the right of the Zoom Control drop-down list box and click 25% in the drop-down list.**

Although highly illegible at 25% of normal, you have an overview of all the data. Why don't you see what is the highest percentage that you can use and still have a view of all the data in this worksheet?

5 **Hold down the Shift key, position the teeny tiny white-cross mouse pointer on the last cell with data in the worksheet, and click the mouse button to select all the almost infinitesimal data in this worksheet.**

If you don't get all the cells with spreadsheet data selected in the first attempt (or you get extra empty ones selected), just continue to hold down the Shift key while you press the arrow keys to either reduce or enlarge the cell selection.

6 **Click the drop-down button to the right of the Zoom Control drop-down list box, click Selection at the very bottom of the drop-down list, and click cell A1 to make this cell current and deselect the other data.**

Note that Excel has applied 44% of normal magnification to show all the selected worksheet data in one screen. At 44% magnification, you still can't make out the data (unless you've got *some* pair of eyes), but you can make out the general layout of the spreadsheet.

7 **Click the first cell in the last column of data displayed on the screen (whether or not you can make out that this is column R) and select 100% on the Zoom Control drop-down list.**

As long as you can tell approximately where you are in the worksheet when zoomed out, you can then select a cell in the vicinity and zoom in on it to check out its data.

Before moving on to the next exercise on creating worksheet titles, try zooming in on the data that's currently displayed at 100% by entering a magnification percentage of your own.

8 **Position the I-beam mouse pointer in front of the *1* in 100% shown in the Zoom Control text box and click the mouse button to select the current percentage before you type *125* and press Enter.**

As soon as you press Enter, Excel replaces 100% with 125% and increases the magnification to 125% of normal (and at this magnification, you don't even need your glasses to read this data).

9 **Press Ctrl+Home to move the cell pointer back into cell A1.**

Exercise 5-5: Freezing panes as worksheet titles

In this exercise, you'll get a chance to use the Freeze Panes feature to "freeze" the column headings in rows 1 and 2 and the row headings in column A on the screen, a phenomenon known as *worksheet titles* (as opposed to the *print titles* that you met up with in Unit 3).

Notes:

1 **Position the cell pointer in cell B3 of the Fuzzy Wuzzy Media-Annual Sales worksheet, just below the Jan column heading in cell B2 and to the immediate right of the Floppy Disk row heading in cell A3.**

When creating worksheet titles, you first position the cell pointer in the cell that's just beneath the row(s) and to the right of the column(s) that you want to remain displayed on the screen, no matter where you scroll to. In this case, that cell happens to be cell B3.

2 **Click Window on the menu bar and click Freeze Panes on the pull-down menu.**

Excel responds by displaying thin, black, intersecting lines along the bottom of row 2 and along the right edge of column A. These lines represent the boundaries of the panes that you've just frozen on the screen.

3 **Click the right-arrow scroll button on the horizontal scroll bar until column I, with the projected Qtr 2 sales figures, is displayed on the screen.**

Because the row headings in column A remain displayed on-screen as you scroll, you can still correlate the various sales figures with their categories.

4 **Click the down-arrow scroll button on the vertical scroll bar until row 15 (with the projected Total Sales) is displayed on-screen.**

Because the column headings in row 2 with the names of the months and the quarters remain displayed on-screen as you scroll, you can still correlate the sales totals with their time period.

5 **Click the right-arrow scroll button on the horizontal scroll bar until column R (with the projected Annual Total sales figures) is displayed at the right edge of the worksheet screen.**

As you scroll through the columns of sales data in this worksheet, the row headings in column A keep you straight as to what you are viewing.

6 **Click the up-arrow scroll button on the vertical scroll bar until row 4 (with the projected sales for Fuzzy's Silly Songs on Floppy Disk) appears under row 2 with the Nov, Dec, Qtr 4, and Annual Total column headings.**

Now you need to return the worksheet display to 100% of normal and then remove the frozen panes from this worksheet.

7 **Click the drop-down button to the right of the Zoom Control drop-down list box and click 100% in the drop-down list.**

8 **Click Window on the menu bar, click Unfreeze Panes on the pull-down menu to remove the panes, and then click cell A1 to make it active.**

Now close this worksheet without saving your changes.

9 **Press Ctrl+F4 and click No if asked to save your changes in the Fuzzy Wuzzy Media-Annual Sales workbook.**

Exercise 5-6: Dividing the worksheet into panes

Instead of freezing panes on the screen to keep specific column and row headings displayed as the worksheet titles, you can divide the worksheet window into separate panes. This method allows you to juxtapose two separate parts of the same worksheet side by side. You can see how this can work for you in the workbook called Simon's Pie Shoppes 96 P&L that contains an income statement for the Simple Simon's Pie Shoppes (another set of companies in the Mother Goose Enterprises family).

1 **Bring up the Open dialog box, locate the Simon's Pie Shoppes 96 P&L file in the Practice folder, and double-click its filename in the Open dialog list box.**

Given all the categories of revenues and expenses in this worksheet, it's currently impossible to see what effect changing the Revenues in cell B3 has on Net Earnings (Loss) in cell B23. However, by dividing the worksheet window into an upper and a lower pane, you can keep the Revenues cell displayed in the upper pane while you scroll the Net Earnings (Loss) cell up in the lower pane.

You can divide a worksheet window into panes either by dragging the split bars that appear at the top and right of the scroll bars to the place in the worksheet where the panes are to appear or by positioning the cell pointer in the worksheet and then choosing the Split command on the Window pull-down menu. First try splitting the window with the split bar.

2 **Position the arrowhead mouse pointer on the small, gray, rectangular button at the very top of the vertical scroll bar. When the mouse pointer changes to a double-headed arrow pointer (with the arrows pointing up and down), click and drag the pointer down. When you've positioned the shaded boundary line that appears from the double-headed arrow pointer between rows 6 and 7, release the mouse button.**

As soon as you release the mouse button, Excel splits the worksheet window into upper and lower panes at the bottom of row 6 and at the top of row 7. Note, also, that each pane has its own vertical scroll bar.

After a window is divided into panes, you can move the cell pointer between the panes by clicking one of the cells in that pane or by pressing Shift+F6.

3 **Press Shift+F6 to move the cell pointer to cell A7, the first cell in the lower pane, and press the ↓ key until you've scrolled up row 23 with Net Earnings (Loss) in the lower pane.**

Next, you'll revise up the Revenues in cell B3 and see how much of an effect this has on "the bottom line" in cell B23.

4 **Double-click cell B3 (with 3,750,000.00) in the upper pane, change this value to 4000000, and click the Enter button on the formula bar.**

When you click the Enter button, the value in the Net Earnings (Loss) cell in B23 in the lower pane increases from $1,620,986.90 to $1,803,486.90.

Use the Undo feature to flip back and forth between these two entries.

5 **Press Ctrl+Z to return the value in B3 to 3,750,000.00 and the value in B23 to $1,620,986.90. Then press Ctrl+Z again to change the value back to 4,000,000.00 and the bottom line to $1,803,486.90.**

Now that you've had some fun playing what-if, you can get rid of your window panes simply by double-clicking the line that divides the window into panes.

6 **Position the white-cross mouse anywhere on the boundary line between row 6 in the upper pane and whatever row you've scrolled up to in the lower pane. When the pointer changes to a double-headed arrow, double-click the mouse button.**

As soon as you double-click, Excel removes the window panes. (You could also have gotten rid of them by dragging the line all the way up to the frame or down to the horizontal scroll bar or by choosing Remove Split on the Window menu.)

Now go ahead and close this workbook before you go on to Lesson 5-3.

7 **Press Ctrl+F4 and click the No button if asked to save your changes.**

☑ **Progress Check**

If you can do the following, you've mastered this lesson:

❑ Use the Zoom feature to zoom out and in on the areas of a worksheet that need editing.

❑ Freeze panes to set up column and row headings as the worksheet titles.

❑ Split the worksheet into different panes and display different parts of the worksheet in these panes.

Lesson 5-3

Inserting and Deleting Cell Ranges

Sometimes in editing the spreadsheet, you will need to add new cells by inserting them into an existing table of data. At other times, you will need to delete cells from the worksheet. Inserting and deleting cells (unlike clearing them) necessarily involves a modification of the spreadsheet's layout. When inserting cells, you can have the cells with existing entries either shifted down or to the right to accommodate the new cells. When deleting cells, you can have existing cells either shifted up or to the left to fill the gap created by the deletion.

At times, instead of just inserting or deleting ranges of cells in the worksheet, you may find it more efficient to insert entire new columns or rows or delete existing ones from the worksheet. When making these kinds of more global column and row edits that affect the entire worksheet, you must take care that they don't disrupt existing data in those columns and rows in parts of the worksheet that are not visible.

Exercise 5-7: Deleting cells

In this exercise, you get some practice in deleting cells from a worksheet. To do this exercise, you'll use the J&J Trauma Centers 96 P&L workbook that you created earlier when doing Exercise 5-1.

1 Bring up the Open dialog box, click the Up One Level button to open the Excel 101 folder icon in the Look in list box, and double-click your personal folder icon in the Open dialog list box to open it. Locate the J&J Trauma Centers 96 P&L workbook in the Open dialog list box and double-click its name to open this workbook.

The first thing to do is to select the cell range A17:B17 that you cleared as part of Exercise 5-3.

2 Use the vertical scroll bar to scroll the worksheet up a few rows so that you can clearly see row 17 at the bottom of your screen.

Now select the cells to be deleted.

3 Click cell A17 and drag the white-cross pointer to the right to select cell B17.

Next, you need to open the Delete dialog box. You can do this by clicking Edit on the menu bar and then clicking Delete on the pull-down menu, or you can choose Delete on the cell's context menu.

4 With the white-cross pointer somewhere in the cell selection, click the secondary mouse button (the right button for you right handers, and the left button for you lefties who've switched the buttons) and click Delete on the cell's context menu.

Excel displays the Delete dialog box that contains four radio button options: Shift Cells Left, Shift Cells Up, Entire Row, and Entire Column. By default, the Shift Cells Up radio button is selected. Because this is the option that you want to use, go ahead and choose OK.

5 Click the OK button or press Enter.

As soon as you choose OK, Excel shifts up the rest of the cell entries in the projected income statement from row 18 on down to row 23 to fill in the gap created by deleting cells A17 and B17. After the program finishes shifting up the cells, the Book Sales heading is shifted up to cell A17, while the amount of 75,500.00 in the cell to its immediate right is shifted up to B17.

Go ahead and make sure that Excel shifted up all the other rows below in the Profit & Loss statement.

6 **If necessary, use the vertical scroll bar to scroll up the rows of the worksheet until you can see at least rows 15 through 22 on your screen.**

As you can see, Excel has not left any gaps when shifting the cells up.

Exercise 5-8: Inserting new cells

In this exercise, you get some practice with inserting new cells and rows in your J&J Trauma Centers 96 P&L workbook. You'll insert a new Other Income category called Watch Your Step Video Sales right above the Book Sales in row 17.

1 **With the cell range A17:B17 still selected in the Jack & Jill Trauma Centers 1996 income statement, click Insert on the menu bar and click Cells on the pull-down menu.**

The Insert dialog box contains the four radio button options: Shift Cells Right, Shift Cells Down, Entire Row, and Entire Column. By default, the Shift Cells Down radio button is selected. Because this is the option that you want to use, go ahead and choose OK.

2 **Click OK or press Enter.**

Excel responds by inserting two new cells and shifting the Book Sales cells (and all those below in the projected Income statement) down one row.

Next, you will enter the new Other Income category, Repair and Maintenance, in the Cost and Expenses category.

3 **With cell A17 still active, press the spacebar twice and type *Watch Your Step Video Sales* before pressing the → key.**

In cell B17, you need to enter the amount of income from the Watch Your Step Video Sales in 1996.

4 **Type *385000* and click the Enter button on the formula bar.**

Next, you need to save your changes to the J&J Trauma Centers 96 P&L workbook.

5 **Press Ctrl+Home to make cell A1 current and then click the Save button on the Standard toolbar or press Ctrl+S.**

Now close the J&J Trauma Centers 96 P&L workbook before going on to Lesson 5-4.

6 **Press Ctrl+F4 to close the J&J Trauma Centers 96 P&L workbook.**

☑ Progress Check

If you can do the following, you've mastered this lesson:

❑ Delete cell ranges by shifting existing cell entries to the left or up.

❑ Insert cell ranges by shifting existing cell entries to the right or down.

Adding Notes to Cells

Lesson 5-4

Excel makes it really easy to add comments to particular cells with its Cell Note feature. Cell notes can be either text notes or, if your computer is equipped with a sound card and microphone, *audio notes* (also called *sound notes*). Text notes that you attach to the cells in your worksheet can be viewed one at a time or can be printed in a group as part of a report. Audio notes, of course, can only be listened to one at a time (whaddya think: that you could put out a "best of the sound notes" CD?). When you attach a cell note to a cell, Excel indicates this attachment by putting a tiny red dot in the upper-right corner of the cell.

Notes:

You can use text notes not only to add commentary to cells, but also as place markers. When you press Ctrl+Shift+?, Excel selects all the notes in the worksheet. While the cell notes in the worksheet are selected, you can then press the Tab (next note) key or Shift+Tab (previous note) key to jump from note to note, no matter how far flung the notes are.

Exercise 5-9: Creating and selecting text notes in cells

In this exercise, you'll get practice adding notes to the Mother Goose Enterprises worksheet in your MGE Quarterly Sales (fmt) workbook. Then, after attaching a couple of text notes to its cells, you'll get a chance to select them and move between them with the Tab key.

1 **Bring up the Open dialog box and then open the MGE Quarterly Sales (fmt) workbook in your personal folder by double-clicking MGE Quarterly Sales (fmt) in the Open dialog list box.**

Now you'll add a text note to cell B7, which contains the January 1996 total pie sales for the Georgie Porgie Pudding Pies company.

2 **Click cell B7 to make it current, click Insert on the menu bar, and then select Note on the pull-down menu to open the Cell Note dialog box.**

To add a text note in the Cell Note dialog box, you simply type the note in the Text Note list box. While creating the note, you can start a new line at any point by pressing the Enter key (you must click the OK button to close the Cell Note dialog box).

3 **Type *Check this total against our Jan 95 total sales* and click the Add button.**

When you click the Add button, Excel attaches the note you just typed to the current cell (B7) and then selects the Cell text box in the Cell Note dialog box.

Next, you'll attach a text note to cell E3 before you close the Cell Note dialog box.

4 **Position the arrowhead mouse pointer on the title bar of the Cell Note dialog box and drag this dialog box down until cell E3 is visible in the worksheet.**

Now you can add the absolute cell address of cell E3 by clicking it in the worksheet.

5 **Use the vertical scroll bar to bring cell E3 into view at the top of the worksheet and click this cell (with the Jack Sprat Diet Centers Qtr 1 Total) to select it.**

When you click cell E3, Excel replaces cell B7 with $E$3 while putting a marquee around the cell in the worksheet. Now all you have to do is type the text in the Text Note list box.

6 **Press Tab twice to select all the text of the first note in the Text Note list box, type *This is the lowest Jack Sprat first quarter total since the company joined Mother Goose Enterprises in Jan 94!*, and click the OK button to add this note to cell E3, while at the same time closing the Cell Note dialog box.**

When the Cell Note dialog box closes, notice the note indicators that now appear in the upper-right corners of cells B7 and E3.

Next, you'll see how you can use your text notes as place markers.

7 **Press Ctrl+Home to position the cell pointer in cell A1 and press Ctrl+Shift+? to select all (both) of the cell notes in this worksheet.**

Excel selects both notes and makes cell E3 active. After all the notes in the worksheet are selected, you can jump from note to note.

8 **Press Tab to make cell B7 active and then press Tab again to make cell E3 active again.**

After a cell with a note becomes active, you can view its text (or listen to it, if it's a sound note) by opening the Cell Note dialog box.

9 **Click Insert on the menu bar and click Note on the pull-down menu to open the Cell Note dialog box.**

The Cell Note dialog box opens with the text of the note attached to cell E3 displayed in the Text Note list box. To view the text of the note attached to cell B7, you simply have to select it in the Notes in Sheet list box.

10 **Click B7: Check this total in the Notes in Sheet list box to select it.**

The Cell Note dialog box now displays the text of the note attached to cell B7 in the Text Note list box.

11 **Click the Close button to close the Cell Note dialog box and then press Ctrl+Home to make cell A1 current and deselect the cells with notes.**

Save your worksheet with the two cell notes in your personal folder with the filename MGE Quarterly Sales (notes).

12 **Click File on the menu bar and then click Save As on the pull-down menu. Click the I-beam mouse pointer between the _f_ and the left parenthesis in the filename MGE Quarterly Sales (fmt), press the Delete key three times to delete the _fmt_ before you type _notes_, and click Save or press Enter.**

Now close your MGE Quarterly Sales (notes) workbook before continuing on to Lesson 5-5 on using the Find and Replace features.

13 **Press Ctrl+F4 to close the MGE Quarterly Sales (notes) workbook.**

☑ **Progress Check**

If you can do the following, you've mastered this lesson:

❑ Create a text note in a cell.

❑ Select all text notes in the worksheet and move from note to note.

Finding and Replacing Data

Lesson 5-5

Excel's Find and Replace commands provide another convenient method for editing spreadsheet entries. You can use Find to locate a particular text or value in the worksheet. You can use Replace to locate specific text and value entries and then replace them with other text or values.

When searching for spreadsheet entries with Find or Replace, you have to keep in mind that Excel normally searches the contents of each cell in the worksheet for the text string or value that you specify. The ramification of this default type of search (referred to as _looking in formulas_) is that, when searching for values, Excel will not consider values returned by formulas to be matches. For example, suppose that you have a spreadsheet with the text _Unit 5_ entered in cell B3, the value 5 entered in cell B4, and the computed value returned by the formula =1+4 entered in cell B5. If you then use the Find feature to search for the number 5 in your worksheet, Excel will stop in cell B3 (with the text Unit 5) and cell B4 (with the value 5), while completely ignoring cell B5 (with the formula =1+4 that returns 5 as the result).

If you want Excel to consider the calculated value 5 in cell B5 as a match, you have to change the Look in option in the Find dialog box from Formulas to Values. If you do that and then search for 5, Excel will stop in cell B3 (with Unit 5), cell B4 (with 5), and cell B5 (with =1+4). Of course, because the program is now looking in values instead of formulas (that is, the contents of formulas) during such a search, a cell containing a formula such as =1+5 would no longer be considered a match.

Exercise 5-10: Finding data entries in the worksheet

In this exercise, you'll get practice using the Find feature to locate different cell entries in the income statement in the Simon's Pie Shoppes 96 P&L workbook.

1 **Bring up the Open dialog box, click the Up One Level button, and double-click the Practice folder before you double-click the Simon's Pie Shoppes 96 P&L file icon in the Open dialog list box.**

Now you'll use the Find feature to search for the occurrence of *cost* in this worksheet.

2 **Press Ctrl+F (or click Edit on the menu bar and click Find on the pull-down menu) to open the Find dialog box.**

To find the occurrence of some text in the contents of the cells, enter all or part of the text in the Find What text box.

3 **Type *cost* in the Find What text box and then click Find Next or press the Enter key.**

Excel moves the cell pointer to cell A5, which contains the heading Costs and Expenses. Because you have not selected the Match Case check box in the Find dialog box, Excel matches *cost* with *Costs* in Costs and Expenses.

4 **Press Enter or click the Find Next button to locate the next match.**

Excel now moves the cell pointer to cell A12, which has the heading Total Costs and Expenses.

5 **Press Enter or click the Find Next button to locate the next match.**

Excel now moves the cell pointer to cell B12 with the formula =SUM(costs). *Costs*, in this case, is a range name assigned to the cell range B6:B11 in this worksheet. Because the Find feature is normally set to look in formulas, the occurrence of *costs* in the contents of the cell, even though its value is displayed as (1,704,470.00) in the cell (you can verify this by dragging the Find dialog box out of the way), is considered to be a match.

6 **Press Enter or click the Find Next button to locate the next match.**

Excel moves the cell pointer back to A5, indicating that no further matches to the search text can be found. Next, see what happens if you change the Look in setting from Formulas to Values.

7 **Click the drop-down button to the right of the Look in text box and click Values in the drop-down list.**

Now use the Enter key to find the next occurrences of *cost* in the displayed values of the cells.

8 **Press the Enter key three times and note where Excel moves the cell pointer each time that you find the next occurrence.**

This time, Excel ignores cell B12 and returns to cell A5 the second time that you press the Enter key.

Next, conduct the same search but this time select the Match <u>C</u>ase check box.

9 **Click the Match <u>C</u>ase check box to put a check mark in it and press the Enter key.**

This time, Excel displays an alert box with the message `Cannot find matching data`. This message appears because no cells whose values match all lowercase letters are in this spreadsheet.

Finally, you'll remove the Match <u>C</u>ase condition and then add the Find Entire Cells <u>O</u>nly condition before conducting the search one last time.

10 **Click OK or press Enter to close the alert box, click the Match <u>C</u>ase check box to remove the check mark from it, and click the Find Entire Cells <u>O</u>nly check box (in the Find dialog box) to put a check mark in it. Press Enter.**

Again, Excel displays the alert box with the message `Cannot find matching data`. This message appears because, in this workbook, no cells exist whose values (regardless of the case) consist of the word *cost* all by itself.

11 **Click OK or press Enter to close the alert box. Then press the Esc key to close the Find dialog box.**

Exercise 5-11: Replacing data entries in the worksheet

In this exercise, you'll get some practice in using the Replace feature to replace some cell entries in the income statement in the Simon's Pie Shoppes 96 P&L workbook.

1 **With the cell pointer still in cell A5 of the Simple Simon's Pie Shoppes 1996 income statement, press Ctrl+H (or click <u>E</u>dit on the menu bar and R<u>e</u>place on the pull-down menu) to open the Replace dialog box.**

The Replace dialog box contains both a Fi<u>n</u>d What text box and a R<u>e</u>place with text box. You will now use the Replace feature to replace Income in the spreadsheet with Revenue.

2 **Type *Income* in the Fi<u>n</u>d What text box. Then press the Tab key to select the R<u>e</u>place with text box and type *Revenue*.**

Note that the Find Entire Cells <u>O</u>nly check box is still selected (from the previous exercise). You need to deselect this check box and select the Match <u>C</u>ase check box.

3 **Click the Match <u>C</u>ase check box to put a check mark in it and click the Find Entire Cells <u>O</u>nly check box to remove the check mark from it.**

Now, you need to select the <u>F</u>ind Next button to locate the first occurrence of the word *Income*.

4 **Press Enter or click the <u>F</u>ind Next button.**

The first occurrence is in cell A14 containing Operating Income (loss). Go ahead and replace this occurrence of *Income.*

5 **Click the <u>R</u>eplace button to replace the first occurrence of *Income*.**

Notes:

☑ **Progress Check**

If you can do the following, you've mastered this lesson:

❑ Locate particular cell entries with Find.

❑ Replace data entries with Find and Replace.

Note that cell A14 now contains the heading Operating Revenue (Loss) and that Excel automatically locates the next occurrence of *Income* in the row heading in cell A16 of the spreadsheet.

6 Click the Replace button to replace the second occurrence of *Income*.

Excel replaces *Income* with *Revenue* in cell A16 and locates the next occurrence of *Income* in cell A19. Skip this replacement by choosing the Find Next button.

7 Press Alt+F or click the Find Next button to locate the next occurrence of *Income*.

Excel jumps to cell A21 containing Income (Loss) before Taxes. Go ahead and replace this occurrence of *Income*.

8 Click the Replace button.

Excel makes the replacement and then selects the next occurrence of *Income*, in cell A1.

9 Click the Find Next button again to leave the spreadsheet title as is.

Excel jumps back to cell A19, the cell you skipped without replacing *Income*.

10 Press the Esc key to close the Replace dialog box. Then press Ctrl+F4 and select the No button to close the Simon's Pie Shoppes 96 P&L workbook without saving your changes.

Lesson 5-6

Checking the Spelling of Spreadsheet Data

The spell-check feature in Excel enables you to rid your spreadsheet of all spelling errors, whether they be the result of making typos, not knowing how to spell a word, or a combination of the two. Of course, the downside of using a spell checker is that many of the proper names that you need to use in a spreadsheet will not be in the dictionary. You can, however, always add special terms and proper nouns that you need to routinely enter in your spreadsheets to Excel's custom dictionary so that the program doesn't pester you about them unless they really are misspelled!

Exercise 5-12: Spell checking the worksheet

In this exercise, you'll get an opportunity to use Excel's spell checker to root out any typos or misspelled words in a spreadsheet. For this exercise, you'll use the Simon's Pie Shoppes Q1 96 Sales workbook in the practice folder within your Excel 101 folder.

1 If necessary, start Excel and bring up the Open dialog box. If necessary, open the Practice folder before you double-click Simon's Pie Shoppes Q1 96 Sales in the Open dialog list box.

To spell check an entire worksheet, you simply click the Spelling button on the Standard toolbar, or press function key F7, or choose Spelling on the Tools menu. To spell check a portion of a worksheet, you have to select the cell range prior to doing one of these things.

2 **Click the Spelling button on the Standard toolbar (or press function key F7) to start spell checking the Sheet1 worksheet in the Simon's Pie Shoppes Q1 96 Sales workbook.**

When you start spell checking a worksheet, Excel opens the Spelling dialog box that highlights the first word in a cell that's not in its dictionary while at the same time selecting that cell in the worksheet.

In Sheet1 of the Simon's Pie Shoppes Q1 96 Sales workbook, this first word is *Simon's* in the title in cell A1. Note that Excel suggests that you might want to change *Simon's* to *Simian's* (yeah, right: Simple Simian's Pie Shoppe — featuring banana cream pies no doubt!).

3 **Click the Ignore button in the Spelling dialog box (or press Enter) to skip this unknown word without adding it to the dictionary.**

Of course, you would use the Add button to add *Simon's* to the CUSTOM.DIC dictionary file if you were to go to work for Simple Simon's Pie Shoppe because otherwise Excel's spell checker would drive you nuts by always stopping at this word.

The next unknown word is the rather quaint spelling of *Shoppe* in the same cell. Again, you can now ignore it, although in real life you would want to add it to the CUSTOM.DIC file.

4 **Click the Ignore button in the Spelling dialog box (or press Enter again) to skip this second unknown word without adding it to the dictionary.**

This time, the spelling checker doesn't know the word *Muffet* in the title in cell A1 and suggests that you might want to change this word to *Muffed* or *Buffet*. Go ahead and ignore this as well.

5 **Click the Ignore button in the Spelling dialog box (or press Enter a third time).**

This time, Excel stops at a real typo in cell D2 where some idiot (me) has misspelled *March* as *Merch*. To see this, you have to drag the Spelling dialog box down a bit. You need to correct this one manually because Excel didn't give you any usable spelling-change suggestions.

6 **Type *March* in the Change To text box (which is already selected in the Spelling dialog box). Then click the Change button or press Enter.**

Excel changes *Merch* to *March* and moves on to the next unknown words, which are *Qtr* and *Sugar'n'Spice* in cells E2 and A5. Go ahead and tell Excel to ignore this word (for which it has no suggestions).

7 **Click the Ignore button in the Spelling dialog box (or press Enter) to ignore the unknown words and move on.**

The next unknown words are *beanstalk* and then another typo in cell A7 where row heading *Total* has been misspelled as *Totil* (drag the Spelling dialog box a little to the right to see this). This time, however, Excel's first suggestion, *Total,* is entered in the Change To text box so that all you have to do is select the Change button.

8 **Click the Ignore button in the Spelling dialog box to ignore *beanstalk*. Then click the Change button in the Spelling dialog box to change *Totil* to *Total*.**

Excel responds by displaying a message dialog box with the message `Finished spell checking entire sheet` to let you know that all the unknown words have been checked.

9 **Click OK or press Enter to close the message dialog box. Then click cell A1 to make it active.**

Spelling button

Notes:

☑ **Progress Check**

If you can do the following, you've mastered this lesson:

❑ Spell check the worksheet.

❑ Add words to the custom dictionary.

Now close the Simon's Pie Shoppes Q1 96 Sales workbook and save your spell-checked version of this workbook in your personal folder as Simon's Pie Shoppes Q1 96 Sales (sp) — for *spell checked*.

10 **Click File on the menu bar and then click Save As on the pull-down menu. Click the Up One Level button to open the Excel 101 folder in the Look in list box and double-click your personal folder icon in the Open dialog list box. Click the insertion point at the end of the filename in the File name text box, press the spacebar, and type *(sp)* before you click the Save button or press Enter.**

Now close the Simon's Pie Shoppes Q1 96 Sales (sp) workbook.

11 **Press Ctrl+F4 to close the Simon's Pie Shoppes Q1 96 Sales (sp) workbook.**

Lesson 5-7 — Editing Worksheets in a Workbook

Before saying farewell to the wonderful subject of editing and moving on to Part III, which is about calculating the worksheet, you need to look at one more aspect of editing: editing the worksheets in your workbook. This type of editing can include renaming the worksheets, adding more worksheets, deleting worksheets from a workbook, and moving worksheets within a workbook or moving or copying worksheets to another workbook.

Exercise 5-13: Renaming worksheets

In this exercise, you'll get some practice renaming the worksheets in your MGE Quarterly Sales (fmt) workbook.

1 **Bring up the Open dialog box. Then double-click Quarterly 1996 Sales (fmt) in the Open dialog list box (make sure that your personal folder is displayed in the Look in list box).**

Now you're going to rename the *Sheet1* worksheet in this workbook to *Q1 96*.

2 **Double-click the Sheet1 sheet tab to open the Rename Sheet dialog box.**

3 **Type *Q1 96* in the Name text box and click OK or press Enter.**

Excel changes the sheet tab for the first worksheet from Sheet1 to Q1 96. Next, you'll rename Sheet2 to Q1 97.

4 **Double-click the Sheet2 sheet tab to open the Rename Sheet dialog box.**

5 **Type *Q1 97* in the Name text box. Then click OK or press Enter.**

Next, you'll rename Sheet3 to Q1 98. (This worksheet contains the sales table that you created in the Part I Lab Assignment.)

6 **Double-click the Sheet3 sheet tab to open the Rename Sheet dialog box.**

7 **Type *Q1 98* in the Name text box. Then click OK or press Enter.**

Now save these changes in a workbook named MGE Quarterly Sales (totals).

8 Click the Q1 96 sheet tab to make the first worksheet active. Click **F**ile on the menu bar and click Save **A**s on the pull-down menu to open the Save As dialog box. Make sure that the name of your personal folder is still listed in the Save **i**n drop-down list box. Then select the letters *fmt* in the filename MGE Quarterly Sales (fmt) in the File name list box and replace these letters by typing *totals* so that the filename is now MGE Quarterly Sales (totals). Finally, click the **S**ave button or press Enter.

Exercise 5-14: Adding and deleting worksheets

In this exercise, you'll get some practice inserting and deleting worksheets in your MGE Quarterly Sales (totals) workbook. First, you'll start by inserting a new worksheet in front of your Q1 96 worksheet.

1 With the Q1 96 Sales worksheet in your MGE Quarterly Sales (totals) workbook active, click **I**nsert on the menu bar and **W**orksheet on the pull-down menu.

Excel responds by inserting a new, blank Sheet1 in front of the Q1 96 Sales worksheet. Rename this new worksheet as Q1 Totals. (You'll actually create these totals as part of the exercises in Exercise 5-16, coming right up.)

2 Double-click the Sheet1 sheet tab to open the Rename Sheet dialog box.

3 Type *Q1 Totals* in the **N**ame text box and then click OK or press Enter.

Next, you'll remove Sheet4 through Sheet16 from this workbook. To delete more than one worksheet from a workbook, you first need to select them all. You'll start this procedure by selecting Sheet4 from the sheet tab scrolling buttons' context menu.

4 Position the mouse pointer anywhere on the sheet tab scrolling buttons. Then click the secondary mouse button to open the context menu and click Sheet4 on this menu.

Next, you'll select all the sheets from Sheet4 through Sheet16 with the old Shift+click method.

5 Click the Last Sheet scroll button (the one with the triangle pointing right to a vertical bar) to display the last few sheets in the workbook; then hold down Shift as you click Sheet16.

Now that Sheet4 through Sheet16 are selected, you can delete them with either the Delete command on the sheet's context menu or the Delete Sheet command on the Edit pull-down menu.

6 Click **E**dit on the menu bar; then click De**l**ete Sheet on the pull-down menu.

Excel responds by displaying an alert dialog box that warns you that `Selected sheets will be permanently deleted. Continue?` Go ahead and select OK.

7 Click OK or press Enter to delete worksheets Sheet4 through Sheet16.

Now the last sheet that you see is the sheet tab for the 3rd Qtr. 1996 worksheet.

8 Click the First Sheet scroll button (the one with the triangle pointing left to a vertical bar) to display the Q1 Totals through the Q1 98 sheet tab.

Notes:

You can verify that these four sheet tabs represent the only four worksheets in your MGE Quarterly Sales (totals) workbook either by displaying the sheets on the sheet tab scrolling buttons' context menu or by shortening the horizontal scroll bar to display more sheet tabs (or the lack thereof).

9 **Position the mouse pointer on the vertical bar on the horizontal scroll bar that's to the immediate left of the scroll arrow button that points to the left. When the pointer changes to a double-headed arrow, drag the left-pointing scroll arrow button and the scroll box to the right. After you've shortened the horizontal scroll bar enough to verify that no more sheet tabs exist, release the mouse button.**

Now you need to activate the Q1 Totals worksheet and save your changes.

10 **Click the Q1 Totals sheet tab. Then click the Save button on the Standard toolbar or press Ctrl+S.**

Exercise 5-15: Rearranging the worksheets in a workbook

In this exercise, you'll get a chance to reorder the worksheets in your MGE Quarterly Sales (totals) workbook by dragging their sheet tabs to new positions. Note that, should you ever need to, you can copy a worksheet by holding the Ctrl key as you drag (analogous to holding down the Ctrl key to copy a cell range with drag and drop instead of just moving the cell range).

You'll start this exercise by moving the Q1 Totals worksheet so that it follows the Q1 98 worksheet (at the back of the bus, so to speak).

1 **Click the Q1 Totals sheet tab. Hold down the mouse button as you drag the arrowhead-plus-sheet-icon mouse pointer to the right until the downward-pointing black triangle that appears at the top of the sheet tab is at the far-right edge of the Q1 98 sheet tab. Then release the mouse button.**

As soon as you release the mouse button, Excel repositions the Q1 Totals worksheet after the other three worksheets in this workbook. Next, try moving the Q1 Totals worksheet so that it's positioned between the Q1 96 Sales and the Q1 97 worksheets.

2 **Click the Q1 Totals sheet tab again, this time dragging the arrowhead-plus-sheet-icon mouse pointer to the left until the downward-pointing black triangle that appears at the top of the sheet tab is positioned between the right edge of the Q1 96 sheet tab and the left edge of the Q1 97 sheet tab before you release the mouse button.**

The Q1 Totals worksheet now appears as the second sheet in this workbook. Finally, drag the Q1 Totals worksheet back to the lead position in the workbook.

3 **Click the Q1 Totals sheet tab again, dragging the arrowhead-plus-sheet-icon mouse pointer to the left until the downward-pointing black triangle appears at the left edge of the Q1 96 Sales sheet tab before you release the mouse button.**

The Q1 Totals worksheet is back where it belongs.

Exercise 5-16: Totaling the worksheets in a workbook

In this lesson, you'll copy the headings from the Q1 98 worksheet into your Q1 Totals worksheet and then create SUM formulas in this worksheet that total the sales figures for all Mother Goose companies in the Q1 96, Q1 97, and Q1 98 worksheets.

1 **Click the Q1 98 sheet tab. Then select the cell range A1:A10 and press Ctrl+C to copy these cells to the Clipboard.**

Now you'll paste these cells into the Q1 Totals worksheet.

2 **Click the Q1 Totals sheet tab and press Enter to paste the headings in the cell range A1:A10 of this worksheet.**

Now you need to widen column A to see the row headings.

3 **Select the cell range A3:A10. Click Format on the menu bar, highlight Column on the pull-down menu, and click AutoFit Selection on the continuation menu to widen column A so that all the row headings are completely visible.**

Note that the spreadsheet heading in cell A1 needs some formatting help.

4 **Select cell A1. Then select the cell range A1:E1. Next, click the Center Across Columns button twice (the first time to remove this formatting, and the second time to reinstate it in the currently selected cell range, A1:E1).**

Now, you're ready to copy the column headings from the Q1 98 worksheet.

5 **Click the Q1 98 sheet tab. Then select the cell range B2:E2 and press Ctrl+C to copy these cells to the Clipboard.**

Now it's back to the Q1 Totals worksheet to paste in the column headings.

6 **Click the Q1 Totals tab, click cell B2 to make it current, and press Enter to make the copies in the cell range B2:E2.**

Next, you need to edit the spreadsheet title in cell A1.

7 **Double-click cell A1, click the insertion point in front of the *1* in *1998,* type *1996-* so that the revised title reads Mother Goose Enterprises 1996-1998 Sales (Projected), and press the Enter key.**

Now you're ready to use the AutoSum button on the Standard toolbar to create a formula in cell B3 that totals the January Jack Sprat Diet Center sales for the years 1996 through 1998.

8 **Click cell B3; then click the AutoSum button on the Standard toolbar.**

Excel enters the formula =SUM() in the cell and positions the insertion point right between the parentheses. Now you need to indicate which cells in the other worksheets are to be totaled.

9 **Click the Q1 96 sheet tab, click B3 in this worksheet, and type a comma (,).**

The formula bar should now display =SUM('Q1 96'!B3,) on it. By typing the comma after selecting cell B3 in the Q1 96 worksheet, you've told Excel that this cell is the only cell to be summed on this sheet. Now it's on to the Q1 97 worksheet.

Notes:

10 Click the Q1 97 sheet tab, click B3 in this worksheet, and type a second comma (,).

The formula bar should now display =SUM('Q1 96'!B3,'Q1 97'!B3,). Next, you need to add the cell B3 in the Q1 98 worksheet to the SUM formula.

11 Click the Q1 98 sheet tab and click B3 in this worksheet.

At this point, the SUM formula on your formula bar should read =SUM('Q1 96'!B3,'Q1 97'!B3, 'Q1 98'!B3). If it does, you're ready to complete the formula and enter it into cell B3 of the Q1 Totals worksheet.

12 Click the Enter button on the formula bar to enter the formula in cell B3 of the Q1 Totals worksheet.

When you click the Enter button, Excel enters the formula =SUM('Q1 96'!B3,'Q1 97'!B3, 'Q1 98'!B3). Now widen column B with AutoFit to see the calculated total in cell B3 of the Q1 Totals worksheet.

13 Double-click the right edge of column B on the frame to use AutoFit to resize column B.

You should now see the calculated total 262,954.72 in cell B3 of the Q1 Totals worksheet. Now use the fill handle to copy this formula into the other cells of this table.

14 Drag the fill handle down to cell B10 before releasing the mouse button.

Now all you have to do is copy these formulas in column B across to columns C, D, and E with the fill handle.

15 Without deselecting the cell range B3:B10, drag the fill handle to the right until you've selected through column E and then release the mouse button.

You'll be finished in a second after you format the numbers in the cell range B3:E10 and widen columns B through E.

16 Click the Currency button on the Formatting toolbar once and then click the Decrease Decimal button twice.

17 Click Format on the menu bar, highlight Column on the pull-down menu, and click AutoFit Selection on the continuation menu before you click cell A1 to deselect the cell range B3:E10.

At this point, your Q1 Totals worksheet should look like the one shown in Figure 5-1. If it does, save your changes in the MGE Quarterly Sales (totals) workbook as you close it.

18 Press Ctrl+F4 and click the Yes button or press Enter when asked to save your changes to this workbook.

Exercise 5-17: Copying worksheets from different workbooks into a single, new workbook

In this exercise, you'll learn how to copy income statements in the Sprat Diet Centers 96 P&L, J&J Trauma Centers 96 P&L, and Simon's Pie Shoppes 96 P&L workbooks into a new workbook so that you can later total them. To copy these income statements in the different workbooks to a single new workbook, you will need to open all 96 P&L workbooks. Then you will need to use the Move or Copy Sheet command on the Edit menu to copy them into a brand new workbook.

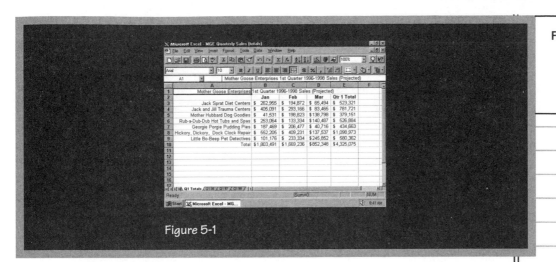

Figure 5-1

Figure 5-1: Here's how the final Q1 Totals worksheet with the totals of the first quarter sales for 1996-1998 should look.

You'll start this procedure by opening the J&J Trauma Centers 96 P&L workbook in your personal folder.

1 Bring up the Open dialog box. Then use it to open the J&J Trauma Centers 96 P&L workbook in your personal folder.

Next, you need to open both the Simon's Pie Shoppes 96 P&L and the Sprat Diet Centers 96 P&L workbooks in the Practice folder.

2 Bring up the Open dialog box again and open the Practice folder. Click Simon's Pie Shoppes 96 P&L file icon. Then Ctrl+click the Sprat Diet Centers 96 P&L file icon so that both files are selected in the Open dialog list box before you click the Open button or press Enter.

At this point, the Sprat Diet Centers 96 P&L workbook should be active in Excel. You will now copy its income statement to a new workbook.

3 Click Edit on the menu bar; then click Move or Copy Sheet on the pull-down menu to open the Move or Copy Sheet dialog box.

Now you'll select the (new book) option in the To Book drop-down list box and select the Create a Copy check box to copy the worksheet with the Sprat Diet Centers 1996 income statement to a new workbook.

4 Click the drop-down button attached to the To Book drop-down list box; then click (new book) in the drop-down list.

Next, you need to select the Create a Copy check box so that Excel copies, rather than moves, the worksheet with the income statement.

5 Click the Create a Copy check box to put a check mark in it. Then click OK or press Enter.

Excel creates a copy of this Sprat Diet Centers 1996 income statement in a new workbook that you will now save in your personal folder.

6 Click the Save button on the Standard toolbar (or press Ctrl+S) to open the Save As dialog box. Open your personal folder by clicking the Up One Level button to open the Excel 101 folder and double-click your personal folder icon in the Open dialog list box. Finally, select the File name text box and replace the temporary filename with *MGE 96 P&Ls* before you click the Save button or press Enter.

Next, rename the Sheet1 worksheet to Sprat Diet Ctr.

7 Double-click the Sheet1 tab, type *Sprat Diet Ctr.*, and click OK or press Enter.

Next, you'll copy the J&J Trauma Centers 1996 income statement into your new MGE 96 P&Ls workbook. First, you have to activate the J&J Trauma Centers 96 P&L workbook.

8 **Click <u>W</u>indow on the menu bar. Then click J&J Trauma Centers 96 P&L on the pull-down menu to make this workbook active.**

Now use the <u>M</u>ove or Copy Sheet command on the <u>E</u>dit menu to copy the J&J Trauma Centers income statement to your MGE 96 P&Ls workbook.

9 **Click <u>E</u>dit on the menu bar. Click <u>M</u>ove or Copy Sheet on the pull-down menu to open the Move or Copy Sheet dialog box. Then select MGE 96 P&Ls.xls in the <u>T</u>o Book drop-down list before you click (move to end) in the <u>B</u>efore Sheet list box and the <u>C</u>reate a Copy check box. Finally, click OK or press Enter to copy the worksheet.**

Now rename this copied worksheet from Sheet1 to J&J Trauma Ctr.

10 **Double-click the Sheet1 tab and type *J&J Trauma Ctr.* in the <u>N</u>ame text box before you click OK or press Enter to close the Rename Sheet dialog box.**

Now you'll select the Simon's Pie Shoppes 96 P&L workbook so that you can copy its income statement into your MGE 96 P&Ls workbook.

11 **Click <u>W</u>indow on the menu bar. Then click Simon's Pie Shoppes 96 P&L on the pull-down menu to make this workbook active.**

Now copy this workbook's income statement just as you did the others.

12 **Click <u>E</u>dit on the menu bar. Then click <u>M</u>ove or Copy Sheet on the pull-down menu to open the Move or Copy Sheet dialog box. Select MGE 96 P&Ls.xls in the <u>T</u>o Book drop-down list before you click (move to end) in the <u>B</u>efore Sheet list box and the <u>C</u>reate a Copy check box. Finally, click OK or press Enter to copy the worksheet.**

Next, rename this new Sheet1 worksheet to Simon's Pie Shoppes before you save your MGE 96 P&Ls workbook.

13 **Double-click the Sheet1 tab. Then type *Simon's Pie Shoppes* in the Name text box before you click OK or press Enter to close the Rename Sheet dialog box.**

Now save your MGE 96 P&Ls workbook before you exit Excel, thereby closing all the open workbook files.

14 **Click the Sprat Diet Ctr. tab to make this worksheet active. Then click the Save button on the Standard toolbar (or press Ctrl+S) before you press Alt+F4 to exit Excel.**

Congratulations! You've come a long way since Unit 1! After you finish the Unit 5 Quiz and Further Exercises and Part II Text and Lab Assignment, you can legitimately consider yourself to be an experienced Excel spreadsheet user.

☑ Progress Check

If you can do the following, you've mastered this lesson:

❏ Rename a worksheet by renaming its sheet tab.

❏ Move a worksheet to a new position in the workbook.

❏ Add worksheets to a workbook.

❏ Delete worksheets from a workbook.

Unit 5 Quiz

Test your knowledge by answering the following questions about working with cell ranges by using the information that you just learned in Unit 5. For each of the following questions, select the letter of the correct response (and remember, I'm not above asking questions where more than one response is correct).

1. **All of the following statements about editing spreadsheet entries are true except:**

   A. To clear a cell entry of everything (its contents, notes, and formats), you can select the cell and then press the Delete key.

   B. To edit an entry on the formula bar, you double-click the I-beam mouse pointer in the entry on the formula bar.

   C. To edit an entry in its cell, you double-click the white-cross mouse pointer in the cell or press function key F3.

   D. When Excel is in Edit mode, the arrow keys move the insertion point in the cell entry instead of moving the cell pointer.

2. **All of the following statements about dividing the worksheet window into panes are true except:**

   A. You can divide the worksheet window into left and right panes by dragging the split bar at the end of the horizontal scroll bar.

   B. You can divide the worksheet window into upper and lower panes by dragging the split bar at the top of the vertical scroll bar.

   C. You can create worksheet titles by selecting the cell in the row right under the one with the column headings and to the immediate right of the one with row headings before you choose Freeze Panes on the Window menu.

   D. The only way that you can remove panes from the worksheet window is to choose Remove Split on the Window menu.

3. **All of the following statements about cell notes are true except:**

   A. Cell notes can consist of either text or, if you have a Macintosh, sound.

   B. To display the text of a note attached to a cell, you double-click the cell.

   C. You can use notes as place holders and then go to each one by selecting them all (with Ctrl+Shift+?) and then pressing Tab.

   D. Excel indicates that a cell has a note attached to it by displaying a little red square in the upper-right corner of the cell.

Notes:

Notes:

4. **All of the following statements about using Find and Replace are true except:**

   A. By default, the Find feature will search the cells' contents for matches to the Find What text.

   B. By default, the Find feature will not worry about matching the case of the Find What text and will consider it a match if the search text occurs in any part of a cell entry.

   C. By default, the Replace feature will automatically replace all the occurrences of the Find What text in the worksheet with the Replace with text.

   D. Normally, when the Replace feature finds a cell with a match to the Find What text, it will replace the entire cell entry with the Replace with text.

5. **All of the following statements about editing the worksheets in a workbook are true except:**

   A. To rename a worksheet, you simply double-click its sheet tab and enter the new name in the Rename Sheet dialog box.

   B. To move a worksheet to a new position in a workbook, you just drag its sheet tab to its new place.

   C. To copy a worksheet to a new place in the workbook, you hold down the Ctrl key as you drag its sheet to a new place.

   D. To delete a worksheet from a workbook, you select its sheet tab and press the Delete key.

Unit 5 Further Exercises

In this further exercise, you'll use the 1996 income statement in the J&J Trauma Centers 96 P&L workbook that you created in Exercise 5-1 to create an 1996 income statement for Mother Hubbard Dog Goodies.

Exercise 5-18: Creating a Mother Hubbard 96 P&L workbook from the J&J Trauma Centers 96 P&L workbook

For this exercise, you'll open the J&J Trauma Centers 96 P&L workbook in your personal folder, edit it to create the 1996 income statement for Mother Hubbard Dog Goodies, and save the income statement as Mother Hubbard 96 P&L.

1. Start Excel and open the J&J Trauma Centers 96 P&L in your personal folder.

2. Edit the spreadsheet title in cell A1 to Mother Hubbard Dog Goodies - 1996 Income.

3. Change the Revenues in cell B3 to 4,250,000.00.

4. Change the Rent cost in cell B7 to (625,000.00).

5. Change the General and Administrative costs in cell B11 to (300,000.00).

6. Delete the row heading Watch Your Step Videos in cell A17 and delete the value 385,000.00 in cell B17. (These two cells will remain blank in this particular income statement.)

7. Change the Book Sales in cell B18 to 125,500.00.

8. Select cell A1 and use the File⇨Save As command to save this revised income statement under the filename Mother Hubbard 96 P&L in your personal folder before you exit Excel.

Part II Review

Unit 4 Summary

- **The easiest way to select a cell range with the mouse:** Click the first cell and then drag through the other cells in the range until all are highlighted.

- **The easiest way to select a cell range with the keyboard:** Move the cell pointer to the first cell, press F8 to put Excel into Extend mode, and then move the cell pointer to the last cell, selecting all the cells in between.

- **To select a nonadjacent cell selection with the mouse:** Select the first range; then hold down the Ctrl key as you select the subsequent cell ranges.

- **To select a table of data with the AutoSelect feature:** Hold down the Shift key as you double-click the sides of the cell pointer in the direction that you want the cell selection extended.

- **To name a single cell or cell range with your own descriptive name:** Select the cell or cell range and then use the Define Name dialog box.

- **To name cells with their column and row headings:** Select the cell range with the headings and cells to be named and then use the Create Names dialog box.

- **To move a cell range with drag and drop:** Select it and then drag it, with the arrowhead pointer, to its new position in the worksheet.

- **To copy a cell range with drag and drop:** Select it and then hold down the Ctrl key as you drag it, with the arrowhead pointer, to its new position in the worksheet.

- **To use cut and paste or copy and paste to move or copy a cell range:** You can move or copy a cell range with cut and paste or copy and paste within the same worksheet as well as to a new worksheet in the same workbook or a different workbook.

- **To replace the formulas in a cell range with their calculated values:** Cut or copy the cells to the Clipboard (Ctrl+X or Ctlr+C) and select the Values radio button in the Paste Special dialog box.

Unit 5 Summary

- **To edit a data entry in its cell:** Double-click the cell and then make the edits.

- **To edit a data entry on the formula bar:** Make the cell current; then click the I-beam mouse pointer in the entry on the formula bar.

- **To complete an edit in the cell or on the formula bar:** Click the Enter box on the formula bar or press the Enter key (you can't use the arrow keys because they only move the insertion point within the cell entry).

- **The easiest way to clear the contents of cell selection:** Press the Delete key.

- **To clear out everything (contents, notes, and formats) from a cell selection:** Choose Edit⇨Clear⇨All on the pull-down menus.

- **To play what-if with an edit:** Use Undo (Ctrl+Z) to undo the edit and then Redo (Ctrl+Z) to redo the edit.

- **To set up column and row headings as the worksheet titles:** Position the cell pointer in the cell to the immediate right of the column(s) and right under the row(s); then select Window⇨Freeze Panes.

- **To display different parts of the same worksheet on the screen:** Position the cell pointer in the cell where you want to split the window into separate panes; then choose Window⇨Split and use the scroll bars to display the different sections of the worksheet in these panes.

- **To delete a cell range:** Select it, choose Edit⇨Delete, and then choose between shifting existing cell entries left or up in the Delete dialog box.

- **To delete entire columns and rows from a worksheet:** Select the columns or rows and then choose Edit⇨Delete. Excel will automatically shift up existing cell entries in rows below or columns to the left.

- **To insert new cell ranges:** Select the cells, choose Insert⇨Cells, and choose between shifting existing cell entries to the right or down.

- **To insert new columns into a worksheet:** Select the columns and then choose Insert⇨Columns.

◆ **To insert new rows into a worksheet:** Select the rows and then choose Insert⇨Rows.

◆ **To rename a worksheet:** Double-click its sheet tab and enter the new name in the Rename Sheet dialog box.

◆ **To locate particular text or values in the contents of the cells:** Choose Edit⇨Find (Ctrl+F) and enter the search text in the Find What text box.

◆ **To replace particular text or values with other text or values:** Choose Edit⇨Replace(Ctrl+H); then enter the search text in the Find What text box and the replacement text or values in the Replace with text box.

◆ **To spell check the entire worksheet:** Click the Spelling button on the Standard toolbar, press F7, or choose Tools⇨Spelling.

◆ **To add an unknown word to the custom dictionary:** Click the Add button in the Spelling dialog box.

◆ **To move a worksheet to a new position in the workbook:** Drag its sheet tab.

◆ **To copy a worksheet into a new place in the workbook:** Hold down the Ctrl key as you drag its sheet tab.

◆ **To add a worksheet to a workbook:** Select the worksheet that is to follow the one you're about to insert and then choose Insert⇨Worksheet.

◆ **To delete worksheets from a workbook:** Select their sheet tabs; then choose Edit⇨Delete Sheet.

◆ **To copy or move a worksheet to another workbook:** Open the other workbook, return to the workbook with the sheets to be copied or moved, and select their sheet tabs before you choose Edit⇨Move or Copy Sheet. Then designate the workbook where you want the selected sheets copied or moved to in the To Book drop-down list box, designate their position in the new workbook in the Before Sheet list box, and (if you're making copies) be sure to select the Create a Copy check box in the Move or Copy dialog box.

Part II Test

The questions on this test cover all of the material presented in Part II, Units 4-5. The first section is True/False, the second section is Multiple Choice, and the last section is Matching.

True   False

Circle the letter of the answer (*T* for True or *F* for False) that best answers the question.

T   F   1. To select a nonadjacent cell selection with the mouse, you can drag through the first range and then hold down the Shift key as you drag through all the other ranges to be added to the selection.

T   F   2. To make a cell selection with the keyboard, you move the cell pointer to the first cell and then press Shift+F8 to get into Add mode before moving the cell pointer through all the rest of the cells to be added to the cell selection.

T   F   3. To select all the cells in the worksheet, you can press Ctrl+Shift+spacebar or Ctrl+A.

T   F   4. To select a cell range with the Go To feature, you select the first cell, open the Go To dialog box, type the address of the last cell, and hold down the Ctrl key as you select OK.

T   F   5. To assign a range name to a constant value, you open the Define Name dialog box and then type the range name in the Names in Workbook text box and the value in the Refers to text box.

T   F   6. To select a named cell range in a workbook, click its range name in the cell address drop-down list on the formula bar.

T   F   7. To move a cell range with drag and drop, select it and then drag it by its fill handle to the new position in the worksheet.

T   F   8. To move a cell range with cut and paste, you can select the range and then choose Edit⇨Cut before selecting the cell range where it's to be moved to and then choosing Edit⇨Paste.

T   F   9. To edit a cell entry, you can either double-click the cell or select the cell and then press the function key F2.

T   F   10. To edit a cell entry on the formula bar, you select the cell and then double-click the formula bar.

T   F   11. Excel's Zoom feature only lets you choose among magnifications of 25%, 50%, 75%, 100%, and 200% of normal and whatever magnification is needed to fit in the current cell selection.

T   F   12. When you delete a range of cells, Excel removes the contents, formats, and notes of the cells without disturbing the other cells around the range.

T   F   13. You can use cell notes as placeholders in a worksheet by selecting all the notes and then using the Tab key to move from note to note.

T   F   14. Normally, when you search a worksheet with the Find feature, Excel matches the search text against just the values of the cells.

T   F   15. To move a worksheet to a new workbook, you just drag its sheet tab to the new workbook.

Part II Test

Multiple Choice

For each of the following questions, circle the correct answer. Remember that there may be more than one right answer to a question.

16. All of the following statements about editing a cell entry are true except:

A. You can replace a cell entry by selecting the cell, just retyping the entry, and then pressing an arrow key to move the cell pointer.

B. You can position the cell pointer in a cell entry by positioning the white-cross cell pointer in the approximate place in the cell and then double-clicking the mouse.

C. You can delete characters (in the cell entry that you're editing) to the left of the insertion point by pressing the Delete key.

D. You can tell that you're in Edit mode in large part because the Cancel, Enter, and Function Wizard buttons reappear on the formula bar and the insertion point is blinking somewhere in the cell entry.

17. All of the following statements about selecting cell ranges in a worksheet are true except:

A. You can select more than one cell range at a time in a worksheet.

B. Cell ranges can include entire rows and columns of the worksheet.

C. The smallest cell range possible in a worksheet is made up of at least two cells right next to each other or right above each other.

D. The largest cell range possible in a worksheet is made up of all the cells in that worksheet.

18. All of the following statements about editing worksheets in a workbook are true except:

A. You can delete all but one of the worksheets in a workbook.

B. You can insert as many new worksheets, after whatever worksheet is active, as you need in your workbook.

C. The way to rename a worksheet is by renaming its sheet tab.

D. You can reorder the worksheets in a workbook by dragging their sheet tabs to new positions.

19. All of the following statements about copying and moving cell ranges are true except:

A. To copy a cell range to a new workbook, you can use the drag-and-drop or the copy-and-paste method.

B. If you're about to overwrite existing cell entries when moving a cell range with drag and drop, Excel forewarns you before replacing the existing cell entries.

C. If you're about to overwrite existing cell entries when moving a cell range with cut and paste, Excel does not forewarn you before replacing the existing cell entries.

D. If you've copied a cell range to the Clipboard with Ctrl+C, you can paste the copy over and over again in different parts of the workbook by pressing the Enter key.

Matching

In the following section, match the items in the first column with the appropriate items in the second column by drawing a line from the item in the column on the left that connects to its counterpart in the column on the right.

20. Match up the following editing icons on the Standard toolbar with the correct function:

A.   1. Undoes the last action you took in Excel.

B. [ABC ✓]   2. Copies the current cell selection to the Clipboard.

C. [icon]   3. Pastes the contents of the Clipboard, using the position of the active cell.

D. [icon]   4. Spell checks the current cell selection or the entire worksheet if only the current cell is selected.

Part II Lab Assignment

In this second lab assignment, you'll get a chance to apply what you've learned about editing the workbook in Units 4 and 5 of Part II. The goal of this assignment is to copy the 1996 income statement in the Mother Hubbard 96 P&L workbook (that you created in Exercise 5-18 at the end of Unit 5) into the MGE 96 P&Ls workbook; then total all four income statement worksheets in this workbook like you did for the first quarter totals in the MGE Quarterly Sales (totals) workbook in Exercise 5-16.

Step 1: Copying the 1996 Mother Hubbard Dog Goodies income statement into the MGE 96 P&Ls workbook

Open the MGE 96 P&Ls and Mother Hubbard 96 P&L workbooks in your personal folder. Then copy the Mother Hubbard Dog Goodies 1996 income statement on Sheet1 of the Mother Hubbard 96 P&L workbook into the MGE 96 P&Ls workbook. Position this worksheet in between the J&J Trauma Ctr. worksheet and the Simon's Pie Shoppes worksheet. Rename the Sheet1 tab to Mother Hubbard and close the Mother Hubbard 96 P&L workbook. Save this workbook in your personal folder with the new filename MGE 96 P&Ls (totals).

Step 2: Adding a new worksheet to the MGE 96 P&Ls (totals) workbook

Insert a new worksheet into the MGE 96 P&Ls (totals) workbook, in front of the Sprat Diet Ctr. worksheet, and then rename this sheet to Total Income. Shorten the horizontal scroll bar until you can see the sheet tabs for all five worksheets in the MGE 96 P&Ls (totals) workbook; then save your changes.

Step 3: Totaling the income statements in the MGE 96 P&Ls (totals) workbook

Copy the spreadsheet title and row headings from the income statement in the Sprat Diet Ctr. worksheet to the Total Income worksheet. Then widen column A in the Total Income worksheet until you can see all the row headings. Edit the spreadsheet title in cell A1 to *Mother Goose Enterprises — 1996 Total Income*. Edit the row heading in cell A17 to *Miscellaneous*.

Select cell B3 in the Total Income worksheet. Then use the AutoSum button to create the following SUM formula in this cell:

```
=SUM('Sprat Diet Ctr.'!B3, 'J&J Trauma Ctr.'!B3,'Mother Hubbard'!B3, 'Simon's
    Pie Shoppes'!B3)
```

After creating this formula, use the fill handle to copy it down column B to cell B23. Then widen column B and delete the contents of all cells in column B that return 0.00 (such as 0.00 in cell B4, which contains a SUM formula that totals the blank B4 cells in all four worksheets). Select cell A1; then save your modified MGE 96 P&Ls (totals) workbook as you exit Excel.

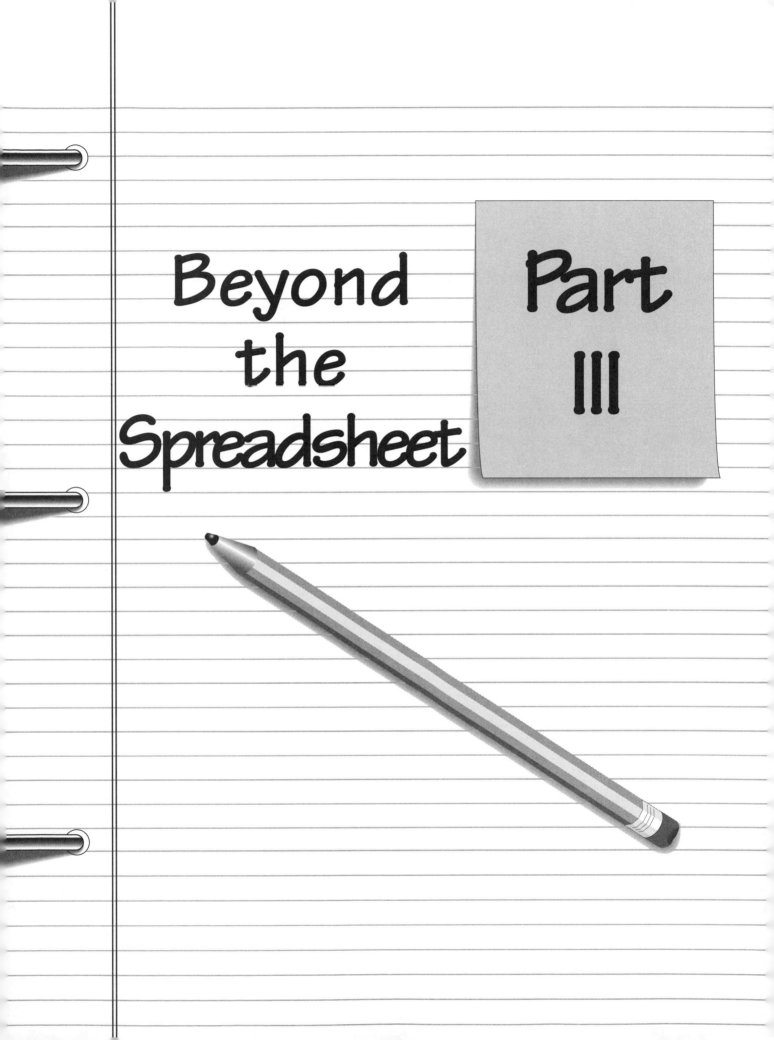

Beyond the Spreadsheet

Part III

In this part . . .

Part III takes you beyond the spreadsheet. This part is made up of two units that expand your skills by introducing you to the art of creating charts and building databases. Unit 6 teaches you how to create cool-looking charts with no sweat at all. Unit 7 teaches you how to create and maintain databases in Excel for Windows 95 with almost as little effort. After you complete the units in this part, you will have greatly increased your Excel skills outside of the traditional spreadsheet.

Charting Spreadsheet Data

Objectives for This Unit

✓ Creating a chart on a worksheet using the ChartWizard

✓ Creating a chart on a separate Chart sheet

✓ Editing the different parts of a chart (including the type of chart and its titles) and formatting its axes

✓ Printing a chart alone or as part of a report with its spreadsheet data

Prerequisites

▶ All lessons and exercises in Unit 5 completed

▶ Unit 5 Quiz and Unit 5 Further Exercises successfully completed

The goal of this unit is to teach you the basics of creating charts from your spreadsheet data. As a result of studying the lessons in this unit, you should be able to create a new chart either on the worksheet with the spreadsheet data used to generate the chart or on a separate chart sheet. You'll also be able to edit the charts that you create in Excel (by modifying such things as the type of chart, the background of the chart area, and the formatting of the chart titles and the y-axis) as well as print the charts that you create, either alone or as part of a report that includes the charted data.

Creating Charts
Lesson 6-1

Charting in Excel is really fun and very easy. The only thing that can be the least bit confusing is the graph terminology that you may not have run across since math class in high school or college.

Excel enables you to choose among a wide variety of two-dimensional and three-dimensional chart types. Most of the 2-D chart types (with the exception of the pie, doughnut, and radar charts) plot the worksheet data against two axes: a horizontal x-axis (which usually shows the categories) and a vertical y-axis (which usually shows the amounts, be they dollars, degrees, or whatever). Most 3-D chart types, with the exception of the 3-D pie chart, add a third z-axis to the normal horizontal x-axis and vertical y-axis. This third axis usually identifies the data series that are represented by some graphic element in the chart, be it a colored bar, area, or ribbon (replicating the function of the legend that identifies the colors assigned to these elements in 2-D charts).

In Excel, you can create a chart as part of the worksheet that contains the charted spreadsheet data (known as an *embedded chart*), or you can create the chart on its own *chart sheet* (a sheet that has its own sheet tab and looks just like a worksheet without having any gridlines). In the exercises in this unit, you'll get practice in creating and editing both an embedded chart and one on its own chart sheet.

Exercise 6-1: Creating a chart with the ChartWizard

The easiest way to create an embedded chart is to use the ChartWizard. To use the ChartWizard, all you have to do is select the spreadsheet data to be charted and then click its button on the Standard toolbar. The ChartWizard then walks you through a series of dialog boxes that enable you to verify the data to be charted, select the type of chart, and add a few of the many possible enhancements to it.

1 **Start Excel. Then open the MGE Quarterly Sales (afmt) workbook in your personal folder.**

This workbook contains two AutoFormatted worksheets: Sheet1 (with the first quarter 1996 sales for Mother Goose Enterprises) and Sheet2 (with Mother Goose Enterprises first quarter 1997 projected sales).

Before you use the ChartWizard to chart the first quarter sales data for Mother Goose Enterprises, go ahead and rename Sheet1 to Q1 96 Sales.

2 **Double-click the Sheet1 tab, type *Q1 96 Sales* in the Rename Sheet dialog box, and click OK or press Enter.**

The next step is to select the spreadsheet data to be charted. When making this cell selection, you select the column and row headings as well as the actual values that will be represented graphically in the chart. In this particular case, you need to select the cell range A2:D9 in the Q1 96 Sales worksheet. (This cell range contains the row headings in cells A3:A9, the column headings in cells B2:D2, and the sales figures in cells B3:D9.)

3 **Select the cell range A2:D9 in the Q1 96 Sales worksheet. Then click the ChartWizard button on the Standard toolbar.**

Chart Wizard
button

When you click the ChartWizard button, the mouse pointer changes to a crosshair with a tiny little column chart appearing slightly below it and to its right. You use this pointer to set the position and the size of the embedded chart that you're about to create with the ChartWizard.

4 **Position the crosshair mouse pointer near the top-left edge of cell A12 (the positioning is approximate, so don't worry too much about it). Then drag the mouse pointer diagonally until the chart outline extends down almost to the bottom of row 26 and is flush with the right edge of column E before you release the mouse button.**

As soon as you release the mouse button, Excel displays the ChartWizard-Step 1 of 5 dialog box, as shown in Figure 6-1. This dialog box displays the cell range currently selected (with a marquee around it) in the worksheet and gives you an opportunity to modify it.

5 **Click the Next> button in the ChartWizard-Step 1 of 5 dialog box (or press Enter) to accept the cell range $A$2:$D$6 as the range to be charted.**

As soon as you click the Next> button, Excel displays the ChartWizard-Step 2 of 5 dialog box, as shown in Figure 6-2. This dialog box selects the Column chart as the chart type and gives you an opportunity to select among 14 other chart types.

6 **Click the Next> button in the ChartWizard-Step 2 of 5 dialog box (or press Enter) to accept Column as the type of chart to create.**

As soon as you click the Next> button, Excel displays the ChartWizard-Step 3 of 5 dialog box, as shown in Figure 6-3. This dialog box selects the sixth Column chart format as the one to use and gives you an opportunity to select among nine other formats.

7 **Click the Next> button in the ChartWizard-Step 3 of 5 dialog box (or press Enter) to accept 6 as the format for the Column chart that you're creating.**

As soon as you click the Next> button this time, Excel displays the ChartWizard-Step 4 of 5 dialog box, as shown in Figure 6-4. This dialog box shows you a preview of how your chart will appear in the worksheet and gives you a chance to modify the orientation of the *data series* (the spreadsheet values being represented as different colored bars in this chart) as well as how many columns in the worksheet are used for the Category (X) axis labels and how rows are used in the Legend text.

Normally, Excel chooses values in the Columns for the data series, which makes the row headings become the category labels and the column headings become the legend text. If you select Rows for the data series, Excel switches this orientation so that the row headings are used as the legend text and the column headings are used as the category labels.

In your initial chart, go ahead and use the default settings for this dialog box.

8 **Click the Next> button in the ChartWizard-Step 4 of 5 dialog box (or press Enter) to accept the defaults.**

As soon as you click the Next> button this time, Excel displays the ChartWizard-Step 5 of 5 dialog box as shown in Figure 6-5. This dialog box enables you to remove the legend and add titles for the chart and the x-axis (category) and y-axis (value).

9 **Click the Chart Title text box and type *Mother Goose Enterprises 1st Quarter 1996 Sales* as the title for this chart. Then press Tab twice to place the insertion point in the Value (Y) text box and type *Dollars*.**

After a few seconds, Excel will add your chart and y-axis titles to the Sample Chart shown in the ChartWizard-Step 5 of 5 dialog box. Now you're ready to create the chart in the Q1 96 Sales worksheet.

10 **Click the Finish button in the ChartWizard-Step 5 of 5 dialog box (or press Enter) to close the ChartWizard dialog box and create the embedded chart in the Q1 96 Sales worksheet.**

When you click the Finish button, Excel closes the ChartWizard and draws the chart over the cell range A12:E26 as shown in Figure 6-6. (Use the vertical scroll bar, if necessary, to view the entire chart.) When Excel creates the chart,

Notes:

Figure 6-1: The ChartWizard-Step 1 of 5 dialog box gives you a chance to change the data to be charted.

Figure 6-2: The ChartWizard-Step 2 of 5 dialog box gives you a chance to select a new chart type.

Figure 6-3: The ChartWizard-Step 3 of 5 dialog box gives you a chance to select a new format for the chart.

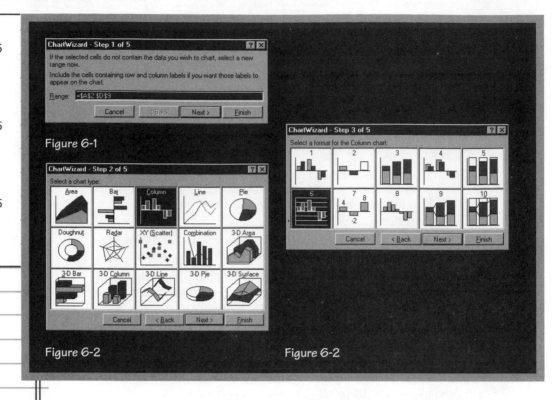

Figure 6-1

Figure 6-2

Figure 6-2

Notes:

you'll notice that the program also opens the Chart toolbar (as a floating toolbar) and that the chart is automatically selected (indicated by the little black sizing handles all around the single-line border around the chart's perimeter). You probably noticed that the Mother Goose company names have been truncated to fit into the current chart size. In Exercise 6-3, you'll learn how to resize this chart so that you can see all the company names.

11 **Click the white-cross mouse pointer in a cell (somewhere outside your Column chart's boundaries) to deselect the chart and hide the Chart floating toolbar.**

Now save your embedded Column chart as part of a new workbook called MGE Quarterly Sales (chart) before going on to the next exercise.

12 **Click File on the menu bar; then click Save As on the pull-down menu. Check to make sure that your personal folder is the last one open in the Save in list box. Click the insertion point in the File name text box between the *t* and the *)* in (afmt) at the end of the filename. Then press the Backspace key four times to delete *afmt* before you type *chart* — making MGE Quarterly Sales (chart) the new filename — and click the Save button or press Enter.**

extra credit

Opening the ChartWizard with the pull-down menus

Instead of clicking the ChartWizard button on the Standard toolbar, you can also open the ChartWizard-Step 1 of 5 dialog box by clicking Insert on the menu bar, highlighting Chart on the pull-down menu, and then clicking On This Sheet on the continuation menu.

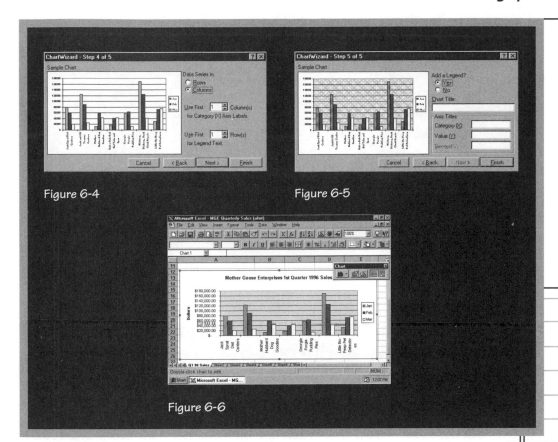

Figure 6-4

Figure 6-5

Figure 6-6

Figure 6-4: The ChartWizard-Step 4 of 5 dialog box gives you a chance to change the orientation of the data series for the chart.

Figure 6-5: The ChartWizard-Step 5 of 5 dialog box gives you a chance to add titles and a legend to the chart.

Figure 6-6: Here's how your embedded Column chart should look after closing the last ChartWizard dialog box.

Exercise 6-2: Creating a chart on its own Chart Sheet

In this exercise, you'll create a chart using the Mother Goose Enterprises first quarter sales data on its own chart sheet.

1 Select the cell range A2:D9 in the Q1 96 Sales worksheet. Then press function key F11.

As soon as you press F11, Excel charts the spreadsheet data in the current cell selection and puts the resulting Column chart on a new chart sheet called Chart1 (as shown in Figure 6-7). Note that this chart sheet is inserted in front of the Q1 96 Sales worksheet (containing the charted spreadsheet data) and that the Chart floating toolbar is automatically displayed in this chart sheet.

Next, you'll rename Chart1 to Q1 96 Chart.

2 Double-click the Chart1 sheet tab. Type *Q1 96 Chart* in the Rename Sheet dialog box before you click OK or press Enter.

Next, you'll move the Q1 96 Chart so that it follows the Q1 96 Sales worksheet in your MGE Quarterly Sales (chart) workbook.

3 Drag the Q1 96 Chart sheet tab until the downward-pointing triangle is positioned between the Q1 96 Sales and Sheet2 sheet tabs; then release the mouse pointer.

Now make the Q1 96 Sales worksheet active and save your changes to the MGE Quarterly Sales (chart) workbook.

4 Click the Q1 96 Sales sheet tab. Then click cell A1 before you save the MGE Quarterly Sales (chart) workbook.

☑ **Progress Check**

If you can do the following, you've mastered this lesson:

❏ Create an embedded chart in a worksheet with the ChartWizard.

❏ Create a chart on its own chart sheet.

Figure 6-7: Here's how your Column chart should look after you create it on its own chart sheet.

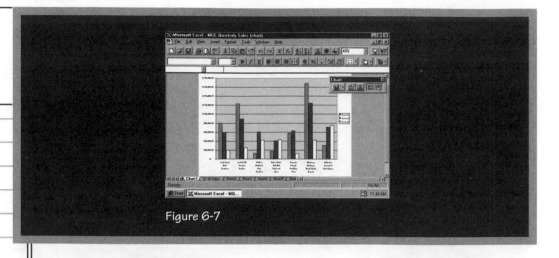

Figure 6-7

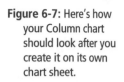

extra credit

Creating a chart on its own chart sheet with the pull-down menus

Instead of pressing F11 to create a chart on its own chart sheet, you can do this by clicking Insert on the menu bar, highlighting Chart on the pull-down menu, and then clicking As New Sheet on the continuation menu.

Lesson 6-2   Editing a Chart

Excel makes it easy to edit the charts that you create with the program. To edit an embedded chart that's part of a worksheet (like the chart that you created on the Q1 96 worksheet), you first need to double-click somewhere on the chart to make it active.

Excel for Windows 95 shows you that an embedded chart is active in one of two ways. If the entire embedded chart is visible on the screen, Excel just surrounds the active chart with a thicker-than-normal chart border with diagonal hash marks. If not all of the embedded chart can be viewed on the screen, Excel puts the active chart in its own editing window with its own title bar, close button, and the whole works.

Excel also automatically displays the Chart toolbar as a floating toolbar as soon as you activate the embedded chart. After an embedded chart is active, you can then select any of its parts (for example, the titles, axes, plot area, and so on) just by clicking them.

To edit a chart that's been created on its own chart sheet, you simply need to select its chart sheet tab. As soon as you do this, Excel automatically displays the floating Chart toolbar, and you can select the part of the chart to be edited by clicking it.

When editing a chart, it pays to remember that each part has its own context menu attached to it. This means that you can often get right to the editing command you need to use by clicking that part of the chart with the secondary mouse button.

In the exercises ahead, you'll get some practice at editing a number of chart elements (including changing the size and position of your embedded chart, the type of chart, and the way the spreadsheet data is charted) and formatting the chart titles and y-axis values.

Exercise 6-3: Moving and resizing an embedded chart

In this first editing exercise, you'll see just how easy it is to move and adjust the size of an embedded chart.

1 **Click somewhere on the embedded Column chart in your Q1 96 worksheet to select the chart.**

Excel shows that the chart is selected by displaying sizing handles and a single-line border around the chart's perimeter and by displaying the floating Chart toolbar.

2 **Use the vertical scroll bar to bring the selected embedded chart up until it's centered vertically on the screen.**

Now you'll use the sizing handle to lengthen the chart so that all the company names are visible at the bottom of the chart.

3 **Position the white-cross mouse pointer on the sizing handle in the middle on the bottom side of the chart border. After the pointer changes to a double-headed arrow pointing up and down, drag the mouse down until the bottom edge of the chart is flush with the lower edge of row 34. Then release the mouse button.**

After you release the mouse button, Excel redraws your embedded Column chart to fit this new length, and you can see (at last) all seven of the Mother Goose company names.

Next, you'll move the embedded Column chart so that it's immediately to the right of the first quarter 1996 sales table instead of beneath it.

4 **Position the arrowhead mouse pointer in the upper-left corner of the selected chart (make sure that you're inside the chart's borders and not on the corner sizing handles). Then drag the chart up (until the top edge of the chart's outline is flush with the bottom of row 1 and the top edge of row 2) and to the right (until its left edge is flush with the right edge of column F and the left edge of column G) before you release the mouse button.**

When you release the mouse button, Excel redraws the embedded Column chart in the new position to the right of the sales table.

5 **Click cell F2 to deselect the chart. Click the scroll button with the right arrow on the horizontal scroll bar until the embedded chart is approximately centered on the screen. Click the scroll button with the down arrow on the vertical bar once to center the chart vertically.**

Now save your MGE Quarterly Sales (chart) workbook again so that the resizing and moving of your embedded Column chart is saved.

6 **Save your changes to the MGE Quarterly Sales (chart) workbook.**

Notes:

Notes:

extra credit

Deleting charts

To delete an embedded chart, click the chart to select it. Then press the Delete key. To delete a chart on its own chart sheet, click its chart tab. Then click <u>E</u>dit on the menu bar and De<u>l</u>ete Sheet on the pull-down menu. Excel will then warn you that the selected sheet is about to be permanently removed. If you then choose OK or press Enter (as opposed to pressing Cancel), the chart sheet and the chart that it contains will be gone forever from your workbook.

If you delete an embedded chart in error, immediately press Ctrl+Z to bring it back. If you delete a chart sheet in error, get ready to re-create the chart all over again. Or, if you haven't saved the workbook since nixing the chart sheet, you can close the workbook without saving your changes (thus getting rid of the chart sheet) and then reopen the workbook (the workbook that still has the chart sheet saved as part of it) from the hard disk.

Exercise 6-4: Changing the chart type and orientation of the data series

Although the Column chart with gridlines is the default chart type, it is but one of many that you can use. In this exercise, you'll get an opportunity to experiment with some of the other chart types. You'll also learn how easy it is to switch the data series in a chart from columns to rows.

1 Click the embedded chart in the Q1 96 Sales worksheet to select it. Then click the Chart Type drop-down list button on the Chart toolbar and click the Line Chart button in the drop-down chart palette (the fourth button down on the left side).

Chart Type button

The chart palette attached to the Chart Type drop-down list button contains icons for the 14 types of charts available in Excel. As soon as you click the Line Chart icon, Excel redraws the embedded chart as a line chart in which the data series are represented by different colored points connected by lines.

Line Chart button

Next, try changing the chart type to a 3-D Column chart.

2 Click the Chart Type drop-down list button on the Chart toolbar. Then click the 3-D Column Chart button in the drop-down chart palette (the third one down in the right column).

3-D Column Chart button

This time, Excel redraws the Line Chart as a 3-D Column chart in which the data series are represented by different-colored three-dimensional vertical bars. Note that (given the small size of this embedded chart) Excel can show only four of the seven company labels on the x-axis. Note, too, that this 3-D chart also shows the legend text as labels along the z-axis (making the legend unnecessary).

Given how tightly packed the information is on this size of the embedded chart in this 3-D format, you'd better change this chart back to the good old default type of (two-dimensional) Column chart.

3 Click the Chart Type drop-down list button on the Chart toolbar. Then click the Column Chart button in the drop-down chart palette (the third one down on the left).

Column Chart button

Excel returns the chart to a good old (boring?) two-dimensional Column chart. Now turn your attention to the Column chart on the Q1 96 Chart sheet.

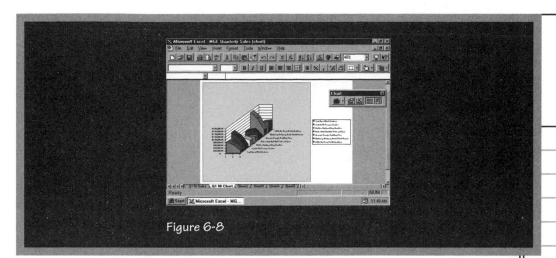

Figure 6-8

Figure 6-8

Figure 6-8: Here's how your 3-D Area chart should look in the 1st Qtr. 1996 Chart sheet after you select rows for the data series.

4 **Click the Q1 96 Chart sheet tab to activate the chart on this sheet.**

As soon as you make this chart tab active, Excel displays the floating Chart toolbar in the window. You will now use it to change the Column chart to a 3-D Bar chart.

5 **Click the Chart Type drop-down list button on the Chart toolbar. Then click the 3-D Bar Chart button in the drop-down chart palette (the second one down on the right).**

When you change the chart type to 3-D, Excel represents the data series as different-colored, three-dimensional horizontal bars.

6 **Click the Chart Type drop-down list button on the Chart toolbar. Then click the 3-D Area Chart button in the drop-down chart palette (the top right).**

When you change the chart type to 3-D chart, Excel represents the data series as different-colored, three-dimensional blocks whose peaks and valleys show the amount of sales at each data point.

Next, instead of changing the type of chart, you will change the orientation of the data series from Columns to Rows. To do this, you must use the ChartWizard button on the Chart toolbar.

When you select the ChartWizard *after* creating the chart, the ChartWizard contains only two dialog boxes: the ChartWizard-Step 1 of 2 dialog box, where you can modify the range of cells being charted, and ChartWizard-Step 2 of 2 dialog box, where you can both switch the data series from columns to rows and change how rows and columns are used for the x-axis and y-axis labels.

7 **Click the ChartWizard button on the Chart toolbar.**

Excel displays the ChartWizard-Step 1 of 2 dialog box with ='Q1 96 Sales'!$A$2:$D$9 shown in the Range text box and a marquee around the cell range A2:D9 in the Q1 96 Sales worksheet.

8 **Click the Next> button or press Enter.**

Excel displays the ChartWizard-Step 2 of 2 dialog box in the Q1 96 Chart sheet.

9 **Click the Rows radio button under Data Series in. Then click OK or press Enter.**

Excel closes the ChartWizard-Step 2 of 2 dialog box, and your 3-D Area chart now looks like the one in Figure 6-8. Having switched the orientation of the data series, your 3-D Area chart now uses the months as x-axis labels; the company names are used in the legend and as z-axis labels.

3-D Bar Chart button

3-D Area Chart button

10 Save the MGE Quarterly Sales (chart) workbook to preserve your changes to the embedded Column chart on the Q1 96 Sales sheet and 3-D Area chart on the Q1 96 Chart sheet.

Exercise 6-5: Editing the chart titles, legend, and gridlines

In this exercise, you'll get some practice at modifying the chart titles, legend, and horizontal gridlines. You'll start by adding a chart title to the 3-D Area chart on your Q1 96 Chart sheet and by removing the chart's legend. Then you'll switch over to your embedded Column chart on the Q1 96 Sales worksheet where you'll modify the formatting of the chart titles, modify the background color of the legend, and remove the horizontal gridlines.

1 With the Q1 96 Chart sheet selected, position the arrowhead mouse pointer anywhere on the 3-D Area chart. Click the secondary mouse button to open the chart's context menu. Then click Insert Titles on this context menu.

Excel opens the Titles dialog box containing check-box options for selecting the kinds of titles that you want to add.

2 Click the Chart <u>T</u>itle check box to put a check mark in it; then click OK or press Enter.

When you choose OK (or press Enter), Excel closes the Titles dialog box and inserts a tiny chart title text box containing the word *Title* in bold. Note that this text box is centered at the top of the chart and that it is currently selected (indicated by the sizing handles all around its border).

3 Type *MGE 1st Quarter 1996 Sales* on the formula bar and click the Enter button to replace *Title* in the chart title text box with the text that you just typed.

After you click the Enter button, Excel replaces the word *Title* with the honest-to-goodness chart title that you just typed. Now, while the title's still selected, go ahead and increase the title's font size by using the Font Size drop-down list box on the Formatting toolbar.

4 Click the Font Size drop-down list button on the Formatting toolbar. Then click 14 in the drop-down list.

Excel increases the size of the chart title text from 12 to 14 points.

5 Click the mouse pointer somewhere on the chart (outside the chart title's text box) to deselect this box.

Now go ahead and remove the legend from this chart because you don't really need a legend in a 3-D chart such as this one, which displays the same labels that appear in the legend along the z-axis.

6. Click the Legend button on the Chart toolbar to deselect it.

As soon as you click the Legend button, Excel removes the legend. You can now move the *plot area* (the gray rectangle that contains all of the 3-D Area chart except for its title) to the right so that it is more centered under the title.

7 Click somewhere on the gray background of the chart (outside the graph itself) to select it. Drag the plot area to the right until you're satisfied that it's now centered under the chart title. Then click somewhere on the gray background (outside the chart area) to deselect the plot area.

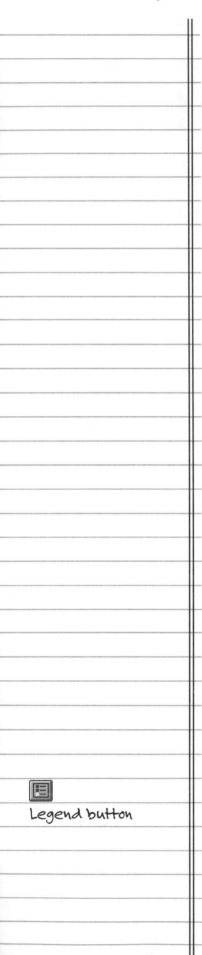

Legend button

Now you'll make some editing changes to the chart title, legend, and gridlines on your embedded Column chart on the Q1 96 Sales worksheet.

8 **Click the Q1 96 Sales sheet tab to make this worksheet with your Column chart active. Then use the horizontal scroll bar to bring the embedded chart into view on the screen. (You should center the embedded chart as best as you can.)**

Note that, currently, the chart title all appears on one line and is a little long. The phrase *1st Quarter 1996 Sales* should be forced onto the second line. To do this, you need to select the chart title.

9 **Position the arrowhead mouse pointer on some part of the Column chart. Then double-click to place the embedded chart into its own editing window.**

When you double-click the chart, Excel puts the entire embedded Column chart in its own editing window for editing.

10 **Click somewhere on the chart title to select it for editing. (You may also need to drag the floating Chart toolbar out of the way.) Then position the I-beam pointer right in front of the *1* in *1st*. Click to place the insertion point before you press the Enter key.**

As soon as you press Enter after placing the insertion point, Excel moves the words *1st Quarter 1996 Sales* down to the second line.

Next, you'll select a new color for the chart area and select a new color for the legend.

11 **Click somewhere on the white chart area (and not on any part of the chart or legend) with the secondary mouse button. Then click Format Chart Area on the context menu.**

Change the chart area color from white to light purple (actually, violet).

12 **Click the purple that's at the right end of the third row of the Color palette in the Format Chart Area dialog box. Then click OK or press Enter.**

Next, change the legend color from white to light gray.

13 **Click somewhere on the legend with the secondary mouse button. Then click Format Legend on the context menu that appears.**

Now select a new color for the legend background in the color palette.

14 **Click the gray that's at the right end of the fifth row of the Color palette in the Format Legend dialog box and then click OK or press Enter.**

Finally, remove the horizontal gridlines from the plot area.

15 **Click the Horizontal Gridlines button on the Chart toolbar to remove these gridlines from the plot area of this Column chart.**

Go ahead and save your changes before going on to Exercise 6-6.

16 **Click the close button in the right corner of the chart-editing window's title bar (or press Ctrl+W) to close the editing window. Click cell F1 to make this cell current and to deselect the embedded chart in the worksheet before you click the Save button on the Standard toolbar to save your changes to the MGE Quarterly Sales (chart) workbook.**

Notes:

Horizontal Gridlines button

Notes:

Exercise 6-6: Formatting the values on the y-axis

In this exercise, you'll learn how to assign a number format to the values that appear along the y-axis of your embedded Column chart. To make the dollar values more legible on this axis, you'll select the Currency format and eliminate the decimal places.

1 **Double-click the embedded Column chart to activate it.**

Next, you need to select the Format Axis command on the y-axis context menu. To open this context menu, you must be careful to position the tip of the arrowhead pointer directly on the y-axis line before you click it with the secondary mouse button.

2 **Click somewhere on the y-axis (the vertical line to the immediate right of the labels $ to $180,000.00) with the secondary mouse button. Then click Format Axis on its context menu.**

Excel opens the Format Axis dialog box, which has five tabs. You'll use the Number tab to assign a number format to the values that appear along the y-axis.

3 **Click the Number tab to make it active.**

Next, you need to select Currency in the Category list box.

4 **Click Currency in the Category list box to display its formatting options.**

The default Currency format code (which is automatically selected) adds a dollar sign, commas, and two decimal places (as evidenced by the $180,000.00 in the Sample area). Go ahead and remove the decimal places and then apply this Currency format to the y-axis values.

5 **Click the down spinner button on the right side of the Decimal Places list box twice, until its list box contains 0. Then click OK (or press Enter) to close the Format Axis dialog box and to assign this new Currency format to the y-axis.**

Excel formats the values along the tick marks of the y-axis by using the selected Currency style without any decimal places. Now that the values on the y-axis all use this Currency style, you no longer need the y-axis title, Dollars.

6 **Position the tip of the arrowhead pointer somewhere on the y-axis title text, Dollars. Then click the secondary mouse button to open its context menu and click Clear on that context menu.**

As soon as you select Clear Excel gets rid of the y-axis title. Now you're ready to deactivate and deselect the embedded Column chart and save your MGE Quarterly Sales (chart).

7 **Click the close button on the title bar of the chart editing window (or press Ctrl+W) to close the editing window. Then click cell F1 to deselect the chart before you click the Save button on the Standard toolbar to save your changes in the MGE Quarterly Sales (chart) workbook.**

Exercise 6-7 Modifying the 3-D View

In this last editing exercise, you'll learn how to modify the view of your 3-D Area chart, the chart that's on its own chart sheet in the MGE Quarterly Sales (chart) workbook.

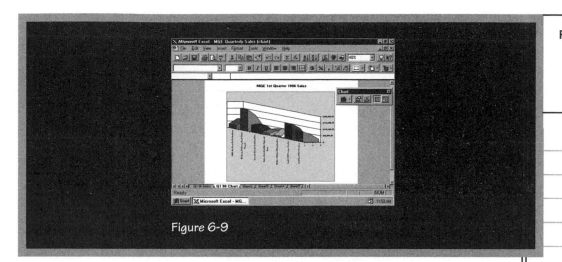

Figure 6-9

1 Press Ctrl+PgDn to make the Q1 96 Chart sheet current.

You can modify the view of a 3-D chart either by using the Format 3-D View dialog box or by clicking on a corner of the 3-D chart and then dragging its wireframe box to the desired position. Using the options in the Format 3-D View dialog box requires a good understanding of 3-D perspective and rotation angles (or at least a lot more understanding than I've got). Because dragging the wireframe box is much more direct, go ahead and use this method.

2 Position the tip of the arrowhead mouse pointer on the corner of the 3-D Area chart that's at the intersection of the x-axis and y-axis (where January meets 0). Then click the mouse button.

Assuming that your mouse pointer was on target, Excel selects the frame of the chart (indicated by selection handles at all the corners), and the mouse pointer changes to a crosshair.

3 Click the corner of the 3-D Area chart where the x-axis meets the y-axis (and January meets 0) and hold down the mouse button.

After you hold down the mouse button for a second or two, the 3-D Area chart suddenly disappears and is replaced by the 3-D wireframe box. This change is the signal that advises you that you can drag the mouse pointer to alter the 3-D view. Go ahead and drag the wireframe box down and to the right until you've actually reversed the 3-D Area chart.

4 Without releasing the mouse button, drag the crosshair mouse pointer slowly to the right and slightly down until the wireframe box is reversed. Then release the mouse button.

When you release the mouse button, Excel redraws your 3-D Area chart so that the company name labels now appear going up the left side of the 3-D chart rather than up the right side (like the one shown in Figure 6-9).

5 Click somewhere outside the plot or chart area to deselect the chart's 3-D box without selecting anything else.

Now you're ready to save your work before you go on to Lesson 6-3.

6 Click the Q1 96 Sales sheet tab to make this worksheet active. Then press Ctrl+Home to select cell A1 before you click the Save button on the Standard toolbar to save your changes to the MGE Quarterly Sales (chart) workbook.

☑ **Progress Check**

If you can do the following, you've mastered this lesson:

❑ Move and resize an embedded chart.

❑ Change the chart type.

❑ Edit chart titles.

❑ Add a number format to the values on the y-axis.

Printing Charts

Printing the charts that you create in Excel is very similar to printing spreadsheet data. To print an embedded chart along with its spreadsheet data, you simply select the worksheet(s) that contains the data and chart before printing. To print a chart that's been created on its own chart sheet, you simply select its chart sheet before printing. To print an embedded chart alone, you need to select all the cells underneath the embedded chart as a single range before you open the Print dialog box where you choose the Selection radio button in the Print What section before starting the printing.

In the following exercises, you'll get practice in printing charts both alone and as part of reports containing their spreadsheet data.

Exercise 6-8 Printing the embedded chart alone and with its spreadsheet data

In this first exercise, you'll print your embedded Column chart on the Q1 96 Sales worksheet, both alone and along with the first quarter 1996 sales table. However, before you start printing, the first thing you should do is to move the Column chart back underneath the first quarter sales table.

1 **Click the Column chart to select it. Drag it so that it's centered horizontally between columns A through F of the worksheet and its top edge is flush with the bottom of row 11 and the top of row 12. Then click cell A1 to deselect the Column chart and make this cell active.**

Now you're ready to print the embedded Column chart. To do this, you must first select the cells beneath the embedded chart. In this case, you will select the cell range A11:E34 to make sure that all of the Column chart gets printed.

2 **Click cell A11, press F5, type *E34*, and hold down the Shift key while you click OK (or press Enter).**

Now you need to open the Print dialog box and choose the Selection radio button in the Print What section.

3 **Press Ctrl+P. Then click the Selection radio button in the Print What area before you click the Preview button.**

When the Print Preview window opens, you'll see the Column chart on the Preview Page 1 of 1. Fortunately, Excel for Windows 95 defaults to print without gridlines, so all you have to do is horizontally center this chart before printing it.

4 **Click the Setup button at the top of the Print Preview window. Then click the Margins tab. In the Margins tab, click the Horizontally check box to put a check mark in it before you click OK or press Enter.**

When you close the Page Setup dialog box, Excel redraws the Column chart and centers it between the left and right margins. Go ahead and print this chart.

5 Click the Print button at the top of the Print Preview window and then click OK or press Enter in the Print dialog box to print the chart and return to the 1st Qtr. 1996 worksheet.

Next, you'll print first quarter 1996 sales data along with the Column chart. To do this, you simply use the print defaults.

6 Press Ctrl+Home to select cell A1 and click the Print Preview button on the Standard toolbar.

This time, both the sales table and the Column chart below appear on Page 1 of 1 in the Print Preview window.

7 Click the Print button in the Print Preview window and then click OK or press Enter in the Print dialog box to print this page and return to the 1st Qtr. 1996 worksheet.

Exercise 6-9: Printing the Q1 96 Chart sheet

In this exercise, you'll get an opportunity to print the 3-D Area chart that's on the Q1 96 Chart sheet all by itself and then with the first quarter 1996 sales data on the Q1 96 Sales worksheet.

1 Click the Q1 96 Chart tab to select this worksheet. Then click the Print Preview button on the Standard toolbar.

In the Print Preview window, Excel displays your 3-D Area chart as Page 1 of 1. Note that Excel automatically selects landscape mode for printing this page.

2 Click the Print button in the Print Preview window. Then click OK (or press Enter in the Print dialog box) to print your 3-D Area chart.

Next, you'll print the first quarter 1996 sales table for Mother Goose Enterprises on the first page of the report and the 3-D Area chart on the second page of the report. To do this, you simply select both the Q1 96 Sales and Q1 96 Chart sheet tabs before printing.

The only problem with printing these two sheets is that when Excel prints the Q1 96 Sales worksheet, it will print the embedded Column chart along with the spreadsheet data in the sales table above. To prevent this, you need to hide the Column chart on the Q1 96 Sales worksheet before printing the report.

3 Click the Q1 96 Sales sheet tab to make this worksheet active.

Next, you'll open the Options dialog box to hide the embedded Column chart.

4 Click Tools on the menu bar. Then click Options on the pull-down menu to open the Options dialog box.

To hide embedded graphics like charts, you need to select the Hide All radio button in the Objects section of the Options dialog box's View tab. (*Objects* here, by the way, refers to *graphic* objects.)

5 Click the View tab in the Options dialog box and then click the Hide All radio button in the Objects section of this dialog box before you click OK or press Enter.

When the Options dialog box closes, you should notice that your embedded Column chart is nowhere to be found.

6 Hold down the Shift key as you click the Q1 96 Chart sheet tab.

Now both the Q1 96 Sales and Q1 96 Chart tabs should be selected.

Notes:

Notes:

✓ **Progress Check**

If you can do the following, you've mastered this lesson:

❑ Print a chart sheet.

❑ Print an embedded chart with its spreadsheet data.

❑ Print an embedded chart all by itself.

7 Click the Print Preview button on the Standard toolbar to preview the printing.

Page 1 of 2 shows the first quarter sales table alone at the top of the page, centered between the left and right margins. Now check out Page 2 of 2.

8 Click the <u>N</u>ext button at the top of the Print Preview window to see Page 2 of 2.

Page 2 of 2 shows the 3-D Area chart in landscape mode. Go ahead and print the two pages in this report.

9 Click the Prin<u>t</u> button at the top of the Print Preview window. Then click OK or press Enter in the Print dialog box to print the report and return to the Q1 96 Sales worksheet.

Now you need to deselect the Q1 96 Sales and Q1 96 Chart sheets and redisplay the embedded Column chart in the Q1 96 Sales worksheet before you quit Excel.

10 Click the Sheet2 sheet tab to deselect the Q1 96 Sales and Q1 96 Chart sheets. Click the Q1 96 Sales sheet tab to make just this worksheet active.

11 Click <u>T</u>ools on the menu bar. Then click <u>O</u>ptions on the pull-down menu. If necessary, click the View tab and then click the Show <u>A</u>ll radio button in the Objects section before you click OK or press Enter.

You should once again see the first part of the Column chart under your first quarter sales data. Now save your changes as you exit Excel.

12 Click <u>F</u>ile on the menu bar. Then click E<u>x</u>it on the pull-down menu. Click the <u>Y</u>es button or press Enter in the alert box that asks whether you want to save changes in the MGE Quarterly Sales (chart) workbook.

Unit 6 Quiz

Test your knowledge by answering the following questions about creating charts in Unit 6. For each of the following questions, select the letter of the correct response (and remember that I'm not above asking questions where more than one response is correct).

1. **All of the following statements about creating an embedded chart are true except:**

   A. To create an embedded chart, you must use the ChartWizard.

   B. You can select the ChartWizard either by clicking the ChartWizard button on the Standard toolbar or by clicking <u>I</u>nsert on the menu bar, Chart on the pull-down menu, and On This Sheet on the continuation menu.

   C. To edit part of an embedded chart, you just click the part of the chart that you want to change with the secondary mouse button and select the desired command from that part's context menu.

   D. To move a chart to a new part of the worksheet, you double-click the chart and then drag it to its new location.

2. **All of the following statements about creating a chart on its own chart sheet are true except:**

    A. Before you can create a chart on its own chart sheet, you must have already inserted a blank chart sheet for it in your workbook.

    B. Whenever you activate a chart sheet, Excel automatically displays the floating Chart toolbar on the screen.

    C. To edit a part of a chart on its own sheet, you can just click the part with the secondary mouse button and then choose the desired command on its context menu.

    D. To create a chart on its own sheet, you select the cell range with the spreadsheet data to be graphed and then press F11 or click Insert on the menu bar, Chart on the pull-down menu, and As New Sheet on the continuation menu.

3. **All of the following statements about editing a chart are true except:**

    A. To remove the gridlines from the plot area of a chart, you click the Horizontal Gridlines button on the floating Chart toolbar.

    B. To change the type of chart, you click the Chart Type drop-down list button and then click the icon for the new chart type in the chart-type palette.

    C. To add or remove a legend from a chart, you click the Legend button on the floating Chart toolbar.

    D. To modify the range of spreadsheet data that's being charted, you first select the new cell range in the worksheet before you click the ChartWizard button on the floating Chart toolbar or the Standard toolbar.

4. **All of the following statements about printing charts are true except:**

    A. To print an embedded chart by itself, click the Chart to select it and then open the Print dialog box and click the Selection radio button.

    B. You can print a chart on its own chart sheet by selecting its sheet tab and then clicking the Print button on the Standard toolbar.

    C. To print an embedded chart with its spreadsheet data, select both the chart and the cell range with the spreadsheet data before you open the Print dialog box and click the Selection radio button.

    D. To print the spreadsheet data in a worksheet without its embedded charts, you need to click the Hide All radio button on the View tab of the Options dialog box before printing the worksheet.

Unit 6 Further Exercises

In these further exercises, you'll get an opportunity to create and print a pie chart on a new chart sheet in your MGE Quarterly Sales (chart) workbook. The pie chart (whether in two dimensions or three) is one of the few types of charts that don't use any axes. This is because instead of comparing a series of values over time by category, the pie chart compares each value in the series to the sum of all the values. It does this by dividing the pie (representing the sum

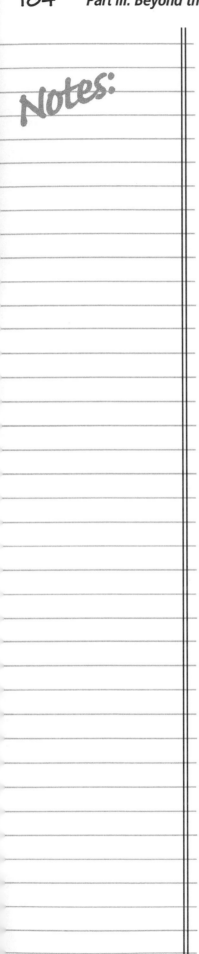

of the values) into sections according to what percentage of the sum each value represents. As such, pie charts are great for showing the relationship of each part to the whole. In these exercises, you will create a pie chart that shows what percentage of the total Mother Goose Enterprises first quarter 1996 sales that each company contributed.

Exercise 6-10: Creating the pie chart

You'll start by opening your MGE Quarterly Sales (chart) workbook and then creating a pie chart on its own chart sheet.

1. Start Excel; then open the MGE Quarterly Sales (chart) workbook in your personal folder.

2. Select the noncontiguous cell ranges A3:D9 and A3:E9 in the Q1 96 Sales worksheet (containing just the company name row headings and the total sales figures for the three months of the first quarter); then press F11 to create a standard Column chart on a new chart sheet.

3. Rename the Chart1 sheet to Q1 96 Pie Chart and then move it between the Q1 96 Sales worksheet and the Q1 96 Chart sheet.

4. Rename the Q1 96 Chart sheet to Q1 96 Area Chart; then make the Q1 96 Pie Chart sheet active again.

5. Click the Chart Type drop-down list button on the floating Chart toolbar; then click the Pie Chart icon (it's the fifth one down in the left column) to change the Column chart into a pie chart.

Exercise 6-11: Enhancing the pie chart

Next, you'll enhance your pie chart by adding a chart title, exploding the pie chart sections, and replacing the legend with data labels that appear next to each section of the pie chart and indicate what percentage to the whole and what company each section of the pie chart represents.

1. Click the chart with the secondary mouse button; then click Insert Titles on the context menu.

2. Click the Chart Title check box, click OK or press Enter, and type *Mother Goose Enterprises Quarter 1, 1996 Sales by Company* before you click the Enter button on the formula bar.

3. Position the insertion point before the *Q* in *Quarter* and then press the Enter key to insert a line break in the chart title so that *Quarter 1, 1996 Sales by Company* is all together on the second line.

4. Click somewhere on the pie chart; then click the Legend button on the floating Chart toolbar to remove the legend.

5. Click the chart with the secondary mouse button, click AutoFormat on both the context menu and in the AutoFormat dialog box, and click 4 in the Formats section (with the exploded pie sections) before you click OK or press Enter.

6. Click the chart with the secondary mouse button, click Insert Data Labels on the context menu, and click the Show Label and Percent radio button in the Data Labels dialog box before you click OK or press Enter.

Exercise 6-12: Printing the 3-D pie chart

Next, print this chart before you close the MGE Quarterly Sales (chart) wordbook.

1. With the Q1 96 Pie Chart sheet still active, click somewhere on the background (outside the plot and chart area) to deselect the pie chart without selecting anything else; then click the Print Preview button on the Standard toolbar.

2. Click the Print button at the top of the Print Preview window; then click OK or press Enter in the Print dialog box to print your pie chart.

3. Click the Q1 96 Sales sheet tab to make this worksheet active; then make cell A1 current before you exit Excel, making sure to save your changes to the MGE Quarterly Sales (chart) workbook as part of quitting the program.

Notes:

Building and Maintaining a Database

Objectives for This Unit

✓ Creating a new database

✓ Adding records to a database using the data form

✓ Using the data form to locate database records

✓ Editing database records with the data form

✓ Sorting the records in a database

✓ Selecting records in a database by using the AutoFilter feature

Sooner or later in your work with Excel, you're going to need to know how to create and maintain long lists of data. In Excel, such lists are technically known as *databases*. Databases consist of a row of column headings (technically known as *field names*) followed by the rows of actual data (technically known as *records*). Each column (technically known as a *field*) contains the same type of information (such as the last name, street address, telephone number, and so on).

The goal of this unit is to familiarize you with Excel's basic features for creating and maintaining a database. As a result of studying this unit, you should know how to create a new database in an Excel worksheet, add and edit the records in the database, reorder the records in a database by sorting them, and select only those records in the database that meet specific criteria.

Lesson 7-1

Creating a Database

Creating a new database in Excel is really easy. All you need to do is enter the row of field names as column headings at the top of the worksheet and then enter the first record with real data in the row-appropriate columns (fields) right below. That's it! After that, you can start using a great little Excel gizmo called the *data form* (which is a custom dialog box that takes field names in the database and uses them as headings next to blanks where you fill in the information required in that field) to enter and edit the rest of the records.

The fields in your database contain text entries (as would the First Name, Last Name, City, and State fields), values (as would the zip code, Birthday, Age, and Item Cost fields), or formulas (as would the Amount Due or Years of Service fields). Fields that contain formulas are referred to as *calculated fields*.

All the field entries that you make in the first record of the database should be aligned as you want them to appear in the *data form,* and all of their columns should be widened sufficiently to accommodate the length of the typical data entry. Calculated fields, as well as those fields that contain values, should be formatted with the number format that you want used in the *data form* and, therefore, applied to those fields in all the rest of the database records.

Exercise 7-1: Creating the field names for a new database

In this first exercise, you'll start creating a new address database that tracks the name, address, and telephone number of each of your clients, suppliers, and new contacts by entering and formatting its field names. You'll set up this Address List database in a new worksheet.

1 Start Excel; then with the cell pointer still in cell A1 of the new Book1 worksheet, type *Mother Goose Enterprises Client and Contact List* **and click the Enter button on the formula bar.**

Next, you'll increase the font size of the database title.

2 Click the Font Size drop-down list button on the Formatting toolbar and then click 14 in the drop-down list to increase the font size to 14 points.

Next, you'll rename the Sheet1 tab to Address List.

3 Double-click the Sheet1 tab and rename it to *Address List* **in the Rename Sheet dialog box.**

Now you're ready to enter the column headings that will act as the field names in your Address database in the second row of the Address List worksheet.

4 Enter *Last Name* **in cell A2,** *First Name* **in cell B2,** *Company* **in cell C2,** *Street* **in cell D2,** *City* **in cell E2,** *State* **in cell F2,** *ZIP* **in cell G2,** *Telephone* **in cell H2, and** *Email* **in cell I2.**

In the next step, you select the field names in the cell range A2:I2 and make these cell entries bold. By assigning a special text attribute such as boldface type or centering, you make it possible for Excel to differentiate the row of field names at the very top of the database from the field entries in the records below.

5 **Select the cell range A2:I2 and then click the Bold button on the Standard toolbar.**

Now you need to widen columns A, B, and H so that you can see all of their field names. You can do this by selecting cells A2, B2, and H2 (remember to hold down the Ctrl key to select the cell H2 after selecting the range A2:B2) and then using the AutoFit Selection command.

6 **Select cells A2, B2, and H2 before you click F̲ormat on the menu bar, highlight C̲olumn on the pull-down menu, and click A̲utoFit Selection on the continuation menu.**

Now save your new address database before you go on to Exercise 7-2 where you'll enter the first record in row 3 of the Address List worksheet.

7 **Make cell A3 current and then click the Save button on the Standard toolbar or press Ctrl+S to open the Save As dialog box.**

You'll name the new database workbook file MGE Addresses and save it in your personal folder.

8 **Make sure that your personal folder is open in the Save i̲n list box and then replace the temporary filename with *MGE Addresses* in the File n̲ame text box before you click the S̲ave button or press Enter.**

Exercise 7-2: Entering and formatting the first record in the Address Database

In this exercise, you'll enter and format the first record of your MGE Addresses database in row 3 of the Address List worksheet. Excel will then use the field names in row 2 and the first record in row 3 to create the *data form* for this database that you can then use in adding all subsequent database records.

When deciding which record to enter as the first one in your new database, you should choose a typical record and not necessarily the first one on your list (you can, as you'll learn in Lesson 7-4, always use the Sort command later on to get the records in whatever order you desire to see them in). A typical record, by the way, is one that has entries for all the fields in the database, which are of average or above-average length.

1 **Type *Cinderella* in cell A3 as the last name; then press the → key to move the cell pointer to cell B3.**

Next, you'll enter Cinderella's first name (and you thought that *was* her first name) in cell B3.

2 **Select cell B3 and type *Poore* as the first name in this cell; then press the → key to move the cell pointer to cell C3.**

Now you need to type the name of her custodial service in cell C3.

3 **Select cell C3 and type *Bibbity-Bobbity Cleaning* as the company name in this cell; then click the Enter button on the Standard toolbar and widen column C with the AutoFit feature.**

Next, you need to enter the street address in cell D3.

4 **Select cell D3 and type *100 Cinder Alley* as the street address in this cell; then click the Enter button on the Standard toolbar and widen column C with the AutoFit feature.**

Now come the City and the State in cells E3 and F3.

Notes:

5 Enter *New London* as the City in cell E3 and enter *ME* (the state abbreviation for Maine) in cell F3; then use AutoFit to widen column E and narrow column F to fit the length of both these entries.

The next entry is for the zip code. In this example, you will enter the five-digit zip code 07890. The only problem with this particular entry is that Excel's default General format will drop the leading zero (thinking that it's unnecessary). In order to prevent Excel from dropping this zero (which the Post Office thinks is *very* necessary), you will preface the number with an apostrophe ('). When you start a cell entry with an apostrophe, Excel accepts the characters that follow as text, even when the characters are numbers; and although the leading apostrophe can be seen on the formula bar when the cell is current, it is entirely invisible in the entry in the cell itself.

6 Select cell G3 and then type an apostrophe — the little single quote character (') on the same key as the double quote (") — followed by *07890* in this cell. Click the Enter button on the Standard toolbar and then use AutoFit to narrow the column so that it's just wide enough for the zip code to be displayed.

In cell H3, you'll enter the telephone number complete with the area code, prefix, and all the rest. You will enter the telephone number for the Bibbety-Bobbity Cleaning service with all its formatting, including the parentheses for the area code and the hyphen to separate the telephone exchange from the rest of the number.

7 Select cell H3 and type *(800)*. Then press the spacebar and type *555-1456* as the telephone number before you click the Enter button on the formula bar and use AutoFit to widen column H sufficiently to display the whole thing.

The last entry you need to make for the first record is Cinderella's e-mail address in cell I3.

8 Select cell I3, enter *Cinderella@bibbob.com* in this cell, and widen column I with AutoFit so that her entire e-mail address is displayed in the cell.

Save your changes to the Address Database workbook before going on to Lesson 7-2.

9 Select cell A3 (with Cinderella in it); then click the Save button or press Ctrl+S to save the MGE Addresses database workbook.

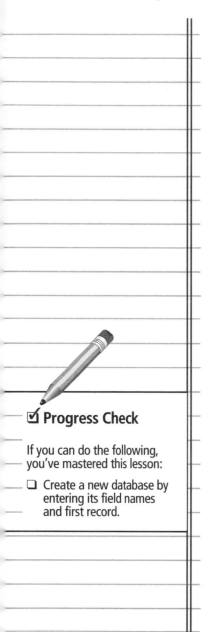

☑ Progress Check

If you can do the following, you've mastered this lesson:

❑ Create a new database by entering its field names and first record.

Lesson 7-2   Adding Records to the Database

After entering the field names and entering the first record for a new database, you can then use the data form to add the rest of the records; or, if you prefer, you can just add them directly to the worksheet cells that make up the database table.

To open the *data form* for a database, you simply position the cell pointer in any one of the cells and then choose Form on the Data pull-down menu. After you've opened the data form for your database, you can use the Tab key to advance the insertion point to the text box for the next field in the record, and you can use Shift+Tab to advance to the previous text box. You cannot, however, press the Enter key or the ↓ key (a natural tendency) because doing this advances you to the next record (which is a new record when you're currently in the last database record).

Exercise 7-3: Adding a record with the data form

In this exercise, you'll see how easy it is to enter records in your new database with the data form by using it to enter a second record, this one for Prince Charming of Dates-R-Us.

1 **With the cell pointer still in cell A3, click Data on the menu bar and Form on the pull-down menu.**

When you select the Data⇨Form command, Excel opens the Address List dialog box created expressly for your Address database (as shown in Figure 7-1) showing Cinderella's record. Note that not only does the program insert the field names as headings in the data form, but it also assigns command letters (the underlined letters you can use with Alt to select its text box) to these field names (except in the case of the Telephone field, where it didn't know what to do).

To enter a new record in the Address database, you can press either the Enter key or the ↓ key, or you can click the New button.

2 **Click the New button in the Address List data form.**

When you click the New button, Excel blanks out all the fields in the Address List dialog box, and the heading New Record replaces 1 of 1 over the New button.

3 **Type *Charming* in the Last Name text box; then press the Tab key to advance the insertion point to the First Name field.**

Next, you need to enter Mr. Charming's first name in the First Name text box.

4 **Type *Prince* in the First Name text box; then press Tab to advance the insertion point to the Company field.**

Now you're going to add the name of his dating service, Dates-R-Us, in the Company text box.

5 **Type *Dates-R-Us* in the Company text box; then press Tab to advance the insertion point to the Street field.**

Okay, now you'll fill in his street address in the Street text box.

6 **Type *75 Castlemont* in the Street text box; then press Tab to advance the insertion point to the City field.**

Next, you need to enter the city in the City text box.

7 **Type *Blueblood* in the City text box; then press Tab to advance the insertion point to the State field.**

Now it's time for you to put the state abbreviation in the State text box.

8 **Type *ME* in the State text box; then press Tab to advance the insertion point to the ZIP field.**

Next, you need to enter the zip code. Because this zip code, like Cinderella's, starts with a zero, you need to preface the digits with an apostrophe to prevent Excel from dropping this zero.

9 **Type an apostrophe (') followed by the digits *08997* in the ZIP text box; then press Tab to advance the insertion point to the Telephone field.**

Enter the 800-telephone number in the Telephone text box.

Notes:

Figure 7-1: The Address List data form dialog box showing Cinderella's record.

Figure 7-2: The Address List data form dialog box showing Prince Charming's record.

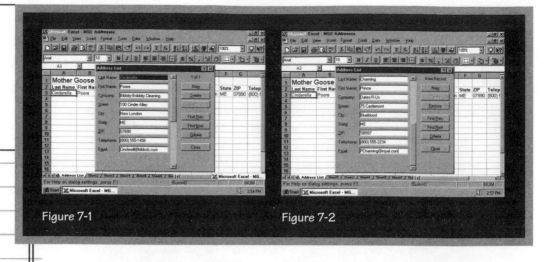

Figure 7-1   Figure 7-2

10 **Type *(800)*, press the spacebar before you type *555-2234* in the Telephone text box, and then press Tab to advance the insertion point to the E̲mail field.**

Finally, enter the prince's Internet address in the E̲mail text box.

11 **Type *PCharming@royal.com* in the E̲mail text box; then check your record against the one shown in Figure 7-2. If everything checks out, click the C̲lose button in the Address List dialog box.**

When you close the data form for the Address List, Excel adds the entries for the various fields of the second record in row 4 of the Address List worksheet.

12 **Save the MGE Addresses workbook by clicking the Save button on the Standard toolbar or press Ctrl+S.**

Exercise 7-4: Adding a record directly to the database table

Although the data form provides a really convenient way to add new records, it isn't the only way to add them to your database. In this exercise, you'll practice adding a new record to your MGE Addresses database by simply entering the information for each field in the appropriate cells in the worksheet. When adding a new record directly to the database table without the data form, you need to take care not to skip any rows (always enter the new record in the very next blank row *immediately* below the last existing database record). You also have to take care to enter the right information in each field (remember that you can make the row of field names into worksheet titles so that they remain frozen on-screen as you scroll down the database records — see Exercise 5-5 for specifics).

Right now, you'll enter a third record in row 5 of the Address List worksheet.

1 **With the cell pointer in cell A3, press Ctrl+↓ to move to the last occupied cell in the Last Name field. Then press the ↓ key again to make the first blank cell in this field (cell A5) active.**

Start this record by entering the first name in the First Name field in cell A5. As you go, be sure to widen the columns as necessary to display the entire field entry.

2 **Type *Stiltskin* in cell A5; then press the → key to move to cell B5.**

Next, enter the last name in the Last Name field in cell B5.

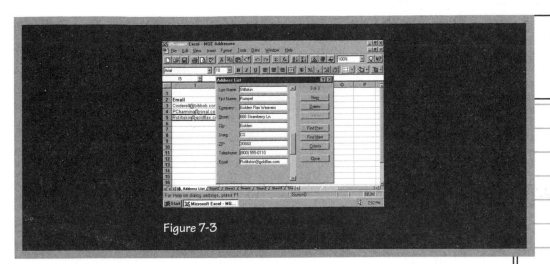

Figure 7-3

Figure 7-3: The Address List data form dialog box showing Rumpel Stiltskin's record.

3 Type *Rumpel* in cell B5; then press the → key to move to cell C5.

Now enter the company for this record in the Company Name field in cell C5.

4 Type *Golden Flax Weavers* in cell C5; then press the → key to move to cell D5.

Next, enter the street address in the Street field in cell D5.

5 Type *666 Strawberry Ln.* in cell D5; then press the → key to move to cell E5.

Now you're ready to make the City field entry in cell E5.

6 Type *Golden* in cell E5; then press the → key to move to cell F5.

Next, enter *CO*, the state abbreviation for Colorado, as the State field entry in cell F5.

7 Type *CO* in cell F5; then press the → key to move to cell G5.

Enter the zip code, 30660, as text in the ZIP field in cell G5.

8 Type an apostrophe ('), type *30660* in cell G5, and then press the → key to move to cell H5.

Now enter his telephone number for this record in the Telephone field in cell H5.

9 Type *(800) 555-0110* in cell H5; then press the → key to move to cell I5.

Finally, you enter Rumpel Stiltskin's Internet address in the Email field in cell I5.

10 Type *RStiltskin@goldflax.com* in cell I5; then click the Enter button on the formula bar to complete this last field entry without moving the cell pointer.

Now open the Address List data form to verify that these entries are recognized by Excel as being part of the third database record.

11 Click **D**ata on the menu bar; then click F**o**rm on the pull-down menu.

The Address List data form dialog box opens, displaying Cinderella's record. Note the "1 of 3" above the New button, indicating that the Address database now has three records in it. Go ahead and view Rumpel Stiltskin's record in the data form.

12 Press the ↓ key twice to display Rumpel Stiltskin's record.

Your record for old, good-as-gold Rumpel should look like the one shown in Figure 7-3. Now you're ready to close and save your MGE Addresses workbook before moving on to Lesson 7-3.

☑ Progress Check

If you can do the following, you've mastered this lesson:

❑ Add a new record to the database via its data form.

❑ Add a new record to the database by entering the field entries directly to the worksheet.

13 Click the Close button to close the Address List data form. Then make cell A2 (with the Last Name field name) current before pressing Ctrl+F4 and clicking the Yes button or pressing Enter to close and save the changes in your MGE Addresses workbook.

Lesson 7-3   Editing the Database Records

You begin to realize the full usefulness of the data form the first time that you need to edit some of the existing database records. You can use the data form to locate the record that needs editing as well as to make the editing changes. These editing changes can include adding entries to blank fields in a record, modifying the contents of particular field entries in a record, or deleting the record entirely.

To help you locate the record that needs editing, you can use the Criteria button in the data form. When you click this button, Excel displays a blank Criteria form where you enter the search criteria in the appropriate field(s). For example, if you wanted to find a record for Butch Cassidy in the database, you could find it by entering *Cassidy* in the Last Name field or entering *Butch* in the First Name field of the Criteria record and then clicking the Find Next button.

You can also use the Criteria form to locate and peruse a bunch of records that share some common characteristic. For example, if you enter *C* in the Last Name field of the Criteria record, Excel will locate only the records in the database where the last name begins with the letter *C* as you click the Find Next or Find Prev button.

In the lesson exercises ahead, you'll practice moving from record to record with the keyboard, locating records with the Criteria form, editing particular field entries in records, and deleting records from the database. For all these exercises, you will use the Bo-Peep Client List workbook that's in your practice folder (you first worked with this workbook when doing the lessons in Unit 3).

Exercise 7-5: Moving from record to record in the database

Excel gives you a number of ways (summarized in Table 7-1) to move from record to record after you've opened the data form for your database. In this exercise, you'll get a chance to use most of these techniques to move between the records of the Bo-Peep Client List as you become acquainted with its contents.

Table 7-1   Moving from Record to Record in the Data Form

To Move To	Do This
Next Record	Press ↓ or Enter or click the Find Next or down-arrow scroll button.
Previous record	Press ↑ or Shift+Enter or click the Find Prev or up-arrow scroll button.
Ten records ahead	Press the PgDn key.

To Move To	Do This
Ten records previous	Press the PgUp key.
First record	Press Ctrl+↑ or Ctrl+PgUp or drag the scroll button all the way to the top of the scroll bar.
Last record	Press Ctrl+↓ Ctrl+PgDn or drag the scroll button all the way to the bottom of the scroll bar.

1 Bring up the Open dialog box. Make sure that the Practice folder is open in the Look in list box; then double-click Bo-Peep Client List in the Open dialog list box to open this workbook.

This database contains 11 fields and 48 records. You can verify that for yourself by opening the data form for the Client List database.

2 Click Data on the menu bar: then click Form on the pull-down menu to open the Client List data form.

Excel opens the Client List data form showing the record for Christian Andersen with the client ID 101-920. As you scan the fields in this database, notice the Years field between the Anniversary and Receivable (Accounts Receivable) fields. This is a calculated field that contains a formula for calculating the number of years the person has been a client of Little Bo-Peep Pet Detectives. (It does this by subtracting the date entered in the Anniversary field from today's date and then dividing that result by 365.) Because the entries for this field are calculated, the Years field does not contain a text box in the data form. (In other words, you can look — but you can't touch — this entry.)

3 Press the ↓ key to move to the next record.

Now you should see Michael Bryant's record, the second one in the Client List database.

4 Press the Enter key to move to next record.

The third record in the Client List is that of Hans Andersen.

5 Press the PgDn key.

The PgDn key moves you 10 records ahead in the database to that of Ben Franklin, whose record is 13th out of the 48 total (must be a descendant, or he'd have to have become a client on 10/21/1787 instead of 10/21/1987).

6 Click the Find Prev button.

The Find Prev button moves you back to the 12th record of the 48, that of Bingo Baggins (how 'bout that!).

7 Drag the Scroll button down the scroll bar until you see 22 of 48 over the New button; then release the mouse button.

Doing this takes you to Kai Dragon's record, the 22nd of the 48 total records.

8 Press Ctrl+↓ key to move to the last record.

You should now see the New Record data form where you can add the 49th record to the Client List database.

9 Press Shift+Enter to move to the previous record.

Now you should see Frodor Gondor's record (what was Mother Gondor thinking?!), which is 48 of 48.

Notes:

Notes:

10 Drag the scroll button in the scroll bar in the Client List data form up until the indicator above the Ne<u>w</u> button reads 6 of 48; then release the mouse button.

You should now see Lu Oow's record in the data form.

11 Press Ctrl+↑ to display the first record in the data form.

You should now be back where you started from, and Christian Andersen's record should be displayed in the data form.

Exercise 7-6: Locating the records with the Criteria form

In this exercise, you'll use the Criteria data form to locate specific records in the Client List database.

1 With record 1 of 48 of the Client List database displayed, click the <u>C</u>riteria button.

When you click this button, Excel clears all of the text boxes, and the indicator, Criteria, appears above the New button.

You'll start by looking for all the records where the first name starts with the letter *A*. To do this, you will click the Find <u>N</u>ext button. Note that when using the search criteria entered into the Criteria form to locate records in a database, you must click the Find <u>N</u>ext or the Find <u>P</u>rev button — pressing the ↑ and ↓ or Enter and Shift+Enter keys just selects the next and previous records in the database, as usual.

2 Press the Tab key twice to place the insertion point in the Fir<u>s</u>t Name text box; then press *A* before you click the Find <u>N</u>ext button.

Excel jumps to Aragon Gondor's record (hey, it's a better name than Frodor), which is the 11th of the 48 records.

3 Click the Find <u>N</u>ext button to find the next record where the first name entry begins with the letter *A*.

Excel now jumps to Anney Oakley's record, which is the 20th of the 48 records.

4 Click the Find <u>N</u>ext button to find the next record where the first name entry begins with the letter *A*.

This time, Excel jumps to Ashley Cinderella's record (Poore's sister, no doubt), which is the 37th of the 48 records.

5 Click the Find <u>N</u>ext button to find the next record where the first name entry begins with the letter *A*.

This time nothing happens when you click the Find <u>N</u>ext button. This lack of response is your signal that Excel has located the last record whose field entries match your search criteria. (If this happens the first time that you click Find <u>N</u>ext, you know that none of the records in the database matches your search criteria.)

6 Click the Find <u>P</u>rev button to review Anney's and Aragon's records; then click the button again.

The third time you click the Find <u>P</u>rev button, as expected, nothing happens because there are no records in front of Aragon Gondor's where the first name begins with the letter *A*.

Next, try searching for the records in the database where the person has been a client 13 years or longer. To do this, you need to enter *>=13* as the search criterion in the Years text box (note that, although you can't modify the entries the Years text box in the data form, you can enter search values in this text box in the Criteria form). Before you do this, however, you first need to clear the current search criteria.

7 **Click the Criteria button to return to the Criteria form. Then click Clear button to clear the *a* from the First Name text box.**

Now you're ready to select the Years text box and enter the new search criteria.

8 **Click the insertion point in the Years text box; then type *>=13* in this text box and click the Find Prev button.**

The search criteria that you enter tells Excel to only select records where the Years field entry is equal to or greater than 13.

After you click the Find Prev button, Excel selects the first record in front of your current position in the database (which is record 11 for Aragon Gondor). This first record happens to be Big Bad Wolfe's record (9 of 48); Wolfe has been a client for 13.5 years.

Now use the Find Prev and Find Next buttons to go through all the records where the Years field entry is 13 or greater. As you have Excel select each new record, be sure to check that the Years entry is 13 or greater.

9 **Click Find Prev again until Excel can find no more matching records in front of Big Bad Wolfe's; then click the Find Next button until Excel can find no more matching records after Big Bad Wolfe's.**

The last matching record in the database is that of Lambchop Wolfe (Big Bad's younger brother, perhaps?), which is record 46 of 48. That's enough fooling around with the Criteria form. In the next exercise, you use it to locate records that need editing so that you can then make the necessary modifications.

Exercise 7-7: Modifying field entries within records

In this exercise, you will make some editing changes to records in the Client List database.

1 **Click the Criteria button to return to the Criteria form. Then click the Clear button to clear out the >=13 criteria in the Years text box.**

Now find L. Frank Baum's record so that you can update his address. Because you're already near the end of the Client List database (record 46 of 48), you'll use the Find Prev button to locate the record after entering the search criteria in the Last Name field's text box.

2 **Click the insertion point in the text box for the Last Name field, type *Baum,* and click the Find Prev button.**

The first record located is Ozzie Baum (L. Frank's brother?), which is 43rd of the 48.

3 **Click the Find Prev button again.**

This time, Excel displays L. Frank Baum's record (16 of 48). Go ahead and start updating his address by editing the Street field entry.

4 **Click the insertion in the S_treet text box. Then drag through the *447 Toto Too* to select this text and type *13 Yellowbrick* so that 13 Yellowbrick Rd appears as the updated street address in this field.**

Next, you need to change the city from Oz to Emerald City.

5 **Press Tab to select *Oz* currently in the City field text box, and type *Emerald City* as the new entry for this field.**

Now when you're in Emerald City, you're not in Kansas anymore, so you'll have to update the State field next.

6 **Press Tab to select *KS* in the State field; then type *CA* as the state abbreviation for this field.**

Finally, update the zip code in the ZIP field text box.

7 **Press Tab to select *65432* in the ZIP field; then type an apostrophe (') before you type *90980* as the new zip code for Emerald City, California.**

Your next editing assignment is to make sure that all clients whose Total accounts receivable are $4,500 or greater are extended credit. Therefore, you will search for all records in the database where the Receivable field contains >=4500 and the Credit field contains No. You will then update the Credit field from No to Yes in these records.

You'll start this editing by moving to the first record of the database so that you only have to rely on the Find Next button to locate all the records that need modifying.

8 **Press Ctrl+↑ to complete the editing change in Baum's record and select the first record in the Client List database. Then click the Criteria button to open Criteria form where you need to click the Clear button to clear *Baum* from the Last Name field's text box.**

Now enter the search criteria in the Receivable and the Credit text boxes.

9 **Click the Receivable text box and type >=4500 before you press Tab to select the Credit text box where you type *No* as the search criteria for this field.**

Now you need to locate the first record that meets your criteria and make the necessary change to the credit status.

10 **Click the Find Next button to locate the first record that needs changing.**

The first record is that of Bingo Baggins, whose accounts receivable are currently $4,560.78.

11 **Drag through the *No* in the Credit field to select the entire text box, and then type *Yes* to change Bingo's credit status before you press the ↓ key to make the change in this record. Then click the Find Next button to locate the next record that needs modifying.**

The next record that needs changing is that of Eros Cupid, who currently owes $4,865.50 to Bo-Peep detective agency.

12 **Drag through the *No* in the Credit field to select the entire text box, and then type *Yes* to change Eros' credit status before you press the ↓ key to complete the edit. Then click the Find Next button to locate the next record that needs modifying.**

The next matching record is that of Balbo Baggins (Bingo's uncle?), who owes $4,890.

13 Drag through the *No* in the Credit field to select the entire text box. Then type *Yes* to change Balbo's credit status before you press the ↓ key to complete this edit. Then click the Find **N**ext button to locate the next record that needs modifying.

The next matching record is that of Venus Cupid (Eros's wife, no doubt), who currently owes a whopping $7,865.50.

14 Drag through the *No* in the Credit field to select the entire text box. Then type *Yes* to change Venus's credit status before you press Enter to complete the edit. Then click the Find **N**ext button to locate the next record that needs modifying.

When you click the Find Next button this last time, nothing happens, indicating that there are no more matching records after this one in the database. Because you began the search from the very first record, you can be sure that you've located all the records that need to be modified.

Go ahead and save your changes to the Client List database with a new filename in your personal folder.

15 Click the Close button to close the Client List data form, click **F**ile on the menu bar, and click Save **A**s on the pull-down menu. Open your personal folder so that its name appears in the Look **i**n drop-down list box, click the insertion point at the end of the current filename in the File **n**ame text box, press the spacebar, and type *(edited)*. Save the file under the new filename, Little Bo-Peep Client List (edited), by clicking the **S**ave button or pressing Enter.

Exercise 7-8: Deleting records from the database

In this next exercise, you'll practice deleting records from the database with the data form. When deleting database records, keep in mind that you can't use the Undo feature to restore a record should you remove it in error. Because of this factor, you should always make sure that you have a backup copy of the workbook containing the database before you start deleting its records.

For this exercise, you can rely on the Bo-Peep Client List workbook in the practice folder as the backup for the Bo-Peep Client List (edited) workbook. If you mess up and delete the wrong records in this exercise, you can open the Bo-Peep Client List workbook and then start the exercise over again.

1 With the Bo-Peep Client List (edited) workbook open in Excel, click **D**ata on the menu bar before you click **F**orm on the pull-down menu.

In this exercise, you will purge the Client List database of records for any clients whose total accounts receivable are less than $50.00 and anniversary date is before January 1, 1983.

2 Click the **C**riteria button. Then enter *<1/1/83* in the Anni**v**ersary text box and *<=50* in the Receiva**b**le text box before you click the Find **N**ext button.

The first matching record is 9 of 48, that of Big Bad Wolfe who became a client on May 28, 1982 and whose total bill is $35.00. Go ahead and get rid of his record.

3 Click the **D**elete button; then click OK or press Enter in the alert box warning that the displayed record is about to be permanently deleted.

When you select the OK button, Excel gets rid of this record, and Poore Cinderella's record takes its place as the 9th record of 47 records.

Now go ahead and see if there are any more deadbeat clients in this database.

Notes:

4 **Click the Find Next button again.**

The next matching record is 35 of 47, that of Doggone Wolfe (a relative of Big Bad, no doubt). His anniversary is December 10, 1982, and he owes only $12.50. Go ahead and get rid of this record.

5 **Click the Delete button. Then click OK or press Enter in the alert box that warns you about the record's deletion.**

When you select OK, Excel gets rid of Doggone Wolfe's record and replaces it with Ashley Cinderella's record, which is now 35 of 46.

6 **Click the Find Next button again.**

The next matching record is 44 of 46, that of Lambchop Wolfe's (these Wolfes are a miserly lot, aren't they?), who became a client on July 12, 1982, and who owes $45.00 even. Go ahead and get rid of his record as well.

7 **Click the Delete button; then click OK or press Enter in the alert box that warns you about the record's deletion.**

When you select OK, Excel gets rid of Doggone Wolfe's record and replaces it with Bella Cinderella's record (the pretty one, no doubt), which is now 44 of 45.

8 **Click the Find Next button again.**

This time, the system beeps when you click Find Next. That lack of action means that you've deleted all the records for clients who've became clients before the beginning of 1983 and who don't owe more than $50.00 to the Little Bo-Peep Pet Detective agency.

Now save this edited version of the Client List under the filename Little Bo-Peep Client List (deleted).

9 **Click the Close button to close the Client List data form, click File on the menu bar, and click Save As on the pull-down menu. Make sure that the name of your personal folder appears in the Look in drop-down list box. Then drag through *edited* in *Little Bo-Peep Client List (edited)* in the File name text box and replace this selected text by typing *deleted* before you click the Save button or press Enter.**

Now close this new workbook before you continue on to Lesson 7-4.

10 **Press Ctrl+F4 to close the Little Bo-Peep Client List (deleted) workbook.**

☑ **Progress Check**

If you can do the following, you've mastered this lesson:

❏ Move from record to record in the data form.

❏ Find a record for editing using the Criteria form.

❏ Change or replace particular field entries for the record displayed in the data form.

❏ Delete a record from the database using the data form.

Lesson 7-4

Sorting the Records in a Database

You can use Excel's Sort feature at any time to change the order in which the records appear in your database. Instead of worrying about the order in which you add the records, you just rely on the old Data➪Sort command to get the records whipped into the order in which you want to see them. This preferred record order, by the way, often changes, depending upon your use for the information. For example, for the printing of regular reports, you may want the records arranged in alphabetical order by the company's or client's name. However, when using database information for preparing a mass mailing, you would then need the records to appear in zip-code order.

To sort the database, you simply need to designate the field or fields (column or columns) in the database according to whose values the records are to be rearranged and indicate whether you want the *ascending* or *descending* sort order applied. When you select *ascending* order, Excel arranges text entries in the designated field(s) alphabetically from A to Z and values from lowest to highest (which puts dates from least recent to most recent). When you select *descending* order, Excel arranges text entries in the designated field(s) alphabetically from Z to A and values from highest to lowest (which puts dates in most-recent-to-least-recent order).

When sorting a database, you can designate up to three fields to be used in a single sorting operation. You only need to worry about designating more than one field for sorting when that one field contains duplicate entries (like a Last Name field where you have a whole bunch of Smiths, Jones, and Abercrombies — Abercrombies??), and you want to tell Excel how to arrange the duplicates (that is, by First Name so that Adam Smith's record is placed in front of Jane Smith, in front of Mortimer Smith). If, however, you are sorting on a field (such as the Social Security Number field) where each entry is unique (or is supposed to be), you use only that one field to get the records sorted into the desired order.

Note that the sorting operation is one of those tasks that is undoable, meaning that, should your screw up royally and sort your boss's database into mush, you can restore the database to its normal order by pressing Ctrl+Z immediately after you perform the ill-fated sort operation.

extra credit

Sorting rows and columns of regular spreadsheet data

You can use Excel's Sort feature to reorder any rows or columns of data entries. To sort rows or columns of spreadsheet data, you need to select the cell range containing the data and then designate which column(s) or row(s) should be used in the sorting. Note that to sort the columns of the worksheet rather than the rows (which is the default), you will need to click the Options button in the Sort dialog box and then click the Sort Left to Right radio button in the Orientation section of the Sort Options dialog box before designating which rows to use in the Sort By and Then By drop-down list boxes.

When sorting the cell selection by rows, be sure that you click the No Header Row radio button at the bottom of the Sort dialog box before starting the sort operation if you've included column headings as part of the current cell selection. This step prevents Excel from sorting the column headings in with the other rows of data.

Exercise 7-9: Sorting the Client List alphabetically

In this exercise, you'll practice sorting the edited version of your Client List in the workbook Bo-Peep Client List (edited), alphabetically by client name.

1 **Bring up the Open dialog box and open the Bo-Peep Client List (edited) workbook in your personal folder.**

Currently, this database is not in any particular order (other than the one in which the records were added). Go ahead and sort the records in ascending alphabetical order.

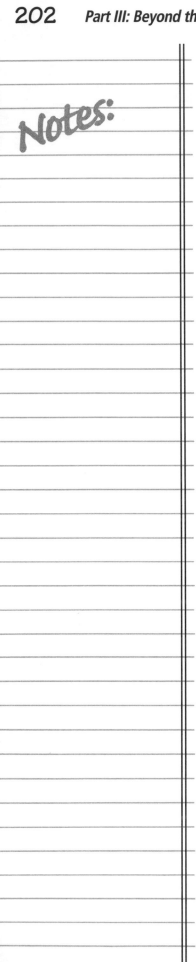

Notes:

2 **Click Data on the menu bar; then click Sort to open the Sort dialog box.**

Excel opens the Sort dialog box and selects the first field, ID No, as the column to sort on and selects Ascending as the sort order. You need to select the Last Name field.

3 **Click the Sort By drop-down button; then click Last Name in the drop-down list before you click OK or press Enter in the Sort dialog box to sort the database records.**

When you choose OK, Excel sorts the database records alphabetically by last name. Note, however, that some of the records with the same last name (most notably the Baggins brothers and the Cinderella sisters) could still be further sorted by their first names.

Go ahead and resort the database, this time sorting both by the Last Name field and then by the First Name field in ascending alphabetical order.

4 **Click Data on the menu bar; then click Sort on the pull-down menu to open the Sort dialog box.**

The Sort By text box stills contains Last Name from the previous sort. All you have to do now is select the First Name field in the Then By drop-down list box right below.

5 **Click the Then By drop-down button right below the Sort By drop-down list box. Then click First Name in its drop-down list before you click OK or press Enter in the Sort dialog box to resort the database records in last-name, first-name alphabetical order.**

That's more like it! Note how the records for the Baggins brothers and Cinderella sisters are now arranged in order of their first name (Balbo before Bingo Baggins, and Ashley before Bella before Poore Cinderella).

Go ahead and save this sorted version of the Client List under the new filename Bo-Peep Client List (sort alpha).

6 **Click the File menu bar and then click Save As on the pull-down menu. Check to make sure that the name of your personal folder appears in the Save in drop-down list box before you drag through *edited* in the filename in the File name text box and replace it by typing *sort alpha*. Then click the Save button or press Enter.**

Exercise 7-10: Sorting the Client List by anniversary date

In this next sorting exercise, you'll practice sorting the Bo-Peep Client List by the anniversary date in descending order (from most recent to least recent). To do this exercise, you'll continue using the Bo-Peep Client List (sort alpha) workbook that you created at the end of the last exercise.

1 **Click Data on the menu bar; then click Sort on the pull-down menu to open the Sort dialog box.**

Excel opens the Sort dialog box with Last Name appearing in the Sort By drop-down list box and First Name appearing in the Then By drop-down list box (from the last sort that you did).

2 **Click the Sort By drop-down button. Then use the scroll bar to locate Anniversary in the drop-down list and click it.**

To sort by Anniversary date from the most recent to the least recent date, you must also change the sort order from ascending to descending.

3 Click the <u>D</u>escending radio button in the <u>S</u>ort By section of the dialog box.

Now you need to remove First Name from the <u>T</u>hen By drop-down list box because you need only to sort on the Anniversary field.

4 Click the <u>T</u>hen By drop-down button. Then click (none) at the very top of the list before you click OK or press Enter to perform the sort.

In order to see if the Client List is sorted correctly by anniversary date (from the most recent to the least recent), you need to see the Anniversary field. The easiest way to do this is by opening the Client List data form and then using it to peruse the records.

5 Click <u>D</u>ata on the menu bar and then click <u>F</u>orm on the pull-down menu to open the Client List dialog box.

The first record that now appears in the Client List data form is that of Big Eaters, whose anniversary date is 9/2/1992.

6 Press the ↓ key to scan the records, paying attention to the date in the Anniversary text box as you move from record to record. When you've seen enough records to convince yourself that the Client List is sorted correctly, press Esc to close the Client List data form.

Now save this version of the sorted database under the filename Bo-Peep Client List (sort date).

7 Click the <u>F</u>ile menu bar and then click Save <u>A</u>s on the pull-down menu. Check to make sure that the name of your personal folder appears in the Save <u>i</u>n drop-down list box before you drag through *alpha* in the filename in the File <u>n</u>ame text box and replace it by typing *date.* Then click the <u>S</u>ave button or press Enter.

Exercise 7-11: Sorting the Client List by city, state, and zip code

In this last sorting exercise, you'll sort the Client List in the Bo-Peep Client List (sort date) workbook by state, city, and then zip code.

1 Click <u>D</u>ata on the menu bar; then click <u>S</u>ort on the pull-down menu to open the Sort dialog box.

Excel opens the Sort dialog box with Anniversary appearing in the <u>S</u>ort By drop-down list box (from the sort that you did in the last exercise).

2 Click the <u>S</u>ort By drop-down button. Then click State in the drop-down list before you click the <u>A</u>scending radio button to its right.

Next, you need to designate the City field as the field to use in sorting duplicate state entries.

3 Click the <u>T</u>hen By drop-down button; then click City in its drop-down list.

Finally, you need to designate the ZIP field as the one to use in the case of duplicate cities in the same state.

4 Click the second Then <u>B</u>y drop-down button, use its scroll bar to locate and click ZIP, and then click the Descending radio button to its right before you click OK or press Enter to perform the sort.

Now check the City, State, and ZIP fields in the Client List worksheet to make sure that the Client List is properly sorted in ascending order (alphabetically) by state and then city and then in descending order by zip code.

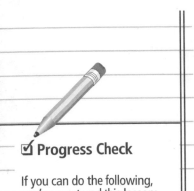

☑ **Progress Check**

If you can do the following, you've mastered this lesson:

❏ Sort a database on up to three fields in ascending or descending order.

5 **Scroll the worksheet to the left just slightly until you can see B through G (fields Last Name through ZIP) on the screen.**

Notice the order of the three Gearings (Dale, Donna, and Shane) who all live in different zip codes within the great metropolis of LaLa Land, California. After performing this sort, their records are now ordered in descending zip code order with zip code 90088 preceding zip code 90055, which precedes zip code 90012.

Go ahead and save this file under the new filename, Bo-Peep Client List (sort zip).

6 **Click the File menu bar. Then click Save As on the pull-down menu. Check to make sure that the name of your personal folder appears in the Save in drop-down list box before you drag through *date* in the filename in the File name text box and replace it by typing *zip*. Then click the Save button or press Enter.**

Go ahead and close this workbook before going on to Lesson 7-5.

7 **Click Ctrl+F4 to close the Bo-Peep Client List (sort zip) workbook.**

Lesson 7-5   Selecting the Records in a Database

The last thing you need to know about working with databases in Excel is how to select their records using different criteria. Excel refers to this selection process as *filtering the records* in the sense that the criteria you apply to the database filter out all the records except for those that meet the criteria. The records that remain after you filter a database are referred to as a *subset* of the database.

Excel makes record selection really easy with its AutoFilter feature. When you turn on AutoFilter by selecting the Data⇨Filter⇨AutoFilter command, Excel responds by attaching a drop-down list button to each of the cells containing the field names for the database. When you click one of these drop-down buttons, Excel displays (All) and (Custom ...) at the top of a list of all the entries in that field (in ascending order). To filter out all the records except for those that contain a particular entry, you simply click that entry in the field's drop-down list. To remove the filter and redisplay all the records in the database, you click (All) at the top of the field's drop-down list. To apply a customized filter that includes a range of values (such as all the records where the gross receipts are between $5,000 and $25,000) or more than one set of values (such as all the records where the state is AZ or the state is CA), you select (Custom) in the appropriate field's drop-down list and then set up the condition in the Custom AutoFilter dialog box. To remove the drop-down list boxes from the fields and to redisplay all the database records, you turn off AutoFilter by selecting the Data⇨Filter⇨AutoFilter command a second time.

Exercise 7-12: Filtering the Client List with AutoFilter

In this first exercise, you'll use the AutoFilter feature to select certain sets of records in the original Client List database in the Bo-Peep Client List workbook.

1 Bring up the Open dialog box; then open the Bo-Peep Client List workbook located in the Practice folder (if your personal folder is the last one open in Excel, you'll have to click the Up One Level button and then double-click the Excel 101 folder to be able to open the Practice folder).

Now you're ready to turn the AutoFilter feature on.

2 Click **Data** on the menu bar, highlight **Filter** on the pull-down menu, and then click Auto**Filter** on the continuation menu.

Excel responds by adding little drop-down list boxes to the field names in row 2 of the Client List database. Go ahead and use the drop-down list box attached to Last Name field in cell B2 to filter out all records except for those where the last name is Cinderella.

3 Click the drop-down list box in the Last Name field; then use the scroll bar to locate and click Cinderella in the list.

As soon as you click Cinderella in this list, Excel filters out all records except for the three dear Cinderella sisters (Poore, Ashley, and Bella). Now remove this filter and redisplay all the records in the Client List.

4 Click the drop-down list box in the Last Name field. Then scroll up the list until you can click (All) at the very top.

As soon as you click (All), Excel redisplays all the records.

5 Click the drop-down list box in the State field; then click CA in the list.

As soon as you click CA in the State drop-down list, Excel filters out all the records except for those where the State is CA. This leaves the records for the three Gearings and a Fudde. Go ahead and filter this subset of the database further.

6 Click the drop-down list box in the Last Name field; then use the scroll bar to locate and click Fudde in the list.

As soon as you do this, all the Gearing records disappear, leaving only Elmer Fudde's record displayed (suffering succotash!). Now go ahead and remove the Last Name and State filters to redisplay all the records in the database.

7 Click the drop-down list box in the Last Name field and then click (All) at the top of the list.

Doing this removes the Last Name = Fudde filter from the database, bringing back the Gearings' records. Note, however, that you still need to remove the State = CA filter to redisplay *all* the records.

8 Click the drop-down list box in the State field and click (All) at the top of the list.

As soon as you do this, Excel redisplays all the records in the Client List database.

Exercise 7-13: Filtering the Client List with an either/or Custom AutoFilter

In this exercise, you'll learn how to use the Custom AutoFilter to select a subset of records in the Client List database, records that fall between a range of values or that have this or that particular value.

The first custom filtering you will do is to select all the records in the Client List where the state abbreviation is either AZ (for Arizona) or CA (for California).

Notes:

1 With the Client List database open and the AutoFilter feature still on, click the drop-down button in the State field and then click (Custom...) in the list.

Doing this opens the Custom AutoFilter dialog box. Note that the first drop-down list box beneath the word *State* contains an equal sign (=). You will now fill in AZ as the first state abbreviation that must be contained in order for a record to be selected.

2 Click the drop-down list button at the right of the first text box that contains the insertion point. Then click AZ at the top of the list.

Next, you need to select the Or radio button (which automatically deselects the And radio button) because you want Excel to select records when the State field contains AZ *or* CA.

3 Click the Or radio button.

Now you need to select the = (equal) sign as the operator in the drop-down list box right below the one with the first equal sign.

4 Press Tab once and then select = at the top of its list.

Finally, you need to select CA as the other state abbreviation to match and then filter the database.

5 Press Tab to put the insertion point in the last drop-down list box. Then click the drop-down button to its right and click CA near the top of its list.

Check the settings in your AutoFilter dialog box against those in the one shown in Figure 7-4. When they match, go on to Step 6.

6 Click OK or press Enter to filter the database using the criteria in your Custom AutoFilter dialog box.

Check your Client List database. You should only see records where the State is either AZ or CA. Go ahead and save the Client List with this subset as a new file called Bo-Peep Client List (filter state) before going on and performing Exercise 7-14.

7 Click File on the menu bar and then click Save As on the pull-down menu. Then click the Up One Level button and double-click the icon of your personal folder before you click the insertion point at the end of the filename in the File name text box. Press the spacebar and then type *(filter state)* before you click the Save button or press Enter.

Go ahead and close this new workbook before you do Exercise 7-14.

8 Press Ctrl+F4 to close the Bo-Peep Client List (filter state) workbook.

Exercise 7-14: Filtering the Client List with a range of values with Custom AutoFilter

In this exercise, you'll use the Custom AutoFilter to select all the records where the amount owed in the Receivable field is between $4,200 and $42,500 (inclusive of the lower and upper values). To set up this filter, you need to set the lower limit of the criteria as >=4200, and the upper limit as <=42500.

1 Open the Bo-Peep Client List workbook that's in the practice folder. Then click Data on the menu bar, Filter on the pull-down menu, and AutoFilter on the continuation menu.

Next, you need to open the Custom AutoFilter dialog box for the Receivable field.

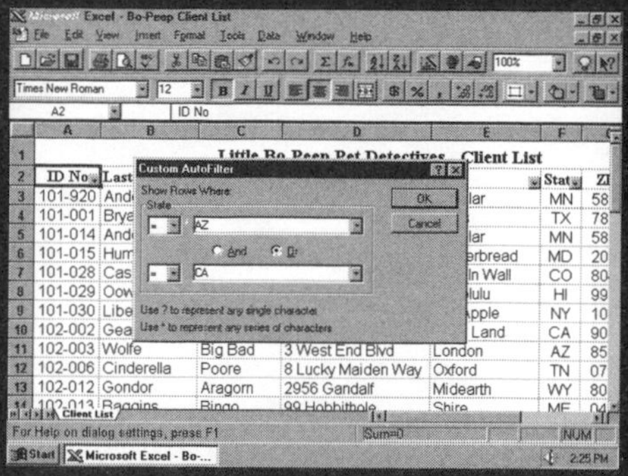

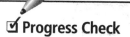

Figure 7-4: The Custom AutoFilter dialog box showing the criteria for selecting records where the State field contains AZ or CA.

Figure 7-4

2 **Scroll the Client List worksheet to the left until you can see the Receivable field; then click its drop-down list button and click (Custom...) near the top of its list.**

Now you need to change the = (equal) operator in the first drop-down list box to >= (greater than or equal to).

3 **Click the drop-down list button to the right of the first box that contains = and click >= in the list.**

Next, you need to enter the lower limit value that a record's Receivable amount must equal or be greater than in order for the record to be selected by this custom filter.

4 **Press Tab to place the insertion point in the text box of the second drop-down list box; then type *4200* there.**

For setting up a condition that involves a range of values, you need to keep the default And radio button selected. Next, go ahead and select <= as the operator to use for the upper limit value.

5 **Press Tab twice to select the third drop-down list box; then press the ↓ key to open the list and click <= in this list.**

Now all that remains to do is enter the upper limit value that a record's Receivable amount must equal or be less than in order for the record to be selected by this custom filter.

6 **Press Tab to place the insertion point in the last drop-down list box; then type *42500* there.**

Check the settings in your AutoFilter dialog box against those in the one shown in Figure 7-5. When they match, go on to Step 7.

7 **Click OK or press Enter to filter the database using this range of values for the amount owed in the Receivable field.**

Scroll through the values in the Receivable field of the filtered database records to make sure that they fall between the range of $4,200 and $42,500.

Now go ahead and save this subset of the Client List database under the filename Bo-Peep Client List (filter rec) before you quit Excel.

8 **Click File on the menu bar; then click Save As on the pull-down menu. Then click the Up One Level button and double-click the icon of your personal folder before you click the insertion point at the end of the filename in the File name text box. Press the spacebar; then type *(filter rec)* before you click the Save button or press Enter.**

Go ahead and quit Excel before you take your Unit 7 quiz.

9 **Click Alt+F4 to exit Excel.**

☑ Progress Check

If you can do the following, you've mastered this lesson:

❑ Use AutoFilter to filter out all records except for those that contain a certain field entry.

❑ Use the Custom AutoFilter to select and filter out all records except for those that contain either one entry or another or a certain range of entries.

Figure 7-5: The Custom AutoFilter dialog box showing the criteria for selecting records where the amounts owed in the Receivable field fall into the range of between $4,200 and $42,500 (inclusive).

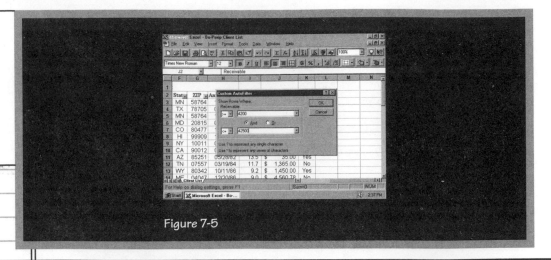

Figure 7-5

Unit 7 Quiz

Test your knowledge by answering the following questions about working with databases by using the information that you just learned in Unit 7. For each of the following questions, select the letter of the correct response (and remember, I'm not above asking questions where more than one response is correct).

1. **All of the following statements about creating a database are true except:**

   A. To create a new database, you need to enter a row of field names at its first row.

   B. To create a new database, you need to enter a single record of field entries in the row right below the one with the field names.

   C. Before using the new database, you need to select all of its cells and assign a range name to them.

   D. After creating the field names and entering the first record in the worksheet, you can open its data form by selecting all the cells and then choosing the Data⇨Form command.

2. **All of the following statements about adding records to a database are true except:**

   A. You can add a record to the database by entering the data as a new row of the spreadsheet.

   B. You can add a record to the database with the data form by pressing Ctrl+↓ and then filling out a New Record form.

   C. You can add a record to the database with the data form by clicking the New button and then filling out the New Record form.

   D. You can add a record to the database with the data form by clicking the Criteria button and then filling out the Criteria form.

3. **All of the following statements about editing database records are true except:**

   A. To change a field entry for a particular record, you must use the data form for that database.

   B. To change a field entry for the displayed record in the data form, you can select its field with the Tab key.

   C. To delete a record from the database, you can display the record in the data form and then click the Delete button.

   D. To clear an entry from a field in the displayed record in the data form, you can drag through its characters in its text box and then press the Delete key.

4. **All of the following statements about sorting a database are true except:**

   A. You can sort a database on up to three fields at one time.

   B. Excel automatically sorts the records added to a new database on its first field in ascending order.

   C. You only need to sort a database on more than one field when that field contains duplicates and you're concerned about the order of those records.

   D. To successfully sort a database on a zip code field, you need to enter the zip codes as text by prefacing their digits with an apostrophe.

5. **All of the following statements about filtering a database are true except:**

   A. When you filter a database, Excel deletes all the records that don't meet the filtering criteria.

   B. To select records where a field contains a single value, you turn on AutoFilter and then select the value in that field's drop-down list.

   C. To select records where a field contains one value or another, you turn on AutoFilter and then select (Custom...) where you enter the first and second values using the Or radio button as the operator between them.

   D. To select records where a field contains a range of values, you turn on AutoFilter and then select (Custom...) where you enter the lower limit and upper limit of the range, using the And radio button as the operator between them.

Unit 7 Further Exercises

In these further exercises you'll get a chance to sort and filter the records of a more complete address list than the one you created in Exercises 7-1 through 7-4. This Address List can be found in the MGE Addresses (final) workbook located in the Practice folder within your Excel 101 folder.

Exercise 7-15: Sorting the Address List by company name

In this exercise, you'll sort the Address List database in the MGE Addresses (final) workbook by the Company field.

1. Start Excel; then open the MGE Addresses (final) workbook in the Practice folder.
2. Sort the Address List database in ascending alphabetical order on the Company field.
3. Save this sorted database as a new workbook in your personal folder with MGE Addresses (sort co) as its filename.

Exercise 7-16: Sorting the Address List by state, city, and zip code

In this exercise, you'll sort the database in the MGE Addresses (sort co) workbook in ascending order (by state and city) and then in descending order (by zip code).

1. Sort the address list database in ascending order by the State and City fields and then sort the same database in descending order by the ZIP field.
2. Save this sorted address database in a new workbook in your personal folder with MGE Addresses (sort zip) as its filename.

Exercise 7-17: Selecting records where the state is NY or CO

In this exercise, you'll set up a Custom AutoFilter that selects only the records where the state is either New York or Colorado.

1. Open the MGE Addresses (final) workbook inside the Practice folder.
2. Filter the address list database with the Custom AutoFilter so that only records where the State field contains CO or NY are shown.
3. Save this filtered address database in a new workbook in your personal folder with MGE Addresses (filter state) as its filename.

Exercise 7-18: Selecting records where the last name starts with the letter C or S

In this exercise, you'll set up a Custom AutoFilter that selects only the records where the last name starts with the letter *C* or the letter *S*.

1. Open the MGE Addresses (final) workbook inside the practice folder.

2. Filter the address list database with the Custom AutoFilter so that only records where the Last Name field starts with the letter *C* or with the letter *S*.

   Hint: Note that you can use the asterisk (*) to stand for an unspecified number of characters in the last name following the initial *C* or *S*.

3. Save this filtered address database in a new workbook in your personal folder with MGE Addresses (filter name) as its filename.

Exercise 7-19: Selecting records where the zip code starts with the number 3

In this exercise, you'll set up a Custom AutoFilter that selects only the records where the zip codes begin with the number 3.

1. Open the MGE Addresses (final) workbook inside the Practice folder.

2. Filter the address list database with the Custom AutoFilter so that only records where the ZIP field begins with the number 3 are shown.

   Hint: Note that you can use the asterisk (*) to stand for an unspecified number of digits in the zip following the initial number 3.

3. Save this filtered address database in a new workbook in your personal folder with MGE Addresses (filter zip) as its filename and then quit Excel.

Notes:

Part III Review

Unit 6 Summary

▶ **To create an embedded chart in a worksheet:** Select the spreadsheet data to be charted and then click the Chart Wizard on the standard toolbar or select the Insert⇨Chart⇨On This Sheet menu command.

▶ **To create a chart on its own chart sheet in a workbook:** Select the spreadsheet data to be charted and then press function key F11 or select the Insert⇨Chart⇨As New Sheet menu command.

▶ **To select an embedded chart:** Click it to display its sizing handles.

▶ **To activate an embedded chart for editing:** Double-click it to display the border with diagonal hash marks.

▶ **To move an embedded chart:** Select the chart; then drag it to its new position in the worksheet.

▶ **To resize an embedded chart:** Select the chart; then drag the appropriate sizing handle until the chart's outline is the size and shape that you want.

▶ **To change the chart type of an embedded chart:** Activate the chart, click the Chart Type button on the Chart toolbar, and click the new chart type in the drop-down chart palette.

▶ **To change the chart type of a chart on its own sheet:** Make the chart sheet active, click the Chart Type button on the Chart toolbar, and click the new chart type in the drop-down chart palette.

▶ **To edit a part of an embedded chart:** Activate the chart; then click the part to be edited with the secondary mouse button and choose the appropriate editing command on the context menu.

▶ **To edit a part of a chart on its own sheet:** Make the chart sheet active; then click the part to be edited with the secondary mouse button and choose the appropriate editing command on the context menu.

▶ **To print a chart on its own chart sheet:** Make the chart sheet active and then click the Print button on the Standard toolbar or open the Print dialog box and press Enter.

▶ **To print an embedded chart alone:** Select all the cells in the worksheet underneath the chart; then open the Print dialog box and choose the Selection radio button before pressing Enter.

▶ **To print an embedded chart along with the spreadsheet data on the same worksheet:** Make the worksheet active and then click the Print button on the Standard toolbar or open the Print dialog box and press Enter.

▶ **To print the spreadsheet data on a worksheet without its embedded chart(s):** Make the worksheet active and then choose the Hide All radio button on the View tab of the Options dialog box before you click the Print button on the Standard toolbar or open the Print dialog box and press Enter.

Unit 7 Summary

▶ **To create a new database:** Enter names for the fields in a worksheet and then format them with some attribute (such as bold or centering) before you make the field entries for a typical record in the row right below.

▶ **To add a new record to the database via its data form:** Position the cell pointer on one of the cells; then choose Data⇨Form and click the New button in the data form.

▶ **To add a new record directly to the database:** Choose the next available blank row right beneath the one with the last record and enter the data for the new record in the appropriate fields.

▶ **To move from record to record in the data form:** Click the Find Next or Find Prev button in the data form or press the ↓ or ↑ key.

▶ **To find a record for editing in the data form:** Click the Criteria button; then enter the criteria for the records to be selected in the appropriate field(s) before you click the Find Next or Find Prev buttons.

▶ **To edit the record displayed in the data form:** Make changes to the appropriate fields; then select the next record in the data form by pressing Enter or the ↓ key to enter the revised record in the database.

Part III Review

▶ **To delete a record from the database:** Display the record in the data form, click the Delete button, and then select OK in the alert dialog box.

▶ **To sort a database:** Position the cell pointer in one of its cells, choose the Data⇨Sort command, select the field(s) to be used in reordering the records, and designate whether to use ascending or descending order.

▶ **To use AutoFilter to filter out all records except for those that contain a certain field entry:** Turn on AutoFilter by choosing the Data⇨Filter⇨AutoFilter command; then select the entry in the field's drop-down list box.

▶ **To use the Custom AutoFilter to filter out all records except for those that contain either one entry or another or a certain range of entries:** Turn on AutoFilter by choosing the Data⇨Filter⇨AutoFilter command, select (Custom...) in the field's drop-down list box, and designate the appropriate criteria in the Custom AutoFilter dialog box.

Part III Test

The questions on this test cover all the material presented in Part III, Units 6 and 7. The first section is True/False, the second section is fill in the blanks, and the last section is matching.

True False

Circle the letter of the answer (*T* for True and *F* for False) that best answers the question.

T F 1. The typical 2-D chart plots spreadsheet values on the vertical y-axis and the categories or time units on the horizontal x-axis.

T F 2. An embedded chart is one that is attached to a regular worksheet.

T F 3. You can use the Chart Wizard to create an embedded chart or a chart on its own chart sheet.

T F 4. To edit an embedded chart, you need to click the part that needs editing with the secondary mouse button.

T F 5. When you create a pie chart, Excel plots the values in the data series as a percentage of the sum of all values.

T F 6. You can create a new database by entering the field names in a row of the worksheet and then opening the data form with the Data⇨Form command.

T F 7. To sort a database alphabetically by last name, you designate the Last Name field in the Sort By drop-down list box and leave the Ascending radio button selected in the Sort dialog box.

T F 8. To sort a database by the order date from most recent to least recent, you select the Order Date field in the Sort By drop-down list box and leave the Ascending radio button selected in the Sort dialog box.

T F 9. To select only the records in a database where the order date was between January 1, 1995 and September 1, 1995 (inclusive), you enter =>as the first operator and *1/1/95* as the first value followed by <= as the second operator and *9/1/95* as the second value in the Custom AutoFilter for the Order Date field.

T F 10. To select only the records in a database where the city is Chicago or New York, you enter = as the first operator and *Chicago* as the first value followed by = as the second operator and *New York* as the second value in the Custom AutoFilter dialog box.

Part III Test

Fill in the Blanks

For each of the following questions, fill in the blanks with the correct answer.

11. When you create a 3-D Bar chart, in addition to the normal x-axis and y-axis, Excel adds a third axis called the ___-axis.

12. The _____ chart is the chart type automatically selected by Excel when you chart a table or spreadsheet.

13. To modify the cell selection with the spreadsheet data that's plotted in a chart that you've created, you need to click the _____ button on the Chart toolbar.

14. The columns of data in a database are known as _____ of the database, while the rows of data in a database are known as _____ of the database.

15. The process of rearranging the data in a database so that its information is presented in a new, preferred order is known as _____ the database.

16. The process of temporarily removing all data from a database, except the data that meets specific selection criteria, is referred to as _____ the database.

17. The data still displayed in a database after applying specific selection criteria using the process referred to in Question 16 is called a _____ of the database.

Matching

In the following section, match the items in the first column with the appropriate items in the second column by drawing a line from the item in the column on the left that connects to its counterpart in the column on the right.

18. Match up the following charting icons on the Chart toolbar with the correct function:

A.   1. Turns off and on the horizontal gridlines in the active chart.

B.   2. Starts the Chart Wizard so that you can modify the contents of the active chart.

C.   3. Turns off and on the legend in the active chart.

D.   4. Changes the chart type of the active chart or selected data series.

Part III Lab Assignment

In this lab assignment, you'll get a chance to apply what you've learned about creating charts and databases in Units 6 and 7 of Part III. In the first part of this lab assignment, you'll create charts for the 1st Quarter 1997 projected sales data on Sheet2 of your MGE Quarterly Sales (chart) workbook. In the second part of this assignment, you'll sort and filter the records in the Client List database in the Bo-Peep Client List workbook.

Step 1: Creating an embedded 3-D pie chart for the 1997 projected sales data

Open the MGE Quarterly Sales (chart) workbook in your personal folder; then select the Sheet2 worksheet and rename this worksheet to Q1 97 Sales so that the first four sheet tabs in this workbook are named Q1 96 Sales, Q1 96 Pie Chart, Q1 96 Area Chart, and Q1 97 Sales.

Use the ChartWizard to create an embedded 3-D pie chart by using the worksheet data in the cell ranges A2:A9 and E3:E9. Position this embedded 3-D pie chart in the cell range A12:E27 of the Q1 97 Sales worksheet. When creating the 3-D pie chart, select the chart format number 7 that includes both the data labels (A, B, and C) and the percentages. Enter *Mother Goose Enterprises Quarter 1, 1997 Projected Sales by Company* as the chart title. Edit the chart so that the chart title appears on two lines with the text *Mother Goose Enterprises* on the first line and *Quarter 1, 1997 Projected Sales by Company* on the second line.

Step 2: Creating a 3-D bar chart on its own sheet for the 1997 projected sales data

With the MGE Quarterly Sales (chart) workbook still open and the Q1 97 Sales worksheet still current, create a 3-D bar on its own chart sheet by using the worksheet data in the cell range A2:D9 of this worksheet. Rename this new Chart1 worksheet Q1 97 Bar Chart and move the chart sheet so that it appears immediately following the Q1 97 Sales worksheet. Shorten the horizontal scroll bar so that you can see all of the first five sheet tabs (Q1 96 Sales through Q1 97 Bar Chart).

Enter *Mother Goose Enterprises Quarter 1, 1997 Projected Sales* as the chart title all on one line. Format the chart's x-axis (in a Bar chart, the x-axis shows the values, and the y-axis shows the category labels) with the first Currency number format with no decimal places so that values appear along the tick marks at the bottom of the chart as $20,000, $40,000, and so on up to $180,000. Use the Zoom Control drop-down list button on Standard toolbar to select 75% as the magnification for the Q1 97 Chart sheet.

Before saving your work in the MGE Quarterly Sales (chart) workbook, deselect the 3-D Bar chart in the Q1 97 Bar Chart sheet, select cell A1 in the Q1 97 Sales worksheet, and make the Q1 96 Sales worksheet active. Then close the MGE Quarterly Sales (chart) workbook.

Part III Lab Assignment

Step 3: Sorting and filtering the Client List in the Bo-Peep Client List workbook

Open the Bo-Peep Client List workbook in the Practice folder within your Excel 101 folder, sort the database in order of the anniversary date from most to least recent, and then filter the database so that only records where the anniversary date is between January 1, 1981, and December 31, 1982 (inclusive), are displayed in the client list.

Check the database to make sure that only records whose anniversary date field entries are between January 1, 1981, and December 31, 1982. Then select cell A2 and save this sorted and filtered version of the database in your personal folder under the filename Bo-Peep Client List (filter date).

Answers

Unit 1 Quiz Answers

Question	Answer	
1.	B	The mouse pointer moves when you move the mouse on the desk, not the cell pointer!
2.	D	The Go To feature (accessed with F5) is by far the easiest way to make such a large move.
3.	A and D	Clicking the sheet tab scrolling buttons, as described in answer A, displays new sheet tabs but not worksheets — you still must click a sheet before Excel displays the worksheet. The Window pull-down described in answer D lets you activate a new open workbook not a new worksheet within a workbook.
4.	A and B	Text entries are always left-aligned when first entered, not centered as indicated in answer A. Text entries can consist of any combination of numbers, letters, and punctuation and don't have to be all letters as indicated in answer B.
5.	C and D	Values can consist of a combination of certain specific characters such as minus signs (-), commas (,), and dollar signs with numbers and don't have to be all numbers as indicated in answer C. Only values that contain formulas appear differently on the formula bar than they do in their cells. If a cell contains a value like -25, it will not appear differently as indicated in answer D.
6.	C	The End key moves the cell pointer only when you press one of the arrow keys after it.
7.	A and B	Excel doesn't know the European system of day, month, year used in answer A (although you can change this), and it doesn't know any dates that use "sts" or "nds" or "ths," as in May 1st, May 2nd, or May 24th.

8.	C	Excel won't calculate this entry because it doesn't begin with the all-important equal sign (=).
9.	B	There is no column IX in an Excel worksheet; therefore, the program will return an error value to this cell.
10.	C	The difference between 500 and 450 is -50 so that Excel will deincrement the next entry by 50, giving you *Item 400* in cell D2.

Unit 2 Quiz Answers

Question	Answer	
1.	C and D	Statement C is incorrect because it's the General tab, and not the Edit tab, of the Options dialog box that contains the Default File Location text box in statement C. Statement D is incorrect because any change that you make to the default file location remains in effect each and every time you start Excel until you edit or delete the path entered in the Default File Location text box.
2.	A	Changes to column widths and row heights in one worksheet don't affect any other worksheet in the workbook unless you have selected their sheet tabs (a technique that you'll learn in Unit 4).
3.	B and C	Statement B is incorrect because Excel will let you center any type of cell entry across columns (although you will seldom find a reason for doing this to values). Statement C is incorrect because the text orientation options on the Alignment tab of the Format Cells dialog box include everything but upside-down.
4.	B	Number formats never have any effect on the values as entered or calculated in their cells. These formats only affect the way the values appear in their cells in the worksheet.
5.	C and D	Statement C is incorrect because a custom style can change both the background color (via the Patterns tab) and the text color (via the Font tab) of the cells to which it is applied. Statement D is incorrect because no Style drop-down list box is available on the Formatting toolbar. (You have to be using Microsoft Word to have this kind of luxury available.) To apply a style to a cell selection in Excel, you have to open the Style dialog box (by choosing Style on the Format pull-down menu) and then select the style in the Style Name drop-down list box.

Unit 3 Quiz Answers

Question	Answer	
1.	B and C	Statement B is incorrect because Excel automatically prints the selected worksheet(s) in the workbook, not whatever cells are selected. Statement C is also incorrect because Excel automatically prints the worksheet name (as it appears on the sheet tab) — not the filename — in the header.
2.	C and D	Statement C is incorrect because you can never make editing changes to the data in the Print Preview window. (To make editing changes, you must return to the worksheet.) Statement D is also incorrect because pressing the PgUp and PgDn keys moves your view back and forth between pages in Print Preview only when it's in full-page view. (When you've zoomed in on the page, PgUp and PgDn move you up and down the page, not from page to page.)
3.	A	You must be in the worksheet, not in Print Preview, to define print titles by selecting cells in their rows or columns.
4.	D	The Fit to Scaling option is the easiest because Excel figures out just how much to reduce the data so that it will all fit on one page.

Part I Test Answers

If you missed more than a few of the questions on the test, you should review the related lessons and exercises before moving on to Part II.

Question	Answer	If You Missed It, Try This
1.	True	Review Exercise 1-1
2.	False	Review Exercise 2-2
3.	True	Review Exercise 2-1
4.	False	Review Lesson 1-3
5.	True	Review Exercise 1-5
6.	False	Review Exercise 2-1
7.	False	Review Lesson 2-6

8.	True	Review Exercise 3-2
9.	True	Review Exercise 3-1
10.	True	Review Exercise 3-11
11.	A and B	Review Exercises 1-8 and 1-9
12.	C	Review Lesson 1-3
13.	B	Review Exercise 2-7
14.	A	Review Exercise 2-1
15.	A and D	Review Exercises 2-1 and 1-22
16.	1 D	Review Exercise 3-8
	2 C	
	3 A	
	4 B	
17.	1 B	Review Exercises 1-3, 1-14, 2-2, and 3-1
	2 A	
	3 D	
	4 C	
18.	1 B	Review Lesson 1-2; Lesson 1-3; and Exercise 2-3
	2 C	
	3 A	
	4 D	
19.	1 D	Review Exercise 2-8
	2 B	
	3 A	
	4 C	
20.	1 D	Review Exercises 2-9 and 2-10
	2 B	
	3 A	
	4 C	

Unit 4 Quiz Answers

Question	Answer	
1.	D	Answer D is false because you must remember to hold down the Shift key as you double-click or all you end up doing is moving the cell pointer from corner to corner on the data table.
2.	C	Answer C is false because Shift+spacebar selects the entire row, whereas Ctrl+spacebar selects the entire column.
3.	B and D	Answer B is false because range names can have numbers in them as long as they don't start with numbers, and answer D is wrong because only DOS filenames are restricted to eight characters maximum
4.	A	Answer A is false because you don't hold down any key (especially the Shift key) as you drag.
5.	B and D	Answer B is false because you select only the first cell of the range (unless you're able to select a range that matches the one that's being moved or copied exactly in both shape and size), and answer D is false because Excel warns you when you're about to replace some existing cell entries only when using drag and drop.

Unit 5 Quiz Answers

Question	Answer	
1.	A and C	Statement A is false because Delete clears only the contents of a cell. You must choose Edit⇨Clear⇨All to clear contents, notes, and formats. Statement C is false because function key F2 puts Excel in Edit mode and locates the insertion point at the end of the cell entry.
2.	D	Statement D is false because you can also remove panes by dragging the pane boundary line all the way to one edge or the other of the worksheet or by double-clicking the boundary.
3.	A and B	Statement A is false because you can add sound notes in Excel, provided that your computer is equipped with a sound card and a microphone. Statement B is false because you must select the cell and then open the Cell Note dialog box (with Insert⇨Note) to display the text of the note.

4.   C and D   Statement C is false because you must choose the Replace All button after Excel finds the first match to replace all occurrences in the worksheet. (The default is not to replace anything but simply to find the next occurrence of the Find What text.) Statement D is false because Excel doesn't replace the entire contents of a cell with the Replace With text unless the Find Entire Cells Only check box is selected when you perform the search and give the word to make the replacement with the Replace or Replace All button.

5.   D   Statement D is false because you must select the sheet tab and then choose Delete Sheet on the Edit menu. (Pressing the Delete key just gets rid of whatever is in the current cell in the sheet that you activate.)

Part II Test Answers

If you missed more than a few of the questions on the test, you should review the related lessons and exercises.

Question	Answer	If You Missed It, Try This
1.	False	Review Lesson 4-1
2.	False	Review Lesson 4-1
3.	True	Review Lesson 4-1
4.	False	Review Exercise 4-3
5.	True	Review Exercise 4-6
6.	True	Review Exercise 4-9
7.	False	Review Exercise 4-11
8.	False	Review Exercise 4-12
9.	True	Review Lesson 5-1
10.	False	Review Exercise 5-2
11.	False	Review Exercise 5-5
12.	False	Review Lesson 5-3
13.	True	Review Lesson 5-4
14.	False	Review Lesson 5-5

15.	False	Review Exercise 5-15
16.	C	Review Lesson 5-1
17.	C	Review Lesson 4-1
18.	B	Review Exercise 5-14
19.	A and D	Review Lesson 4-3
20.	1 C	Review Exercise 4-12
	2 D	Review Lesson 5-6
	3 B	Review Exercise 4-12
	4 A	Review Exercise 5-3

Unit 6 Quiz Answers

Question	Answer	
1.	C and D	Statement C is incorrect because you must first double-click the embedded chart before you can click the secondary mouse on a part of the chart to open that part's context menu. Statement D is incorrect because you only have to click the chart once to select it before dragging it to its new location.
2.	A	Statement A is incorrect because Excel automatically creates a new chart sheet as part of the process of creating the chart, and no command for inserting a new chart sheet ahead of time is available in Excel!
3.	D	Statement D is incorrect because you must select the ChartWizard button on the floating Chart toolbar or the Standard toolbar before you select the new range of spreadsheet data. If you select the data range first, the ChartWizard uses this range to create a new chart in the worksheet.
4.	A and C	Statement A is incorrect because you must select the cells underneath the embedded chart before choosing the Selection radio button in the Print dialog box. Statement C is incorrect because you only need to select the worksheet with the spreadsheet data and embedded chart and then print either with the Print button on the Standard toolbar or from the Print dialog box.

Unit 7 Quiz Answers

Question	Answer	
1.	C and D	Answer C because you never have to give the cells with a database a range name to use it. Answer D because, to open the data form, you only have to position the cell pointer in any cell of the database (including those with the field names) before you choose the Data⇔Form command.
2.	D	Answer D because anything you enter in the Criteria form is used only for locating existing records in the database.
3.	A	Answer A because you can always edit a field entry in a database record by editing its contents directly in its cell or on the formula bar just as you would any cell entry in the worksheet.
4.	B	Answer B because Excel always leaves the records in a new database in the order in which they were added.
5.	A	Answer A because Excel only hides the records that don't meet the filtering criteria. It never deletes them.

Part III Test Answers

If you missed more than a few of the questions on the test, you should review the related lessons and exercises.

Question	Answer	If You Missed It, Try This
1.	True	Review Lesson 6-1
2.	True	Review Lesson 6-1
3.	False	Review Lesson 6-1
4.	False	Review Lesson 6-2
5.	True	Review Unit 6 Further Exercises
6.	False	Review Lesson 7-1
7.	True	Review Lesson 7-4
8.	False	Review Lesson 7-4

9.	True	Review Lesson 7-5
10.	False	Review `Lesson 7-5
11.	z-axis	Review Lesson 6-1
12.	Column chart	Review Lesson 6-1
13.	ChartWizard	Review Lesson 6-2
14.	fields: records	Review Lesson 7-1
15.	sorting	Review Lesson 7-4
16.	filtering	Review Lesson 7-5
17.	subset	Review Lesson 7-5
18.	1 D	Review Lesson 6-2
	2 C	Review Lesson 6-2
	3 A	Review Lesson 6-2
	4 B	Review Lesson 6-2

Index

Symbols

A

B

T

Tab, 18, 19
table formats, predefined, 74
table headings
   changing the alignment of, 58–59
   changing the font and font size, 57
tables, increasing vertical space between, 54
Taskbar, starting Excel from, 10
telephone number format, 65, 66
Telephone style, creating, 71
text, entering numbers as, 190
text data, 23–24
Text Note list box in the Cell Note dialog box, 142
text notes
   adding to cells, 141–143
   creating and selecting in cells, 142–143
   as place markers, 142
times, entering as values, 29
titles
   centering vertically, 63
   editing in charts, 176
toggles, 57
Total Pages button in the Footer dialog box, 90

U

unchanging address, 21
Undo, changing between pane entries, 139
Undo button, 135
Undo Clear on the Edit menu, 35
Undo/Redo, switching between, 135
Unfreeze Panes command, 138

V

values, 23–24
   calculating with formulas, 32–36
   displaying negative in red, 70
   entering dates and times as, 29
   entering from the numeric keypad, 28
   formatting on the y-axis, 178
   looking for, 144
Values radio button in the Paste Special dialog box, 128
vertical scroll bar, 16
vertical y-axis, 167–168

W

white-cross mouse pointer, 15
Width command on the
   Column continuation menu, 53–54
Window menu, opening, 13
window panes. *See panes*
Windows Explorer, opening Excel from, 12
workbook, 10
  closing, 14
  copying worksheets into a new, 152–154
  editing worksheets in, 148
  merging styles into a new, 73–74
  moving around and between worksheets in, 15
  moving between the sheets of, 22–23
  opening an existing to start Excel, 12
  opening blank, 13
  opening for formatting, 50
  opening a new, 12–13, 73
  opening new within Excel, 12–13
  printing an entire, 84–85
  rearranging worksheets in, 150
  switching between open, 13–14
  totaling worksheets in, 151–152
worksheet gridlines, removing, 60
worksheet titles, freezing panes as, 137–138
worksheet window, dividing into panes, 138–139
worksheets
  adding, 149
  cells available in, 20
  copying into a new workbook, 152–154
  deleting, 149–150
  dividing into panes, 138–139
  editing in a workbook, 148
  finding data entries in, 144–145
  inserting, 149
  moving around and between in a workbook, 15
  paging, 80
  printing, 83–84
  printing a range of cells in, 86–87
  printing selected, 85–86
  rearranging in a workbook, 150
  renaming, 148–149
  replacing data entries in, 145–146
  scrolling, 16
  selecting entire with the keyboard, 112
  selecting entire with the mouse, 110–111
  selecting next, 23
  selecting previous, 23
  spell checking, 146–148
  totaling in a workbook, 151–152
  zooming in and out on, 136–137
Wrap Text option, 63–64

X

Y

Z

IDG BOOKS WORLDWIDE LICENSE AGREEMENT

Installing the Dummies 101 Disk Files

To use the files on the disk that comes with this book, you first have to *install* them on your computer. Follow these steps to do so:

1 Insert the *Dummies 101* disk in your computer's 3¹/₂-inch floppy disk drive (the only drive in which the disk will fit).

2 Double-click on the My Compuster icon.

3 Double-click on the Control Panel icon.

4 Double-click on the Add/Remove Programs icon.

5 Click on the Install button.

6 Follow the directions on-screen.

Unless you *really* know what you're doing, accept the settings that the installation program suggests. If you decide to forge into the unknown and change the folder in which you install the files that you'll use with this book, write the pathname of that folder here:

Folder in which this book's files reside: _____

(Problems with the installation process? Call the IDG Books Worldwide Customer Support number: 800-762-2974.)

IDG BOOKS WORLDWIDE REGISTRATION CARD

Title of this book: **Dummies 101:™ Excel For Windows® 95**

My overall rating of this book: ❏ Very good [1] ❏ Good [2] ❏ Satisfactory [3] ❏ Fair [4] ❏ Poor [5]

How I first heard about this book:

❏ Found in bookstore; name: [6] _____

❏ Advertisement: [8] _____

❏ Word of mouth; heard about book from friend, co-worker, etc.: [10] _____

❏ Book review: [7] _____

❏ Catalog: [9] _____

❏ Other: [11] _____

What I liked most about this book:

_____

_____

What I would change, add, delete, etc., in future editions of this book:

_____

_____

Other comments:

_____

_____

Number of computer books I purchase in a year: ❏ 1 [12] ❏ 2-5 [13] ❏ 6-10 [14] ❏ More than 10 [15]

I would characterize my computer skills as: ❏ Beginner [16] ❏ Intermediate [17] ❏ Advanced [18] ❏ Professional [19]

I use ❏ DOS [20] ❏ Windows [21] ❏ OS/2 [22] ❏ Unix [23] ❏ Macintosh [24] ❏ Other: [25] _____
(please specify)

I would be interested in new books on the following subjects:
(please check all that apply, and use the spaces provided to identify specific software)

❏ Word processing: [26] _____

❏ Data bases: [28] _____

❏ File Utilities: [30] _____

❏ Networking: [32] _____

❏ Other: [34] _____

❏ Spreadsheets: [27] _____

❏ Desktop publishing: [29] _____

❏ Money management: [31] _____

❏ Programming languages: [33] _____

I use a PC at (please check all that apply): ❏ home [35] ❏ work [36] ❏ school [37] ❏ other: [38] _____

The disks I prefer to use are ❏ 5.25 [39] ❏ 3.5 [40] ❏ other: [41] _____

I have a CD ROM: ❏ yes [42] ❏ no [43]

I plan to buy or upgrade computer hardware this year: ❏ yes [44] ❏ no [45]

I plan to buy or upgrade computer software this year: ❏ yes [46] ❏ no [47]

Name: _____ Business title: [48] _____ Type of Business: [49] _____

Address (❏ home [50] ❏ work [51]/Company name: _____)

Street/Suite# _____

City [52]/State [53]/Zipcode [54]: _____ Country [55] _____

❏ **I liked this book!** You may quote me by name in future IDG Books Worldwide promotional materials.

My daytime phone number is _____

IDG BOOKS

THE WORLD OF COMPUTER KNOWLEDGE

 **YES!**
Please keep me informed about IDG's World of Computer Knowledge.
Send me the latest IDG Books catalog.

SECRETS™

...FOR DUMMIES™
COMPUTER
BOOK SERIES
FROM IDG

MACWORLD
MW
AUTHORIZED
EDITION

AUTHORIZED
PC WORLD
EDITION

- -

NO POSTAGE
NECESSARY
IF MAILED
IN THE
UNITED STATES

BUSINESS REPLY MAIL
FIRST CLASS MAIL   PERMIT NO. 2605   FOSTER CITY, CALIFORNIA

IDG Books Worldwide
919 E Hillsdale Blvd, STE 400
Foster City, CA 94404-9691